TEACHING THE MOTHER TONGUE IN A MULTILINGUAL EUROPE

Teaching the Mother Tongue in a Multilingual Europe

Edited by

Witold Tulasiewicz and Anthony Adams

CASSELL

Cassell
Wellington House
125 Strand
London WC2R 0BB

370 Lexington Avenue
New York
NY 10017 - 6550

First published 1998

British Library Cataloguing-in-Publication Data
A catalogue record for this book is available from the British Library.

ISBN 0-304-33490-1 (hardback)

Typeset by Sam Merrell, Bath, England
Printed and bound in Great Britain by Redwood Books, Trowbridge, Wiltshire

Contents

Acknowledgements

The editors owe special thanks to Peter Gannon, who as HMI was secretary of the Kingman Inquiry into the Teaching of English; Dan Taverner OBE, formerly Chief Inspector of Schools in the London Borough of Newham; and Lionel Elvin, Honorary Fellow of Trinity Hall, Cambridge, for reading the manuscript and offering suggestions and corrections. We also benefited from discussions about the mother tongue in the changing socio-political situation in several countries, not only with those named above, but also with colleagues from a study group on Language Awareness, including George Labercane of the University of Calgary; Frieder Kron of the University of Mainz; Printz Påhlson, Fellow of Clare Hall, Cambridge; and Jerzy Nikitorowicz of the University of Warsaw. We are also grateful to Alison Manson, the Graphics Unit, School of Education, University of Leeds, for providing the maps and to Martine Jago, Research Fellow of Christ Church College, Canterbury, for reading the proofs.

The authors of the case studies in Part Two have been responsible for making the book a European study of the mother tongue, in which everyone concerned had a share in a number of bilateral and multilateral discussions. It is also a pleasure to recall a number of stimulating conversations with friends in several places, particularly with Keith Spalding of the University of Wales about vocabulary and vocabulary change, the Misses Wood of Kirby le Soken about the languages of the Channel Islands, and Uschi Kron of Mainz about computer technology.

With a bibliography covering more than ten countries using words from many mother tongues requiring dozens of diacritics, we were greatly helped by the professional expertise of Ken Turner, Fellow of Hughes Hall, Cambridge, a member of our original European Union-funded research into multicultural classrooms in Europe, Sheila Hakin, librarian and Gavin Courtney, technical officer, at the University of Cambridge Department of Education.

The book would not have appeared in the form it has without the expert services of Ruth McCurry, commissioning editor, Seth Edwards, editorial assistant, and Helena Power, desk editor, at Cassell, and Mervyn Thomas of Thomas Editorial Services. The index was compiled by Martin Hargreaves.

While acknowledging thanks to all those mentioned and others, the 15 contributors alone are responsible for omissions in what has always been intended to be a provocative book.

Witold Tulasiewicz
Anthony Adams

The Contributors

Anna Berlińska is Assistant Professor in Polish at the University of Białystok and is currently Lecturer in Slavonic Studies, University of Toulouse.

Françoise Convey is Principal Lecturer in French at Trinity and All Saints College, University of Leeds.

Elżbieta Czykwin is Assistant Professor in Education at the University of Białystok.

Nikolas Coupland is Professor and Director of the Centre for Language and Communication Research at the School of English, Communication and Philosophy, University of Wales, Cardiff.

Antonia Ruíz Esturla was formerly Coordinator of Spanish Mother Tongue Teaching in London at the Spanish Embassy Education Office and is currently Senior Teacher of English, Granada.

Peter Garrett is Senior Lecturer at the Centre for Language and Communication Research, School of English, Communication and Philosophy, University of Wales, Cardiff.

Anne Holmen is Assistant Professor in the Department of Nordic Philology at the University of Copenhagen.

J. Normann Jørgensen is Assistant Professor in the Department of Nordic Philology at the University of Copenhagen.

James Muckle was formerly Senior Lecturer in Russian at the University of Nottingham and is currently researcher in Russian Studies at the University of Nottingham.

Ingelore Oomen-Welke is Professor of Education at the Higher College of Pedagogy, Freiburg.

Mary Rose Peate is Researcher at the Centre for Language and Communication Research, School of English, Communication and Philosophy, University of Wales, Cardiff.

Robert Protherough was formerly Senior Lecturer in English Education at the University of Hull.

Guido Schmitt is Assistant Professor at the Higher College of Pedagogy, Freiburg.

Witold Tulasiewicz and **Anthony Adams** are Fellows of Wolfson College, Cambridge.

List of Maps

Part I

Mother Tongue: Definitions and Teaching Implications

Chapter 1

What Is Mother Tongue?

INTRODUCTION

Throughout the writing and editing of this book the authors have been bedevilled by its title and the use of the term 'mother tongue'. Although we have tried to achieve some consistency in the editorial work we have done on the chapters in Part II, it will be seen that our various contributors have interpreted the term in different ways. This is to be expected since the historical and social linguistic situation which affects the status of the languages spoken in each of the countries discussed is very different. The term 'mother tongue' has been retained by us because it is a familiar one and one that most readers will intuitively understand.

As with much else in the realm of language, what is intuitive is often misleading. By 'mother tongue' we understand what linguists usually refer to as L1, that is the language first acquired by a child and the first one to find expression developed from the Language Acquisition Device posited by Chomsky (1965). It may, however, also be the preferred language in a multilingual situation, which presupposes a choice made from two systems or more, and means it is no longer the mother tongue as defined above. For example, many immigrants to the USA will use English as their first language even though their mother tongue may be altogether different. Our own researches in the London Borough of Newham, funded by the European Union and conducted in 1989–91, revealed many occasions when the preferred language of school pupils was English even though their mothers might speak no English at all. On such occasions the oldest male child would frequently act as an interpreter negotiating between his parent and the school on such occasions as parents' evenings. By contrast, in a demographically very similar area, in the City of Peterborough, a large number of pupils in one of the primary schools we studied saw little point in learning English at all, as they lived in a community where it was possible to survive without seeing or hearing a single word of English. Although they lived in a large city, English was for them – paradoxically – more of a foreign language than a second language (L2) of study.

Perhaps it is because of the complexities surrounding the concept that comparative studies of the teaching of the mother tongue, which is usually also the nation state's language, have been relatively few. One specific work of which we are aware in the area is that of Ten Brinke (1976), entitled *The Complete Mother Tongue Curriculum*. This was extensively researched but highly theoretical. Recent developments in the European Union and the work of the Council of Europe have led us to believe that there would be some benefit to all teachers of L1, and those interested in language generally, which includes teachers of second (L2) and modern foreign languages, of a study of language issues and the teaching of language across a representative range of European countries, such as is attempted in the present volume. An investigation into the teaching of the English language in England began at the time of the Kingman Inquiry, whose secretary collected information on how the mother tongue was taught in a number of other European countries as part of the evidence received by the committee (Kingman Report, 1988). In France, the Chevalier and Janitza Report (1989) worked to a similar brief: the purpose and nature of language education. The necessity to meet the educational needs of a multilingual Europe in a mixed ability context has stimulated a European Union funded comparative study of the teaching of the mother tongue in France, England, Germany and Spain. Most recently, there has been the initiative to set up an International Association for the Improvement of Mother Tongue Education (IAIMTE), which held its first conference in Amsterdam in 1997. As part of the inquiry into teaching the mother tongue, the authors have also been involved in international discussions on the nature and purpose of language awareness.

SOME DEFINITIONS

The *Oxford English Dictionary* defines 'mother tongue' as 'one's native language', the language into which one is born. This dispels the Romantic notion of being born *with* a language. Before the present period of mass migration that language was most likely the first, though not necessarily the only, language of everyday communication. The exact equivalent of the term 'mother tongue' is found in many European and non-European languages, *Muttersprache* or *langue maternelle*, although in some Slavonic languages the terms 'father tongue' (as in Polish *język ojczysty*) or 'native language' (as in Russian *rodnoi yazyk*) are used instead. Since Medieval Latin had the term *lingua materna*, it is possible to accept that, in European societies at least, it was the mother who was assumed to pass on her language to her children. In languages whose standard form was not consolidated until the nineteenth century 'mother tongue' is probably a *calque* of its use in the European languages in which nineteenth-century philological research, which came up with a variety of mother language models, was conducted. 'Mother tongue' as a term was not documented in modern European languages until after 1000 AD. Twelfth-century Northern Germanic *modersmål* is attested earlier than the Medieval Latin version found in the Wetterau collection of 1366; Middle Low German *modersprake* (1424) in turn predates the High German use of *Sprache* which had attested the related *mutterliche Zunge*, 'native tongue', before 1350. Luther uses the term *Muttersprache* in 1523 (Luther, 1883).

In English 'mother tongue' is first found in Wyclif in 1380 (reprinted by the Early English Texts Society), and refers to the 'admissibility of the native language in court pleadings' clearly intended to facilitate communication for speakers without Latin versed only in vernacular English. The legal dispensation illustrates the recognition of the 'mother tongue' as an official language of the courts and confirms the acceptance of the regional dialect of the population as a language, both spoken and written, likely to be understood beyond its immediate region. The Central Midlands Dialect, which was to become the basis for the standard version of English, had not begun to assume general currency throughout the country until the fifteenth century.

A 1541 Zürich dictionary translates *Muterspraach*, which is also called the *Landspraach*, as the Latin *patrius sermo* and shows a similar legal and 'regional' application. *Landspraach* identifies it as the regional, later to be called the 'national', language medium. These could be different languages, as documented in Polish Lithuanian Commonwealth usage – *gente Ruthenus, natione Polonus* – with their different languages. The Polish *język ojczysty* is also first found in a legal text before the sixteenth century and shows the link between mother tongue and legal language.

Language and environment

It is the language community of the mother tongue, the language spoken in a region, which enables the process of enculturation, the growing of an individual into a particular system of linguistic perception of the world and participation in the centuries old history of linguistic production (Pocock, 1971). One of the mother tongues of the Inuits, which allegedly has dozens of words for 'snow', enables users to distinguish among many varieties of 'snow', while the English have to do with a mere three or four ('slush' or 'sleet' for example). However, it is the language users who find what they consider the appropriate words for the phenomena in their environment, as do the Inuits in the case of snow, or the French who see the 'foot' (*pied*) of a table while the English prefer its 'leg'. The Russians have a separate single word (*sutok*) to denote the whole period of twenty-four hours in addition to the two words for 'day' and 'night' which does not divide the period of time in terms of a twenty-four hour 'day', as does the English. The seven-day week is used throughout monotheistic communities which have adopted the idea of a 'sabbath'. But it has been maintained by Aitchison in her 1996 Reith Lectures on BBC radio that this division of time into a unit of seven days (a week) is purely arbitrary, even though it constrains our thinking. She points out that, by contrast, 'an Inca week had ten days, nine working days, followed by market day, on which the king changed wives'.

While language is closely linked with our customary way of thinking, the now accepted view is that different languages only *reflect* the different environments in which their speakers live, modifying the Whorfian hypothesis of linguistic relativity that it is language which influences the way in which its speakers actually perceive the world, thus determining their cognitive functioning (Whorf, 1956). Vygotsky's (1962) emphasis on the link between speech and thought reflects his view of the interplay of the two in children's concept formation. Where two words are available they 'divide up' a concept in a different way from that which happens when there is only one word available. Trier's 1931 *Wortfeldtheorie* (Trier, 1973) is applied to a group of related concepts which border on each other, so that each word has a fixed meaning with any changes in it affecting the whole structure. It goes back to de Saussure's structuralist concept of language. The *Wortfeld* itself was used to illustrate the division of abstract concepts such as 'intellect', as well as concrete terms like 'horse' into qualifying subunits. Concepts expressed in one language are accessible with the linguistic resources of another but the process may involve the creation of sub-units.

It is tempting to consider the post-modern arguments about the power of language convincingly phrased by Barthès – *la langue est fasciste* – against the background of eighteenth- and nineteenth-century views of the mother tongue as the prime stimulus of human activity. Further pursuing the topic of language as worldview, we note the exaggerated nationalist claims made particularly by eighteenth-century German scholars, such as Hamann (quoted in

Baron, 1947), who were among the first to equate mother tongue with national language in the sense of a 'nation's tongue'. It was Humboldt in 1836 (Humboldt, 1979) who linked language with the 'spirit of the nation' that speaks it, a view curiously not dissimilar to the one expressed about a hundred years later in the Newbolt Report (Board of Education, 1921) on the teaching of English about the relation between 'the English language' and the concept of 'Englishness':

> English is not merely the medium of our thought, it is the very stuff and process of it. It is itself the English mind, the element in which we live and work . . . It connotes the discovery of the world by the first and most direct way open to us, and the discovery of ourselves in our native environment.

The association of mother tongue with national language assumed a more sinister dimension in Nazi Germany, which associated the 'power' of the language with the *Volk* and its territory. Cementing the identity of linguistic tradition with the nation's speakers deliberately severed the personal link of the idea implied in the term 'mother tongue' with the individual's actual mother. Thus Weisgerber in 1939 (Weisgerber, 1949) spoke of the *volkhafte Kräfte der Muttersprache* ('the native dynamic of the mother tongue'), giving rise to notions of 'inferior' and 'superior' languages linked to the idea of superior and inferior nations and races.

It is possible in the first instance to identify the three following uses of 'mother tongue': that of a 'private' language used among intimate groups of speakers; that of a vernacular which may be used as a 'regional' language; and that of a language which achieves national status and is used on all public occasions of the nation state. 'Mother tongue' comes to be seen as the distinguishing mark of ethnicity which accounts for the often made claim that independent states must have their own language. Such a claim brings in the concept of the 'official language' of government where a language may be imposed upon an entire state. This can be seen in the example of Slovakia where laws have been passed restricting the public use of Hungarian. Relegating language as the distinguishing mark of ethnic identity to the more narrowly instrumental function of communication used by a community opens up the consideration of the more symbolic characteristics of an ethnic group. The argument whether language is the distinguishing mark of nations cannot be said to have been conclusively settled (Edwards, 1984 and 1985; Giles, 1977).

Mother tongue and national language

A rapid count reveals that there are many more 'mother tongues' than there are sovereign independent states in Europe. In the United Kingdom alone, in addition to English, there are the other 'territorial' languages: Welsh, Scottish Gaelic and Irish Gaelic spoken at one time by the Welsh, Scots and Irish settled in their territories for periods longer than the English. Though no longer so widely spoken they are still regarded as the mother or native tongues of some British Celts. It is possible to add other languages to this list, for example Cornish and Manx, which can be seen as languages to be studied rather than used, perhaps a little like Latin, which was itself once a mother tongue. Scottish English is a later arrival which has created a territory where it is spoken and is often seen as more of a language than a dialect. Within the boundaries of Germany, Danish and Sorbian are the territorial mother tongues of some 160,000 of those who use them instead of, or in addition to, the official language of the Federal Republic of Germany spoken by more than eighty million Germans. The term 'official' language (*Amtssprache*) is used in Germany more frequently than in other countries.

This shows a concern by the government to elevate the national language to an official status.

The regional mother tongues just mentioned are numerically small when compared with the official languages of communication, administration and education. English in the United Kingdom was, until relatively recently, the only language of compulsory education although Welsh can now be taught before English in the Principality and there are Danish classes available in Germany.

There are, however, several numerically much bigger additional mother tongues in Europe. These include Catalan with nearly ten million users and at least two other mother tongues besides Castilian within the borders of the Kingdom of Spain. Alternative mother tongues like Luxembourgeois are at least as strong as the other two official languages (French and German) of the Grand Duchy (Lepschy, 1994).

Although for some natural speakers of the dialect designated as the state, or official language, the two, mother-tongue dialect and national language, may to a large extent coincide, not all the different mother-tongue dialects enjoy the status of a country's official language. One of the main reasons for this is that in most cases there are no 'nations' distinguished as politically separate from the main nation, which could recognize them as the main or official medium within their territory. Thus, East Anglian English qualifies as a dialect, while Kashubian is classified as a language by German and a dialect by Polish scholars. Since neither region is politically independent this may determine the rationale behind the use of the term dialect. Historically, Catalan is a language which is separate from Spanish, spoken in a region which enjoyed independence during the middle ages. Before political autonomy was granted to the region in 1978 it was popularly taken, outside Catalonia, to be a dialect of Spanish. The fifteen variants of Italian, if that is what they are, such as Sicilian, Piedmontese or Venetian, used only in certain regions of Italy, differ sufficiently from national Italian, based on the dialect of Tuscany, as well as from each other to be regarded by some as separate languages. Taken together, the fifteen are regarded as mother tongues by 57 per cent of all Italians; 85 per cent of whom, however, can also use the national language. For most of them, therefore, 'national' Italian is a second language (Grimes, 1988). A number of modern states will accept several national languages: they may all be 'official' as in Switzerland, or one may be 'more official' as is Russian in some of the regions of the former Soviet Union. A nation may have more than one language as a medium of communication although one may be designated the 'national' or 'standard' language, as is the case with English in England. This is not so in the Irish Republic, Wales or Canada which, like many other countries, are officially designated as bilingual and where law or custom may require those working in administration or teaching to be fluent in both the official languages.

Taking the 'mother tongue' as the first language of communication, there are as many different kinds of mother tongues as there are languages so used; some of them may be referred to as dialects or 'home languages'. 'Home language' is the term preferred by some linguists to denote the usually small, uncodified, spoken varieties of dialects used in domestic speech situations which are frequently unacknowledged as distinctive dialects, so as to emphasize their mainly oral character. Indeed some home languages are just that: unwritten variants of dialects used by small groups of speakers living rather isolated lives during most of which they use their 'home language' to communicate only with each other. Like the small regional mother tongues which, by virtue of belonging to a different language family or because they are spoken in a politically independent region, are styled languages, such as Welsh or Catalan, 'home languages' or 'home dialects' function *alongside* the national or official language, to which they may or may not be related. They have to make way for it when the use of a more widely understood, formal and 'educated' speech is required. Occupational jargons do not qualify since they are not the first language of communication and are used for transactions only within one specific area of human activity. The term 'natural language' has the ring of 'first language', a spontaneous medium whose exact relation to the majority national medium is left undefined. 'Preferred language' emphasizes the choice of a user who can choose between at least two languages, although this choice may be restricted as a consequence of the context of communication in which one language may be more useful. A narrowing of the sphere in which the 'minor' regional languages are used results in their being demoted to the status of 'home language' which, as we have argued earlier, may also be regarded by their users as their mother tongue. Local variations of spoken Belorussian and Ukrainian in Poland which are not clearly distinguished from neighbouring variants, or have no version delimited by writing, are called by their users 'the language of here'(*język tutejszy*) – as good a definition of a home language and mother tongue as any.

Languages or dialects whose territories enjoy a degree of political and cultural autonomy are not usually referred to in this way. In Switzerland, the tiny Romansch, the next smallest language after Italian, and in Spain, Basque (*Euskera*) or Galician, are used for most purposes in a compact region. The limited extent of Romansch, however, makes it necessary for speakers to use another of the Swiss languages for everyday transactions, limiting its function to being the mother tongue of its 40,000 users. The term *Ausbausprache* was coined by Kloss in 1952 (see Kloss, 1987) for minor languages which would not normally be classed as national languages but which, because of the way they have been codified, have perfected the linguistic tools necessary to function in all areas of communication and have acquired the status of national languages without which they would have a more limited validity, relegated, like the 'home languages', to intimate spheres of communication. Prestigious languages in a region where they are not the mother tongue of all inhabitants, may be awarded the status of a 'cultural' medium, as is seen in the case of French in many countries of the African continent.

FUNCTIONS AND STATUS OF THE MOTHER TONGUE

The 'mother tongue' may be the user's first language but for a number of reasons it may not remain so. Each variety of language just discussed can be the chosen medium of communication by some users in some contexts. Depending on the actual circumstances, user preference may be taken as the means of determining whether the language qualifies as a mother tongue rather than just as the main medium of communication. It is the mother tongue which is seen as the refuge of a nation under linguistic threat which may have to yield to the realities of efficient commercial communication. This affects the position of the smaller languages in areas where other languages are also used. Some territorial languages, like Sorbian in Germany, Belorussian in Poland, and the Celtic languages in the British Isles have, to a varying extent, been rediscovered as a piece of cultural heritage, the language of folkloristic and cultural expression (Sorbian) or the language of the chapel (Welsh). They may also of course be used in a small number of administrative transactions, often restricted to certain domains or to certain parts of the country only. They are, however, rarely used as the medium in commercial transactions. On the other hand, given the right political climate, they may qualify to be recognized as fully fledged national, or at least regional languages, a situation in which politics rather than size is often the deciding factor. This can be seen by comparing the recently restored status of Welsh with that of Breton (Temple, 1994). In examples such as

Welsh and Irish, languages may on occasion be employed in politics as the language, not of administration, but of protest. Both Welsh and Irish may be used in court, but often not as the first choice of language, thus limiting their roles as 'official' languages. Irish Gaelic has been identified as a mark of protest in Northern Ireland when it is used in Catholic church services and Irish songs. Precisely this development may lead to languages being called national or even 'nationalistic' when they are used as a tool to reconquer a territory, leaving the other language to be used as the official instrument of business and administration. The continuing use of two languages, Belorussian and Russian, in the Republic of Belarus demonstrates this development where both languages are used by about the same number of speakers. Many speakers in these groups are 'secondary bilinguals' who do not use the mother tongue at all regularly.

The reasons for using a language may be socio-political: the language is identified with some political and social classes of the population but not with others; cultural and religious: the language is used in predominantly artistic or denominational contexts; commercial: the language of business transactions; domestic: the language of the home; and linguistic: the language is small and not distinct enough, yet is different from the official language and has been used for a long time by people who are reluctant to change to another. In this they may be supported by experts who look upon such a language as a cultural inheritance and object of study. Though one's choice of mother tongue may be a personal decision, the opportunity for using it is largely dictated by societal considerations. This can result in language conflict. An illustration was the wholescale riots in Belgium thirty years ago over the language dispute between the users of French and Flemish. The outcome of such conflicts may be resolved by the size and the status of the language involved (Weinreich, 1953). In the case of Belgium, while the struggle, after the division of the country on mother-tongue lines, is no longer so bitter it is probably true that it still has force as seen in the bilingual status of the Brussels area today.

The intimate and the public spheres

The question put to one of the authors during a discussion of the use made of Belorussian by Polish citizens living in the north-eastern borderlands of the country who declared themselves ethnic Belorussian was: Is the language (Belorussian) used in intimate situations among relatives and close friends the mother tongue ? After an affirmative answer, the author then asked another question: Do all ethnic Belorussians use that language in similar situations? The answer to this was: 'No'. The discussion then ensued to explore whether two different languages can be used in a near identical intimate situation and convey the same emotional message? The referendum held in Belarus in the summer of 1995 showed that, in their own country, Belorussians were equally divided on whether to use Russian or Belorussian as the official language of the country, a dilemma solved by the closer economic union between Russia and Belarus concluded the following year. Thus there will always be an official place for both, unless the use of one becomes forbidden, a sanction many languages have survived.

In the referendum intimate speaking situations were not, of course, addressed. However, in such circumstances obtaining in the Republic of Belarus, Belorussian cannot qualify as the only mother tongue of the people since Russian is currently used by several million (mainly town dwellers) as their main or only medium; nor indeed is it accepted as the only national and official language of political and business transactions in the country. It is estimated, however, that more speakers will use Belorussian in the more private spheres of their lives.

With all the different circumstances taken into account it is not possible to separate a definition of 'mother tongue' from that of 'national', let alone 'official', language. Such a definition must consider the linguistic, socio-political, economic, cultural and personal factors involved in the territory where the language is used. This has implications for mother tongue education and government policies which relate to the status of the official languages and the dialects used. In the case of a world language like English, these factors assume a dimension not so far considered. Not only are the majority of those who speak 'English' not first-language users of British English nor users of the many American, Australian or other 'English' varieties of it, but users of the different 'Englishes' spoken in Asia and Africa, as well as in Europe, using them as a second or foreign language. All languages have varieties used as mother tongues by some sections of the population which may be referred to as dialects. However, because of the wide expansion of English, which has been allowed to develop independently, there are more regional variants of 'English' regarded as national or official languages of sovereign states. American-English has assumed a particularly important international status and has developed its own living features. In the context of English as a world language, it has been suggested that 'English' has in a way been 'stolen' from its original speakers. This growth of many different varieties of English worldwide is discussed in Hayhoe and Parker (1994) and is clearly more noticeable than is the case with Spanish or French, widely seen as the second and third 'world languages'. In practice such a distinction may or may not be made: for example Germans, Poles and others use the term 'American', not the hyphenated, 'American-English' when speaking of the language of the USA.

Major world languages are increasingly being used for commerce and international communication in countries where they are neither the original mother tongue nor an additional regional language or dialect in the sense discussed earlier. This may reduce the role of, and so displace, the original mother tongue or national language, a process analogous to the displacement of home languages by the 'stronger' national language, leaving the former with fewer mother-tongue speakers or relegated to the status of an 'associated' language not used for communication (Eastman, 1984; Eastman and Reese, 1981). English is the most prominent modern example of a strong language in this sense. In the past, such languages as Latin enjoyed similar international roles. Their roles were not identical, however, since their spread, territory, number of users, and the uses made of the languages by them were considerably smaller. Latin certainly did not affect as many people in so many countries as modern English, or even French or Russian, do today (Ammon, 1989).

This must change further the appropriate definition of the term 'mother tongue' and returns us to the question: Can languages which no longer serve the users as the sole interpreter of their worlds be called their mother tongues? Can languages acquired later in life be called mother tongues? In Malcolm Bradbury's novel *Rates of Exchange*, various non-native English users (posing politically as 'communist'), speaking their own varieties of English, acknowledge the impact of English on both *their* English and their original mother tongues, especially since, as a result of political circumstances, the intrusion of the English and American realities into their lives made them acquire new definitions for many words used. In the same way the 'Western' definition of 'democracy', or concepts such as the sense of give-and-take ('fairness') in the Welsh colloquialism, 'fair play' (*chwarae teg*), can affect people's worldviews, without affecting the actual reality.

An individual's mother tongue, if it is of the standard variety, may also be a national language; one dialect user's national language may be another's mother tongue yet used as a national tongue by another. This accounts for the unequal distribution and status of languages in different countries. British English is the mother tongue and preferred language of business transactions of more people than German, which is, however, the mother tongue of more people than French. This is because German is only associated with a few ethnic nationalities often classed as German, such as the Austrians. French is used by many nationalities, Belgians as well as Swiss, Luxembourgeois and Monegasques, to name those nearest to France. There may be fewer people who are 'English' than those who are 'German', but English has a much greater number of non-ethnic users. These include the millions of people of Irish descent, or indeed non-Europeans, such as Nigerians, for many of whom English is their first mother tongue, and who, more than the 'Germans', are distinguished from each other by such features as religion or political culture (Parry *et al.*, 1994; Ammon, 1991).

Therefore there is another mother-tongue category represented by users of the non-regional languages of immigrants before they decide to jettison them in favour of the language of their host country. This process may often never be complete (Tulasiewicz, 1994). In the United Kingdom, immigrant languages such as Panjabi, Hindi or Caribbean English are linked predominantly with Asia and the West Indies, in Germany, Turkish with Turkey and Turkish Kurdistan. They may in some circumstances, as in India, also include English as the language of expatriate Britons. Such languages have only a short historical and territorial base in their host countries, though they may be widely spoken in the areas where many of the immigrants have settled. As mother tongues or home languages, they may have a wide domestic circulation in their own countries; as the home languages of immigrants their role in the host country may be marginal. However, though confined to the often very lively and pulsating intimate and religious spheres of human intercourse, they may satisfy the mother tongue criteria more readily than minor territorial languages whose areas of use are only more extensive because they are the preferred languages in a number of official and commercial transactions. But they are used less widely and by fewer speakers in the intimate spheres. Such 'home languages' are especially subject to displacement but may be supported by the mother country if it is politically minded so to do. The users themselves can be very much attached to their languages, a phenomenon which can ensure them a greater security than that of the smaller territorial languages – especially if under threat from an entrenched major language, as in the case of Sorbian, Irish, or West Greenlandic. The Kurds in Germany receive no official support from the Turkish government to help maintain their mother tongue, which is not recognized as official. By contrast, Lithuanians in Poland are strongly supported by their government. The fact that Romany and Yiddish speakers have no compact linguistic territory in their host countries has added to their difficulties when asserting their identity. Again, English, French or German make up a very different category, in these respects.

Major languages may be differently affected. The repatriated Germans (*Aussiedler*) enjoy full government support in Germany. Abroad, German language lessons are readily available. However, the original German mother-tongue dialects of the *Aussiedler* are not the *Hochdeutsch* spoken and currently taught in Germany so that, unlike the foreign immigrants (*Ausländer*), who may receive lessons in their mother tongues, the *Aussiedler* are faced with the socio-psychological problems of the likely loss of their mother tongue (Hamburger, 1994). The socio-economic pressure on them to adopt standard German is especially strong and is frequently not resisted. This is also the case with 'official' French in countries where the standard form of the language is usually more influential than any dialect version or the native language of the people. In the case of English, support for the language which cuts across all the categories considered above is ensured by virtue of the combined commercial and political strengths of the United States and of the United Kingdom, and by the fact that variants of the language are widely used as mother tongues by millions of non-native English speakers throughout the world. Only the less popular and prestigious variants of English mother tongue may be affected by loss of currency to another language. This is very likely to be the standard version of English itself, an issue discussed at the 1995 New York international convention on the teaching of English organized by the International Federation for the Teaching of English (IFTE).

Variants of other languages may play a similar role to that of variants of English, though less readily so in the case of the smaller languages not used so widely as languages of commerce and administration. As a result of a policy of language 'purity', the French advocated in the francophone states of Africa is the French of metropolitan France. There is thus less likelihood of the emergence of a distinctive new (in addition to Canadian) official French as is British English from 'Australian' or 'American' English. This phenomenon of language purity may lead to the existence of a single variety of language – for example, the French spoken by the educated classes in some African and Asian countries. Contrasting with this is the French of Quebec, an old dialect subject to its own rules and with a distinctive vocabulary, which retains, for example, the use of dipthongs in its spoken version. In this respect it resembles, in the case of French, the situation of the different 'Englishes'. Such dialects and home languages as Creoles, '*patois*' or 'pidgin', though they may change by the addition of new words, are not affected since the pressure is to learn standard English or French and not to modify the patois or Creole. Teaching mother-tongue English may employ the '*patois*' partly as a part medium of instruction but the intention is to learn the 'standard'. South American Spanish is sufficient as the *lingua franca* of Cuban refugees in the United States since its only rival is English and not another variant of Spanish.

Attitudes as indicators

Despite the influence of socio-political factors outside the user's control in respect of the choice of the national language of communication, the choice of mother tongue, particularly in the domestic sphere, is entirely the user's own. Of documented language variants the one predominantly used as both mother tongue and national language in a given society will also be perceived as the most familiar and useful. It will also be the one most users will wish to learn at school and one which may, in any case, be imposed upon them. Ordinary users do not as a rule switch dialects for what may be described as purely linguistic reasons – for example to use a historic or dialect version. Apart from the well attested personal and national loyalties to one's mother tongue, people's attitudes to other official languages and dialects are usually closely linked with their perceived social status and vitality and their resulting usefulness to the users (Giles and Johnson, 1981). The decision to keep or jettison the language is invariably affected by the user's education and social awareness. Indeed, some dialect speakers are reluctant to learn the corresponding standard language of the region, preferring to learn the official language of the country even if, as a foreign language, it is unrelated to their 'mother tongue'. The choice of the foreign language is perceived as providing a more convincing tool for communication and social advancement. For example, in the Irish Republic, many users will prefer, apart from English, to learn a more widely spoken second 'European' language than the officially supported Irish. Switching to another dialect of the same language may even be seen as more of a loss of one's identity, a betrayal of one's linguistic loyalty to the first mother tongue, than taking up what is a foreign language. This is demonstrated by the lack of appeal of the less well codified Vigo standard to speakers of other Galician variants who may prefer to learn and use Castilian instead. Official language approval may prove to be ineffective in such cases.

To be complete, a definition of 'mother tongue' needs to include the fact that some users, having the choice, may employ more than one language on occasion. These are the bilingual speakers who may attain different degrees of linguistic ambidexterity, especially if they have a preference for, or are restricted to, a particular specialist area of discourse. Different areas of linguistic transactions in which the languages are used, and the prestige and importance attached to them, play an important role in motivating people to take up another language. For educated users, in most cases, the mother tongue is the national language. Languages, in a minority situation, which have additional functions, for example when they are used as the language of religion, such as Arabic or Hebrew, are in a stronger, more protected position. There needs to be a climate of ready acceptance to make the choice a genuinely 'free' one. It can also be a case of expedience, such as the availability of users of the language in a particular context.

Some linguistic pluralism exists in all countries, multilingualism being the most frequent companion of multinationalism. Because dialect speakers are designated as bilingual (or bidialectic) if they also use the national or standard language, pluralism is an almost universal phenomenon. The 'free' choice of a preferred alternative 'mother tongue' for all transactions is at least partly determined by language policies and accessibility. It is less frequent and depends upon the strength of the language and the protection afforded to it. It is the classical case of mother tongue having to be identified with the national language, a process assisted by schooling, and one which may result in language conflict.

Chapter 2

Mother Tongue and Identity

LANGUAGE AS MARKER

It is generally assumed that all users of a particular mother tongue can be identified by the language they use inasmuch as that language distinguishes them from users of other mother tongues, other dialects, foreign languages, indeed other home languages. In a very real sense, however, each mother tongue user is also different from all the other users of the 'same' mother tongue. This is so because, except under the constraint to conform on a public or official occasion, such as making a speech or writing a dissertation, and sometimes not even then, their language used freely is never 100 per cent identical with that of any of the other users of the 'same' language, if variations of accent, pitch, intonation, the use of favourite words and expressions, metaphors and turns of phrase, let alone grammatical 'inaccuracies' and syntactical 'oddities' are taken into consideration. It is possible to identify the authorship of a text on the evidence of word frequency and word order. The language taken as a marker of identity at the level of the individual user, however, his or her ideolect, is not 'the words or structures of the language as such but the skills with which they are used which vary from society to society and from individual to individual' (Waldron, 1985).

If what has been said about the individual user's language is applied to that of the ethnic group or entire nation, the language marker becomes even less firm. Although national languages differ from dialects in a number of ways it is difficult to make an appeal to them to draw explicit ethnic boundaries that would hold in every case, unless once more we reduce the definition to refer to the prescriptive languages and their rules. This view is not incompatible with Habermas' (1974) thesis that humans are different 'by virtue of the different impact of their language on their development' and distinguished by the language they use.

An additional qualification is that the language of a user which 'emerges' on contact with that of another user will be subject to further variation. As the instrument of all human communication and processes which then lead to action, a language need not be identical in every respect in order to enable such interaction, albeit in the process of communication languages are 'adapted' to some degree to improve comprehension. Access to language is universal but the type and quantity of language which is acquired and available at the user's disposal varies. Thus, all language users have acquired a much larger vocabulary than that relatively small selection of their total lexicon that they generally employ; all have both an active and a passive vocabulary.

Even so, language as the visible and audible mark of ethnic identity through which the wider community of users of the 'same' language emerges as a group distinguished by its language is easy to accept. Though a distinction must be made between an individual identity and the collective identity of a group or community, language has been seen as one of the features which is jealously guarded as a distinguishing marker of identity.

In the following sections the terms 'instrumental' language, in the sense of the language actually used in the processes of communication, and 'symbolic' language in the sense of a 'hidden language' which is not used as such but which affects the users' instrumental language because of their linguistic and non-linguistic experiences, will be introduced. We would add that Halliday (1973) has a narrower use of the word 'instrumental'.

The increasingly more frequent questioning of the view of language as the sole marker of identity, particularly in respect of ethnic and national identity (Almond and Verba, 1963) has led to the emergence of other markers, such as cultural and religious differences, which can also serve individuals as well as groups wishing to distance themselves from others. Durkheim's phrase: 'the totem is the flag of the clan', clearly identifies religion as a marker of identity, and Fishman's (1977) view of language as the 'quintessential symbol of ethnicity' refers to it as more than a mere instrument of communication. Paradoxically, it is language in an instrumental, communicative sense that is used to signal the distinction.

In his historical discussion of the concept, Smith (1991) sees nationalism as not appearing until after the break up of an imperial period, when large heterogenous units split up into smaller, homogenous 'national' units characterized by a number of common features, language being one, which separate them from each other. The separatist, militant type of nationalism was less in evidence where there was less opportunity to demonstrate differences because they were already included within a common political and social setup. Groups of different language users existed side by side without emphasizing their separate identities, even though they may have been distinguished by markers such as religion and, indeed, their language. The earliest politically independent nation states of Europe, France and England among them, assumed a political identity in a context in which more than one language was spoken. On the other hand, in societies where attempts by ethnic units to proclaim their difference in order to free themselves from a global dominance took longer to realize, with periods of struggle for independence lasting into recent history, languages often played a prominent part as the marker of the separate identity of their users.

In Britain, the English language was only one of several factors leading to a unifying dominance; institutionalized religion and monarchy, as well as geography, playing an important part. Though religion was also a factor elsewhere, in the case of the already English-speaking Irish and Scots, language was emphasized somewhat less strongly than it was in the politically more heterogenous conditions of central, eastern and southern Europe where to this day a separate language is prominently identified with nationhood (Barbour, 1994).

By locating national identity within a cultural and political identity supported by the possession of power which makes it possible for the society to define itself in terms of nationhood, Smith suggests two models: the *rational* (Western) characterized by the territorial and political civic components of the constructs of state; and the *mythical* (Eastern) which relies on a remembered genealogical and ethnic model of descent. In his examination of class, religion, culture, territory and of a civic legal system, as well as ethnicity, as elements of national distinctiveness, he emphasizes the possession of common values passed down in historical memories as the principal hallmark of identity. Among these language finds relatively little mention.

That, among the agreed historical elements of identity, language may be one of the weaker markers is demonstrated by such claims as Steiner's (1975) who, in *After Babel*, declares himself 'perfectly trilingual'. If this is so, can all his languages be his mother tongues? Which language determines his identity? Or does he in fact possess three? The view that rather than language it is the historical, ancestral links, values and customs which determine ethnic identity is gaining acceptance, so that writers like Eastman (1984) argue for the permanence of ethnic identity as opposed to evanescent language. This is despite the fact that religion is expressed through instrumental language – an argument in favour of linking language and identity since religious identity usually includes more than one ethnic group.

Identity changes with the change of shared cultural patterns. These are made up of a combination of factors of which religion is particularly important, and which has been more frequently quoted than the large variety of civic cultural characteristics and customs, all of which aspire to the status of 'national'. What is referred to as 'high culture' in Williams' (1981) definition has always been more readily accepted as a marker of identity than mere custom. All these, including language, can change. Language or dialect is an instrument of communication which can be adapted easily and readily, as demonstrated by bilingual speakers or those learning to master another language in order to switch codes; even so it has to be recognized as more than just an instrument of communication to qualify as an enduring and exclusive marker of identity.

The two-sided reason for this can be summed up in that there are hardly any national states where the national language is the only one used and that, on most occasions, humans use a language which is peculiar to themselves. This somewhat static view of language as a characteristic of ethnic identity has been challenged by Ross's (1979) more dynamic view which distinguishes between language as something derived from ethnicity and language as a marker of distinction which, to be accepted, has to be negotiated or fought for by communities or minority groups. Thus the individual, or collection of individuals, existing outside another larger and stronger group may seek to retain a separate linguistic identity in order to mix, or not to assimilate with it. To what extent this is done will depend not just on the wish of the outside individual or group alone but also upon the attitude of the larger group as to whether or not to accept them. All moves towards assimilation have to be seen in terms of reciprocity. Ross's thesis can be seen to have similarities with Mead's argument that 'identity is *learnt* through language identity' (Mead 1973).

The concept of mother tongue and identity may also be explored in a different way: the loss of language alone cannot entail total loss of identity. Non-linguistic distinguishing and compensating factors, such as customs and religion, whose role in communication goes beyond the mere instrumental one of human interaction, survive as stable identification criteria long after the loss of language, proved by the surviving identity of persecuted religious communities, and replicated on the individual level by the example of the Irishman proclaiming his Irishness with or without the ability to speak Irish Gaelic.

What, then, are the markers that distinguish an Irish person from an English one, and why do some ethnic groups fight harder to retain their distinctive identities than others? When does an Irishman cease to be Irish and become identified as Irish-American? Indeed, when does he become American? This dynamic encourages us always to go beyond the conventional meaning of 'symbolic' as 'token-sign' to the fully representational, typifying use of the term. This is not just 'an interest in roots which could . . . persist for generations' (Gans, 1979) but the genuine manifestation of one's roots as identity out of reach of the changing realities of ethnic mobility and 'the painless acceptance of another language' (Gellner, 1964).

SYMBOLIC LANGUAGE

The national and individual distinguishing characteristics other than language, some of which have already been identified, do not exist in isolation, but combine to produce a compound effect of identity which may also be called 'language'. 'Language lifts out of the social process a situation which is logically or implicitly there' (Mead, 1973). We take it that this language is 'important as a symbol of an underlying image of group purpose' (Connor, 1978), that is for self definition. Symbolic language can be defined as a private language which is not used for the purpose of interactive communication, but which, because of its composition, can endow an individual or group with a distinctiveness of their own which is particularly difficult to lose. The term 'associated language' was used by Eastman and Reese (1981) to designate the non-instrumental language, identified by what is left after the instrumental language has been lost, that gives rise to a symbolic (only partially linguistic) identity to all those members of a language community who no longer use their original language for their transactions and interactions with others. Its linguistic relics may amount to a few phrases of the old language or a distinctive style of using the new language which marks the speakers off as being different and is their instrumental language. This 'language', together with the other markers of identity, has to be interpreted by non-users of it in a way similar to the language which would be necessary to deal with users of a foreign language; except that in the former case the language of communication is believed to be the 'same' or nearly the same as their own. It is like comparing the conversation of an Irishman with an Englishman in English rather than with a German who would be using German. Though there is no doubt that communication between two ethnic groups using the 'same' language can become more fluent than if they use different languages, problems can arise if the two dialects differ significantly from each other. Misunderstandings can be the result of different emphases or of different words and structures being used by different speakers and becomes especially serious if the conversation includes a discussion of values and cultural shibboleths. This is also the case when misunderstandings arise because of different conventions involving gesture or body language. Ralph Schneller's research reported orally in 1993 showed how, after the airlift of the Ethiopian Jewish community to Israel, much misunderstanding occurred because, although their Hebrew was impeccable, their body language was essentially African, frequently resulting in their bodies 'saying' something that was at odds with their spoken discourse.

Our definition of 'symbolic language' goes further. We are guided here by the duality through which all language processing may be viewed; for example, 'the meaning of a sentence is more than what is acquired by studying the surface structure of the sentence' (Carroll, 1986). Language goes beyond our total conscious inspection. We attempt to penetrate through the words to the structure of ideas. This is the effect of the impact of that language which is responsible for the development of a human being, the language that ultimately elucidates, defines, and affects one's *persona* which can be idiosyncratic, an ideolect in fact. It needs to be placed alongside the external phenomena of dialect or accent in language which, while separating individuals and groups using the same language from non-users of that language, are no more than different instruments used for communication. To put it another way: the paralinguistic features which survive the imposition of another language as the medium of communication have to be detached and identified as markers of a distinct personality and identity. It is they that remain as the enduring marker while the instrumental language which serves as the medium of communication has changed.

In this sense it is possible to be bilingual, or multilingual, although, depending on the strengths of the permanent marker and the communication medium, it may be more appropriate to speak of a 'second' or even a 'preferred' language used in addition to the first or mother tongue. Each can create an identity, but only the latter provides the accepted main definition of an ethnic or national identity. This happens irrespective of whether a separate language exists; however, where such a language can be identified it reinforces the instrumental language of communication (the ethnic or national dialect) and adds a further dimension to the symbolic identity. The 'symbolic' language is thus the silent mother tongue, the language which is 'part of us', not an 'exterior' collection of words and structures to be used. The greater the extent of the loss of the first language, the mother tongue, the more of a 'symbolic' role is assumed by the second language, which is peculiar to its natural user and which becomes a more enduring marker of national identity. To return to the Irish example, it would be his Irish version of English used by an Irish speaker. In mainland Europe there are many examples of this phenomenon in the border areas of Germany, Poland and Belgium as well as many other countries, where the way some users handle their instrumental language 'gives them away' as belonging to one side of the border rather than to the other.

Language is important even when it is no longer an instrument of communication, since 'man cannot converse with others that belong to that community without taking on its peculiar attitudes' (Mead, 1973). The dialogue called by Mead that of being 'with one's self' is one which determines ethnic identity and consciousness of one's self.

Language skills are related to the instrumental use of language while ethnic behaviour is more the result of the values and cultural beliefs held. Without insisting on this point, we suggest that the former may be used as a convention; the latter determines identity in a more significant way. Human behaviour is determined by language, but it is 'symbolic' language that is involved. This can be felt particularly convincingly when using a language other than one's own which goes on to assume a role more significant than that of the simple language instrument used. Because the vocal and the gesture signals and the different behaviours and attitudes manifested are linked, the new medium is rich with symbolic remnants of the old which are more than the 'visible' matter left behind by the 'associated' language consisting of distinctive styles and patterns of speech or accents. The cultural and religious features add to this creation of a complex and distinct 'linguistic' identity. While economic conditions may impose the use of English on foreigners, for example, when they are communicating with others, many of the 'old' values and beliefs remaining as characteristics of their identity, precisely those which prevent them from becoming English, show up in their use of English. The old language remains as the symbol; the new language, affected by extra sets of values which are the values of the original users of that language, becomes the medium of communication. The language behaviour of Bradbury's 'communists' provides material for thought.

Identity thus becomes more subjective and dynamic than something derived from the assumed passive possession of a language alone. Those who use it can *dictate* the way the language is handled, as the Irish may do with their English. Earlier views of group identity were much more likely to name language as the only distinguishing marker. Condillac's assertion made in 1746 that 'no nation can have a binding link which expresses its distinctiveness unless there is a language which has prepared for it' (Condillac, 1970) is typical of the eighteenth-century view in which language was identified with the static subjects of national identity rather than with the activity of language users. The view persists because language is not only the distinguishing mark of ancestral ethnic links but also the vehicle for communicating and recording them.

Direct support for the instrumental language becoming recognized as the vehicle of identity is provided by such factors as the fact that there are fewer religions than languages, with many more countries sharing the same religion than share a common language. However, like languages, religions, too, adapt to national cultures as seen in the case of Celtic Christianity or English Buddhism. This extends their use as a criterion of ethnic diversity and increases their contribution to the symbolic language, which in every case, whether the language as an instrument of communication has or has not been lost, is the identity marker, a 'passion which drives man on', to paraphrase the words of philosopher David Hume in his *Natural History of Religion*.

LANGUAGE AND OTHER MARKERS

There are therefore national characteristics expressed in a distinctive linguistic sub-stratum which may affect practically the entire nation, seen as a collection of active, creative users of a mother tongue, or preferred language, which serves to distance them from others. There are also features which are shared by some members of the nation only. For example, the Welsh-speaking Welsh are distinguished from the English-speaking Welsh, the two taken together representing the entire Welsh nation as distinct from the English. The distinction can be made despite the fact that both Welsh groups retain some Celtic features: the cultural, religious and linguistic symbolic quality in their speech, which in the two cases blend in a different degree with the English features. This can also be seen in the Lowland Scots variant of English, Lallans, which lays claim to being a full-grown separate language because of the existence of the symbolic elements.

'Home' languages are not usually regarded as equally strong markers of national identity because they are spatially and temporarily more restricted and more likely to be replaced in communication by the speech of other national language users than are the more established dialects. They can, however, characterize individuals. Home language features are particularly well placed to reveal the creative and symbolic contribution made by language users with no formal education, whose language is a vehicle of self-identification going beyond communication. This is exemplified by the distinctive features of dialects which can be allegedly described as dynamic or colourful; and are more easily detected in a smaller language group. This love of language is shared and advanced more consciously by 'educated' individual language users who, unlike the spontaneous actions of the 'home language' group, often use more deliberate, 'second-hand' devices to achieve the effect of moulding their language so as to enable it to become a defining and distinguishing phenomenon. When extended to the entire community or nation, local authorities, given the power, can play a part in language planning, asserting the home language, dialect or national standard language as the marker which becomes a national symbol.

The 'spirit of language' suggested by nineteenth-century philosophers, which transcends communication, retranslated into the language activity of its users, becomes the collective link of identity which can ensure survival of identity, particularly for the new, or resurfacing nations. This is the element which characterizes the 'continuity' of Irish English or Welsh English and distinguishes their 'Englishes' from English English or British English. Language symbolism, or symbolic language, the use of it in an interaction which is creative, is not easily organized and channelled to purposes which are extrinsic, such as serving purely as an instrument of communication.

Symbolic language is the language outside the regulatory bonds of efficient communication. The latter may in fact degenerate into a 'language ritual', stereotyped signals sent out and responded to in conformity (Habermas, 1974), unlike the symbolic language which is the emancipatory medium of its users. Mead (1973) put forward the concept of 'symbolic interaction' in which the individual's language plays a role as the social medium of interpreting oneself. It may not have to be expressed vocally as other symbols, gestures and paralinguistic practices can also achieve this. It can be described as a manifestation of human existence expressed in media other than speech, and is the symbolic aspect of language serving to demonstrate identity, individual and group, for the everyday expression of which instrumental language will be used (Kron, 1996). Together they make up the creative use of language.

In making language a symbol, its users demonstrate the role of language as going beyond that of an instrument, discovering in it a uniting factor for identity which often may not be used for instrumental communication at all. This can be seen most clearly in the individual use of language. The creative aspect of language as the distinguishing mark of a person which can be placed alongside other manifestations of identity is particularly true of the concept of the symbolic function of language. Writers who use language creatively do so by virtue of relying on the 'hidden' resources of language, including the 'symbolic', which prompts their creation with the linguistic material available. Those who have lost their original language often show amazing linguistic creativity in manipulating their new language medium because they can also draw on the remaining resources of their old one.

SOME USERS AND THEIR LANGUAGE

The vernacular is the object of interest and care of politicians and government as well as of pressure groups. Irish Gaelic, despite official and financial support, has not been able to achieve the desired comeback. Other languages, such as Hebrew, have been more successful. A language used in religious ritual has a greater chance of survival, though in a frozen form (Joos 1967), than one that is not so used. This situation is familiar to those who may be said to have more than one mother tongue or at least to have a preferred language in addition to the mother tongue. Their preference may result in one of them being weaker, not regarded as a language, a state of bidialectism bordering on diglossia. By accepting their language the work of creative writers may contribute to language restoration.

Jewish (Yiddish and Hebrew) symbolism surfaces in the artistic creations made in Yiddish, for example, in the form of humour whose characteristic ingredient is the presence of two elements fighting for expression: the self-deprecatory humour that pokes fun at those Jews who ape the Gentiles yet know in their hearts of hearts that they are equal and perhaps surpass them. The silenced vying with the articulate results in the use of speech patterns containing the two elements, relying on word play, parody and irony for a powerful effect (Ziv and Zajdman, 1993). In the Celtic communities, too, political and linguistic movements have been linked with creativity in the production of literature going back at least to the time of W. B. Yeats and 'the Celtic twilight'. In some cases this has been associated with a kind of sentimental nostalgia attaching to the language, but in many other cases, especially with Anglo-Irish, Anglo-Scottish and Anglo-Welsh writers, it is an attempt to stretch the 'foreign' language, that is English, to its limits, as can be seen with varying degrees of success in the work of Macdiarmaid, James Joyce and Dylan Thomas among many others.

This may happen in the case of language loss. It is then as if the writing is done in a foreign tongue. Even if, like Thomas, the writer is not a Welsh speaker, he is forced to find new modes of expression to explore a different culture and, through this, the target language is itself transformed. It is difficult to imagine, for example, Joyce's Dublin being described in anything other than the variety of Anglo-Irish that he consciously created in *Ulysses*. The same would be true of the Edinburgh writer, Tom Scott, in his use of Lallans for his long epic poem, *Tales of Robert the Bruce*. This can perhaps be best of all seen in the work of the Irish writer, Beckett, who wrote much of the time in French and translated his own work into English and who is, arguably, one of the greatest literary-linguistic innovators of the century.

The linguistic prowess of authors writing in a 'new' language, such as the English Pole Joseph Conrad, the Jew and Pole Julian Tuwim, the already mentioned Anglo-Welsh Dylan Thomas and the fact that five of the winners of the Nobel Prize for Literature written in English were Irish shows the grasp of language available to those who wish to make it their medium of artistic expression. Their language is nourished by the symbolic quality of their original mother tongue which permeates the new language, endowing it with new linguistic creativity in a process where the user is aware of the two media so as to produce a varied richness which may on occasion degenerate into an over-profusion.

An example of compensatory language as a creative medium is the dynamic and highly articulate use of Yiddish language segments, but incorporating Hebrew elements, originally generated by diaspora Jews which have meanwhile been adopted by generations of other language users, perhaps especially so those of American English, exposed to a language contact. Their language can be used not simply to communicate information in the neutral fashion of an instrument but as a symbol which goes on to define its particular identity in a distinctive economical, word-saving, way. Jewish jokes use the narrative technique of the parable story known from the Bible and the Torah. In these the end of the story takes the reader back to the beginning often retold with a cumulative 'back to front' effect to draw home the point. The word 'Torah' in fact means 'teaching' and 'instruction'. Listeners to the important but highly amusing religious messages of Rabbi Lionel Blue on BBC Radio Four may be familiar with the humorous effect technique.

The ability to be at home in two media at once allows for a great degree of language flexibility: for example, Herzl called Palestine *Altneuland*, a term which requires no further commentary to put the message across. The headline of an article in the Guardian of 23 April 1996 BAFTA SCHMAFTA, reporting on films awarded distinction by the British Film Academy is a good illustration. Rhyming with the unknown and untranslated second word encapsulates much of the comment made about the particular BAFTA ceremony. The use of the phoneme (*sh*) in combination has an effect familiar to users of Yiddish as well as to Jews and those who have experienced their culture. If we consider that *shmo* means a 'fool' and *shmok* equates to 'penis' in Yiddish and Hebrew then it is possible to savour the dismissive implications of neologisms, such as used in the article to criticize the awards. The article 'teaches', although the interpretation may also take in *shmuosn*, which refers to the ritual of 'consolation of the bereaved by talking'.

The references in the above text to 'quantifying the unquantifiable', 'objectify the subjective', and to 'live happily with the crass and arbitrary assessment systems that have been imposed . . .' [by the verdicts] show the masterful command of this language polarization to make the criticism announced by the headline to anyone willing to look at a strange new word.

Word and sound play is not, of course, confined to Yiddish. The English text itself shows a creative use of the English medium. Alliteration and vowel harmony can also be used to achieve an effect illustrating a new language direction from the customary one taken by the writer on the base of the common Language Acquisition Device with an application of Language Awareness, both topics dealt with in more detail in the 'Teaching the Mother Tongue' chapter. The multicultural argument is made by showing how creators of language with a deep-rooted ethnic sense can express their identity through their own dexterity in using a major ('non ethnic'!) language for their purpose. In order not to run the risk of over-interpreting no further comments will be made about this occasion.

CONCLUSION

Modern nation states are distinguished by the possession of a national language, usually the mother-tongue language of the largest and dominant ethnic group, which in its codified standard form is the language of schooling. The symbolic language is not usually part of the normal language instruction but may be referred to in the teaching of various other parts of the national heritage, its art or its history. Since it can affect individual users' language when introducing expressions and turns of phrase, it may, subjected to fresh influences, contribute to language change.

There are a large variety of attributes associated with national identity. Polish nationalism is often ethno-religious, the Catholic image of redemption and suffering being an important marker in addition to the language. It is here that the peculiar terms of language and symbolism which are especially characteristic for Polish nationalism can be seen. The language abounds in expressions characteristic of this suffering stance which can also constitute an element of the structure of its literature, especially that of the Romantic period. The combined effect of several supporting factors, as in the case of Catholicism and language in Poland and Lithuania, in the latter nation with a strong admixture of pagan elements, or the political loyalty to Catholicism and republicanism in Ireland may also be taken as an illustration of symbolic language waiting to be expressed as identity. The Swiss are not German because their beginnings and commonality are rooted in a revolt against feudal practice which involved their separation from the larger German whole (Watts, 1991), Swiss German reinforcing the republican freedom concept of the Swiss.

Religious reformers, and particularly those linked with translations of Holy Scriptures, have contributed to strengthening the link between language and belief and values. The new religious language was more easily identified with the popular language, the language as instrument of everyday communication, which because of the Church–State connection helped to make language the marker of nationalism, shown in the proudly displayed translations of holy texts as an integral part of a country's literary identity. If instrumental language has been more closely identified with national identity then this is because of nation-state policies towards language maintenance and linguistic distinctiveness, as seen in the recent language laws introduced by the administration in Quebec for example, or language purity policies. However, all these actions are 'external' to the symbolic, private language which cannot easily be exterminated and serves as the best marker of identity.

Chapter 3

Mother Tongue Standards

THE EMERGENCE OF THE STANDARD

Among the number of more or less closely related dialects spoken in a given territory as the first language of everyday communication, of which the 'standard' is one, not counting variants of linguistically unrelated regional or immigrant mother tongues which are also used, there are some which become the widely used medium of communication of the majority of language users. These languages achieve a superordinate function in relation to other dialects in the communication processes of the entire territory. Over time, accessibility and ease of communication, made up of comprehension and flexibility of expression, become linked with other attributes, such as prestige, which enable the 'chosen' dialect to emerge as the preferred, in some conditions imposed, language of the nation state. As the language of government and administration, that dialect becomes dominant in the political, educational and commercial transactions of the majority and may be designated as 'standard', often also referred to as 'correct' language, against which the other dialects may be measured. For that usually major national group inhabiting the nation state that dialect is its national language in the fullest sense of the word.

'The standard language is one which is subject to minimal variation of form while being capable of a maximum variation of functions' (Joseph, 1987). To achieve this it has undergone a more rigid process of codification and standardization than other dialects. Most of this is a spontaneous language change in use, with both ordinary users and authorities on language aligned in favour of or rejection of some of the changes. As the language of all official agencies of the nation state and used for its international transactions, it is generally employed in writing and, to a large extent, in speaking by educated users in formal contexts, with others expected to use it at least in writing also. This highly codified and cultivated language, designated the 'official' or national language of the state, may be explicitly referred to as such in written state constitutions It may be the only permitted language of compulsory state education, even if not always used in classrooms, and a core school curriculum subject: often called mother-tongue education. A good knowledge of it, attested in examinations, is a prerequisite for entry to posts in the civil service as well as the more prestigious jobs in business and commerce. To a lesser extent the national language is also acknowledged as the dominant cultural medium in the territory, a position which lends it and its speakers an additional currency. Policy on the maintenance of the 'purity' of the standard language and whose responsibility this is varies in different countries. However, both the spoken and written and the 'private' and the 'official' dialects and idioms can grow further apart as a result.

The other languages used in the territory, as is the case with Welsh in the British Isles, may undergo a similar process, especially if the language has become the language of education, as in bilingual Wales, although the rules may be interpreted in a more relaxed way and the use of dialects tolerated more widely. The problems associated with this have been recorded in the case of less rigidly enforced languages such as Belorussian. However, School Danish in Germany, conforms to the 'standard' used in the Kingdom of Denmark, even if the spoken dialect does not.

Time, geography, economics and politics are the factors responsible for changing what is referred to as a dialect into a language. That the process of change is measured in several decades rather than years is clear, what with the distribution of competing dialects and their prestige together with the socio-psychological forces underlying all inter-ethnic relations in which language is involved (Ross, 1979; Giles and Johnson, 1981). In the case of an absence of a mechanism responsible for propelling the process forward due to a weak economy or a weak government, or the absence of national independence not all languages will develop an agreed dominant standard in the same period of time, as seen in the late national language arrivals of south-eastern Europe.

The so-called standard English was identified with a small number of users. The majority were not expected to master it until relatively recently when increasing governmental concern with economic failure was attributed to their inability to handle the standard form. This went some way to reduce the class differences of users. In most activities involving language after the Bolshevik Revolution and the setting up of the German Democratic Republic, uniform variants of Russian and German respectively were expected to be used for the same reasons. Dialects remained the object of folklore. Indeed, post-revolutionary societies in a number of countries, such as France, have decreed one dialect as the national medium of communication.

The dialect accepted as a standard language will have undergone a process of refinement. The model of language standardization set up by Haugen (1972) demonstrates the processes of selection, codification and elaboration of the emerging dialect before it is recognized as a standard and used for the appropriate functions. This cannot be a prescriptive, deliberate inter-ference, since the emergence of a standard is usually due to its widespread acceptance by users in all sectors: socio-political, economic, cultural, civic, although education and language planning policies may intervene in this process, as is the case with the English standard. The language model established by individual leaders, spiritual and temporal, can play a decisive role in language acceptance. This may result in a dialect becoming the standard language of a particular diocese in secular business as well as in the church, a good example of it being the diocese of Trier, whose German dialect differs in small but significant respects from that used in the neighbouring territories. The secular and religious spheres combine particularly effec-tively in the earliest stages of language development, the court and church reinforcing each other. Translations of sacred texts make an important contribution which may result in 'freez-ing' language change, as seen in the fate of Bible translations, with Protestant Welsh faring better than Catholic Gaelic (Durkacz, 1983).

The accepted standard national language remains the dialect understood by the widest number of users and tends to place the other dialects at the peripheries of communication. Some of these may proceed to assume an independent existence as locally preferred or official languages in their territories if sufficient cultural and political autonomy, as in the case of Scottish English or Luxembourgeois, allow it. Media use is divided between the local and the national variety. The variants of Italian, current 'national' Italian being one of them, have enjoyed a long period of prestigious independent existence because, in the absence of a unifying cultural and political centre, they have assumed a role close to what would eventually be a territorial national language, now seen to some extent in the re-emergence of the political north-south divide as a result of economic differences. The continuing process of codification and elaboration by authority, as in France, or by influential individuals, the most prominent of such being Dr Johnson in England, ensures easier universal comprehension. Meanwhile its rival non-standards, though more frequent and less well documented, also change, freer to create variety and achieve vitality. The language of education, for linguistic as well as socio-political reasons, has a designated role to play in this process which discourages diversity, resulting in the home languages and dialects being regarded as 'incorrect', banished to a role in spontaneous or intimate discourse.

THE ACCEPTANCE OF THE STANDARD

The acceptance of the standard depends on its status within a territory, such as newly installed Galician in the Autonomous Spanish Community of Galicia. The degree of recognition and interpretation of conditions for acceptance, such as those recently being made by the French *Académie* or the Spelling Reform Commission in Germany, may also have to await finding favour with users. The combined effect is what has been identified as 'power of language' (Fairclough, 1989). Except in countries which have an 'academy' the standard forms 'grow into the national language rather than being decreed as the standard' as they become increasingly used as the medium of communication and artistic creation. The moves where they do occur may be 'official' or 'educational' in character: the Qualifications and Curriculum Authority (QCA) in England can lay down school syllabuses, the French *Académie* has a wider socio-political brief and influence. A weak authority at the political centre enables dialects and home languages paradoxically, at the same time, to assume a *bigger* (for example in artistic production) and a more *limited* (confined to intimate or artistic discourse) role in communication which affects the acceptance of the remaining, non-standard dialects. The currency of all languages is enhanced and their status confirmed if they fulfil their expected roles: their clarity and precision in official speech or flexibility and inventiveness in the personal and cultural domains. This intention is often forgotten when official texts are published in obscure language so that their meaning is not immediately apparent. In the case of English in particular, this has led to the Campaign for Plain English in England and the powerful wʳ on Doublespeak conducted in North America by the National Councils for the Teachinɡ English in both America and Canada. Such movements started a very long time ago. We r note the work of Herbert (1935), a prominent reforming independent Member of Parlⁱ and Gowers (1973), a senior civil servant who urged his colleagues to write in wʳ easily understood by the public at large. Language education is divided on this: clⱥ contend with inventiveness. In practice these processes cannot be kept entirely ser outcry over the imposition of Standard English in many circles of England ⸮ demonstrated.

Factors that contribute to the establishment and recognition of an aut′
impose rules concerning the form and position of the standard natiᴄ

appeared in many societies, usually as sanctions for 'incorrect' use in education. But they have also combined with economic and technical factors used to monitor and control language, such as access to media and the raising of such questions as to whether French should dispense with its diacritic signs. In Britain the moves for spelling reform have been private initiatives, such as George Bernard Shaw's one-man campaign, and movements which became linked with commercial interests, as in the case of Pitman's campaign for simplified spelling on a phonetic basis, following the undoubted success of his invention of a system of shorthand based entirely on phonetic principles. These campaigns have failed to gain official acceptance. They would, if adopted, however, totally obscure the history of the language which is encapsulated in the spelling system. In Britain these considerations were regarded as less important than the almost contemporaneous simplification of Russian spelling decreed after the Bolshevik Revolution. This, too, was to some extent dictated by the 'genius of the language': since Russian was already far more phonetically based than English, the change inflicted by adopting spelling reform was far less than it would have been in the case of a language where spelling was based not so much upon phonetics as upon etymology.

The acceptance of a variant as standard is not a question of language adequacy although such abstract considerations may be present and help to secure, under the right socio-political and economic conditions, the maintenance of a selected dialect. In the majority of cases it is the influence of a class of important users, such as London merchants or influential writers in Poland, which may, as in France, be reinforced by the authority of an academy. Ordinary users may help or hinder the process of the supremacy and 'correctness' by their attitude to the dominant dialect by dint of using or rejecting it, since there is no such absolute as a 'correct' language. However, the transfer of ideas and discoveries made in one language area to another territory may require the language used to adapt its vocabulary and grammar to accommodate the new arrivals into the process of communication. Suitability and appropriateness in particular contexts and transactions are legitimate conventions, although this practice may discriminate against those dialect users whose dialect is the least favoured or distant, in socio-political or cultural terms, from the standard. The social prestige of some variants of English and the labelling of some languages as 'primitive' because they have a different way of counting or indicating plurality, such as some African languages, are part of the same attitude.

The Galician speakers' strong attachment to their own home dialects is an important reason for the slow progress made with the codifying process, enabling the Vigo dialect to emerge as the regional 'national' language of the Autonomous Community. Political and economic transactions are likely to be more influential than *belles lettres* although mutual reinforcement and the role of influential writers and other media cannot be discounted, for example in the case of Swiss German or Bavarian. Dialects and their speakers frequently become the butt of jokes: French jokes are often located in the dialect areas of Provence, Germans make fun of the Prussians and Bavarians. English dialects on the mainland have, with some exceptions, such as those associated loosely with 'the north', or, more accurately, with Yorkshire, Liverpool or Newcastle, lost their 'independent' existence, unlike the Scottish and Welsh ones, but are still often used in exaggerated forms for the purposes of comedy.

The adjectives used to identify the standard language reflect the priorities in each country towards the national language: national (in France the link with the nation), general (in Poland to mark its acceptability throughout the country), high (in Germany to refer to a dialect), standard (in England to connote distinction status), as well as common which is used to describe s size, the extent of its linguistic dimension compared with other dialects, as well as official many countries to emphasize its use by governmental agencies).

Although it is widely accepted that the standard is appropriate and suitable in formal and official transactions and that its command will enable the user to advance socially and professionally, referring to the standard as the 'correct' dialect or language is mostly confined to educational circles in which particular language agendas operate, and by those who do not wish to confuse 'correctness' with 'acceptability'. However, general acceptance does discriminate against those sections of dialect speakers whose dialect is considered sub-standard or less than 'correct', though the linguistic basis for such decisions is very dubious. The notion of 'sub-standard' generally has more to do with fashion and social prejudice than any rational grounds and varies as between nations, for example, French is particularly attached to quality practice (*bon usage*). In England more than elsewhere the standard is regarded as the language of those aspiring to jobs in which they can influence others, while in Poland the national language has been closely identified with national independence. Users are attached to their native languages, but the way in which they express their feelings has much to do with the status of the language throughout its history.

English 'standard', a term documented only in 1836 for the 'correct and accepted' version of English (in the *Oxford English Dictionary*), goes back much earlier to a local Midlands dialect which has triumphed by virtue of its supremacy in the political and economic conditions and its location in and around the capital city of a centralized state. Thanks to a combination of further political developments, it has spread beyond the British Isles, to assume in turn new forms as independent national languages, with additions from other dialects and a combination of other circumstances as in American English. In the past decade Standard English has become a key concept in the National Curriculum where it has been, through deliberate policies of central government, privileged above all other dialects. Many teachers of English regret this, feeling it stigmatizes the language actually used by their pupils thereby devaluing both it and them (Cox, 1995). Cultivated Parisian French enjoys a similar status in France, a position not matched, because of the federal structure of the country, by a wholesale adoption of the German *Hochdeutsch*, where even in schooling there is a more tolerant attitude to variants. Other countries have their own standard or 'correct' national language policies for use in school and administration.

DEVELOPING THE STANDARD

Language change is an autonomous continuous process, with academies in those countries where they exist only having the authority to monitor the maintenance, practice and change in the standard. The role of the academy is not that of an author of change but of a codifier of change who seizes the initiative in adjudicating in matters of spelling and the admissibility of foreign borrowings, as recently in the case of lexical items and their spelling in France and Germany. Such agencies can be said to define the standard whose maintenance is then continued by reputable authors writing in the language, 'official' authors or the producers in other media, who in the case of absence of an academy may themselves set the model for language, as in Poland, Germany or Russia.

The standard does not stand still for long, however, having to adapt to changed functions. For example, today the wider use of American spelling is being dictated by computer technology just as earlier independent publishing houses adopted their house style which imposed a particular form of spelling on their authors. Luther's Bible proved to be more influential in setting language standards than the Catholic versions published in the south, once the political centre of the (German) Holy Roman Empire had moved east. French as vernacular French may have been used for popular sermons but when French became the language of philosophical and theological discourse it had to transform itself into a more sophisticated medium of expression, using its own components in a different way or borrowing or coining new words and phrases. When the late president of the Ivory Coast, Senghor, described French as the *langue de la culture* this was a value he set upon the French standard to protect it against the encroachment of English as the international language, since the language itself could not be described as any more or less cultured, except in the sense of culture as a power indicator which helps to diffuse a version of someone's mother tongue enabling it to become established as a national medium.

Schooling did not initiate the process of standardization but joined the process by helping to determine the 'correctness' of a language. Long before French became widely taught in schools in the nineteenth century, its use was beginning to be encouraged for political ends through a process of codification and elaboration as early as 1539 (Lodge, 1994), which led to the establishment of the *Académie Française* in 1635 to make the language into a vehicle of 'advanced communication'. English did not begin to be codified until the seventeenth century, the process, some would say, not untypically helped by influential individuals. Dr Johnson reported on events such as the rise of the London business class and its impact on the emergence of an English language. Of particular significance here was the foundation of the Royal Society in 1660, which placed an explicit importance upon the development of plain and clear English for scientific discourse and changed the language from the more baroque Elizabethan and Jacobean prose that had preceded it (Sprat, 1667). If the seat of political power encourages the maintenance of the dialect spoken there, decentralized states like Italy and German show greater tolerance to dialectal diversity.

This is most likely to happen when language status is conceded to the dialect of an entire territory in receipt of a degree of political autonomy. The process itself may prove difficult if, as in the Galician case, the new standard is almost identical with the national language of another country. A merger with Portuguese could involve the loss of a political frontier. The clash with individual users' dialect preferences, as it involves learning another dialect, is a prospect which may be no less daunting than learning a foreign language because of the confusion of similarities. The existence of the Republic of Ireland serves to protect a written standard of Irish Gaelic, a dialect resented by mother-tongue speakers, but which happens to be the co-official language of the country with English (Edwards, 1977; Breatnach, 1964).

A comparison with Luxembourg is interesting since, in this case, the majority of users rally behind the Luxembourgeois dialect. Any objective analysis would, of course, be much coloured by the personal preferences of the analyst, although there are some objective facts which enable comparison such as different historical development. In the case of the Grand Duchy, with its political independence, the proximity of France and the authority of its language have made themselves felt; the absence of German political control, except for periods of occupation which were very much resented, prevented *Hochdeutsch* from becoming the official language as opposed to the dialect which is the co-official medium. A dialect related to other varieties of language and which is a mother tongue may be repartitioned among several states but remains in the territory, unless dispersed as in the case of Polish dialects of the former Polish East or the Central Eastern German dialects after World War Two.

There are several criteria used for distinguishing between language and dialect, with the outcomes not necessarily identical, a problem recognized by many. It is possible to use linguistic criteria, which involve tracing the development of the parent language and its break up into a number of varieties. Socio-political together with cultural and economic criteria accept the existing differences but may exaggerate them to make a 'variety' look like a separate construct. Personal preferences play a role but tend to be swept aside especially by socio-political considerations which apply the strategy of language is power. The examples of Galician or Kashubian or Luxembourgeois can be replicated in many other countries.

Dialects of an established written language, such as East Anglian or Cockney, differ from standard in many aspects: lexis (as the most 'open' system offering the widest variety), morphology, phonology and indeed syntax. When it comes to writing it down, a dialect allows for greater freedom, enabling a variety of forms not accepted by the standard. Dialects can in certain conditions be regarded as distinctive national languages, their status in the community being an important consideration. Thus the Lowland Scots dialect (Lallans), spoken by some 40 per cent of Scotsmen, is almost on the point of being accepted as a 'national' language, along with the many other varieties of English such as Caribbean which create a standard within their own territory. As such, Lallans is not just the vehicle of general everyday communication but also, within limits, the language of instruction and administration, and that includes using its written form.

Chapter 4

Teaching the Mother Tongue

LANGUAGE IN SCHOOLING: A SOCIO-HISTORICAL OVERVIEW

With schooling in the hands of the Church or established on the ruler's personal initiative, Latin (in the West) or Greek (in the East) were the languages of instruction at all but the most elementary levels, both foreign languages for most learners. The use of Latin, Greek or Church Slavonic in religious services gave the non-academic learners who would follow the liturgy an acquaintance with the languages; the better educated they were, the greater their knowledge of the languages could become.

Putting the mother tongue as national language on to the school curriculum became a reality when the governments of nation states assumed responsibility for schooling. Instruction in the mother tongue was determined by the new socio-political and cultural-economic priorities of the rulers, both secular and spiritual, and the school pupils' own status. For the sons and sometimes daughters of the gentry, the future civil and military servants, teaching in the successor states of the Western Roman Empire and their neighbour states had been in Latin, which was also the language of all higher education. However, an ability to 'handle' the mother tongue was expected of those professionals who in the course of their duties had to deal with those who had no Latin. A number of translations of professional manuals into French was made in the early fifteenth century for the purpose of making 'technical' knowledge more widely available. In several other European countries such manuals did not appear until a century or more later. However, Latin texts were read with a Spanish pronunciation at least three centuries earlier.

Rulers saw the need for the mother tongue in schooling to keep lower army ranks, workers and peasants in check, to convert them or to strengthen their religious beliefs, and to enable them to play their part in the work they were required to do. The Church would add the ability to preach in the vernacular, for which rhetoric was also a subject of education, although members of the mendicant orders, like the friars, would use the spoken form of the mother tongue, including dialects, without much formal education. Higher level theological education which was identified with the clerical profession as well as a vocation, as opposed to the lower status of preaching, was until recent times taught exclusively in Latin (Brock & Tulasiewicz, 1988). When the mother tongue became used more widely, after sharing a place with Latin, lawyers also needed an education in the spoken use of the mother tongue. The ability to write in the mother tongue was soon required by those called in to draft documents, to prepare instructions and certificates. Unlike the earlier priorities the more recent emphasis on teaching the national versions of mother tongues was associated with the emancipation of the population, the view of education as an entitlement and as a necessary condition for a prosperous economy. This ensured a firm place in the curriculum for the teaching of the mother tongue, although its introduction to different types of pupils spread over some three centuries. In Prussia under Frederick the Great, future soldiers were instructed in German at elementary level; in Poland, elementary education in Polish was introduced in 1793. In France, under the Jules Ferry laws, French was made compulsory at the elementary and secondary levels but, albeit exclusive and in a less systematic way, it had been taught since before the Revolution.

Over the centuries more nationalistic overtones have crept into some school curricula including mother tongue education in mainland Europe as a means of rallying the young generation against enemies of the mother country. Between the wars German teaching insisted on a version of the language free from foreign elements as a demonstration of 'independence', while many of the patriotic poems in French and Polish course books would have to be learned by heart. In the England of the 1990s, the role of English in the National Curriculum contrasts with the absence of the subject in many independent schools until relatively recently.

There are those who hold that the situation when one language, English rather than Latin, could be shared by large sections of the population throughout most of Europe may be about to return in the supranational bodies of the twentieth century such as the European Union.

CHOOSING THE LANGUAGE AND TEACHING METHOD

Which language?

The national language version of the 'mother tongue', which for most will not be the mother tongue dialect they were born into, is the accepted medium of modern schooling, or it is available, if there are other officially recognized regional languages, as the principal one. Its dialect versions or home languages, widely used in informal and private situations, are handed down in family and community, a function in which custom and religious ceremony can play a significant part (Paulston, 1992; Corson, 1993). In many classrooms children can still be rebuked for using dialect, the policy being enforced more vigorously in some countries than in others; for example in France and Russia more so than in much of Germany. The status of dialects as cult languages which can be formally taught has emerged as a recent phenomenon.

The 'standard language' of formal teaching is the product of a process which is the outcome of accepted usage being supported by a recognized authority, not necessarily the government, and by a regulating agency, where one exists, for the school curriculum. It finds expression in the preparation of school board and ministry of education-approved grammar and spelling textbooks and readers, as in France and Germany, an enterprise in which commercial publishing interests are also involved. This policy is beginning to make itself felt in England and Wales, where study aids written by examiners can be purchased by pupils intending to sit some school leaving examinations.

A dialect may, in some circumstances, become the medium of instruction once it is identified as a national rather than as a local medium of communication, as in the case of Swiss German (*Schwyzerdütsch*) or Luxembourgeois (*Letzeburgesch*), where it is the local dialects and not the *Hochdeutsch* standard which may be accepted in a number of official transactions besides the *Schuldeutsch*. In both countries the local dialect cultivated as the mother tongue enables users to distance themselves from the standard version of German, demonstrating more than their linguistic independence. Pupil motivation can play a useful part by enlisting the usually positive associations with using one's mother tongue dialect to help the learning process. The opportunity to demonstrate their distinctive nationality is denied to the Swiss French, who look to the French of France as their standard for regular school instruction. *Plattdeutsch* functions more as a heritage language. With the existence of 'home languages' in addition to the dialects the choice of the accepted and 'right' mother tongue as a school subject and using it with the appropriate teaching method, is an important mechanism for widening learners' linguistic repertoire.

The learning process

The first or mother tongue is acquired in an informal predominantly oral learning process chiefly through the family, reinforced by what are described as 'grooming gestures' to facilitate mutual comprehension. The language actually transmitted may vary from a version close to, or identical with, the national standard language to a strongly differentiated dialect. It is difficult to discover with any precision whether it is easier to learn the matching standard language version if one is already familiar with the dialect than it is for someone who uses a language that is completely different from that standard to do so, since the 'language transfer and interference' processes work both ways (Johanson, 1993). Vygotsky (1962) suggests that in a first encounter with what in his terminology are 'spontaneous concepts', such as 'brother', the word functions as an introduction to the concept and 'plays the role of the means in forming a concept and later becomes its symbol'. It has in fact been established that, except for the 'basic' language and the simple spontaneous concept formation of Vygotsky's definition acquired very early, all the 'advanced' language and scientific concepts, indeed some spontaneous ones also, have to be learned or unlearned, as the case may be, during the process of formal schooling. Often these are apparently 'easy' lexical items describing family relationships like 'cousin', colours like 'purple', or foods like 'marmalade', met with early on. Even deceptively simple non-spontaneous concepts such as 'fair' or 'just' may require redefinition. This means that though a very early start is made with mother tongue acquisition the process is a continuing one, which in later years confronts the mother tongue user with the need to learn much of the language anew, a component of 'mother tongue' education often neglected in favour of the study of literature.

This has implications for all language study in school. Traditionally, the mother tongue and modern foreign languages used to be taught in two separate classroom contexts even in countries, such as Belgium, with a largely tri- or at least bilingual Flemish, French and German-speaking population before the linguistic separation which placed French or Flemish on a par with what are referred to as school modern foreign languages. This separation takes insufficient account of the chronology of the process of language learning which at a later point of a child's language development, when the more spontaneous early mother tongue acquisition assumes a closer similarity to language learning, becomes a more deliberate activity with users beginning to check their choice of words or grammar. The study of second and of foreign languages is even more affected by this conscious activity since learners' speech and understanding are determined by the level of linguistic mastery already attained in the mother tongue. In the case of the learner of a foreign language, the 'overlap in linguistic rules between two languages and (linguistic) interference' could be brought to help in this task (Sachs, 1976). The interference between the two is a subject of debate (Gass and Selinker, 1991). As an example of a concept which also in the mother tongue is likely to be met as a lexical item *before* being assigned a concept role Vygotsky suggests the term 'exploitation', a concept not easily grasped even by advanced language users. The implication of this is that in the case of new 'advanced' concepts being acquired as lexical items before they are placed in their relevant conceptual contexts in the mother tongue, the process of modern foreign language vocabulary learning, which is the first language activity, is replicated. The processes of learning the mother tongue and a modern foreign language become more similar since concepts appear as 'words' in both instances, though as it is the first language of communication the words are likely to be used more quickly as concepts in the mother tongue. Not only lexical items but morphological and syntactical concepts can be learned just as explicitly. The teaching of 'traditional' grammar in the mother tongue, which included parsing, is a reminder of the ways of studying one's own language as if it were Latin. The point being made here, however, is that it is language 'in use' that may be studied in this way, if that approach helps to inspire confidence leading to improved competence. It is not suggested that grammatical terminology should be presented first, that is before the actual 'text' appears or is used which is then made to fit in a scheme or table.

It has been argued that enlisting the help of dialects or exposing mother tongue learners to some items of a foreign language in school, or conversely using the child's first language to help when teaching a second or a foreign language, apart from developing pattern recognition and lexical skills can lead to an understanding of the various forms of language role and language change, which can stimulate the learners' overall linguistic conceptualizing capacity. This is made possible by making use of learners' common 'universal grammar' language facility as a base from which to direct their subsequent 'transformational' experience of two or more languages using the languages as it were as media to assist in spotting similarities or differences where this is, in fact, possible. The timing will depend on the learners' age and linguistic circumstances. Such early experience of language 'confrontation' enables non-native users to compare words, expressions and structures in the mother tongue or modern foreign languages and especially to delimit more precisely the concepts encountered. An early case for this in the school context was made out by Hawkins in 1984. Many later bilingual language users who can compare their two languages, though less so the immediately spontaneous more fluent early bilingual speakers who have had less opportunity for this, have had linguistic encounters which allow them to manoeuvre between two language worlds. In such situations teachers would ideally be expected to deal with two speaking media: the dialect and the standard or the standard (or dialect) and the modern foreign language to direct their pupils. The findings of Krashen (1981), who proposes the need for a formal as well as an informal stimulus when learning a foreign language, bear a certain similarity to our own views.

Language acquisition and teaching methods

The individual's growing into a particular mother tongue is made possible by the Language Acquisition Device (LAD) plus, as he or she gets older, the intervention of an input, in the form of an expanding lexis, encountered in the process of communicating with others. This activity is responsible for developing one language to the exclusion of potential others, unless this possibility is enabled by the administration, simultaneously or near-simultaneously with it, of an alternative input. The 'continuity' theory of language acquisition which assumes the two components, the LAD and the input, as put forward by Clahsen (1992) offers a more exciting and dynamic interpretation of the child's use of the universal grammar after exposure to an increased lexical input than does the alternative theory of 'maturity' which takes no account of the contribution made by the input (Weissenborn *et al.*, 1992). The universal grammar, in the Clahsen view, can be said to 'react' when reactivated by the child's own memory, skills and intelligence faculties over and above the linguistic development alone. The lexical input provides the child with a way to 'set' the universal grammar principles at the appropriate value without this teaching affecting the purely innate language faculty. Using this device, the input received at the learner's appropriate level of discourse is responsible for 'restructuring' a 'less developed', not firmly set grammar, involving linguistic and general intelligence factors, to give access to a second language. It is tempting to enlist Vygotsky's 'learning support theory' of activating the child's 'proximate zone of development' which triggers off and advances the child's own development potential when stimulated by the teacher, to support the two-way process of combining universal grammar, which is present from the start of language acquisition, with the environmental input which appears in the course of time. As Clahsen (1992) puts it: 'the availability of the principles is activated during the process of performance . . . Development is essentially data-driven . . . [and] by the child's changing perceptions of external linguistic evidence.' Chomsky (1986) puts it differently when he says that the 'Language Acquisition Device receives positive data as input and produces a cognitive subsystem as output' that allows 'use' to account for the continuity of language development.

Teaching can thus be regarded as a systematic attempt which the parents are not necessarily capable of providing if they are unable to help the process. They may be taking insufficient account of distracting factors, such as the noise of misdirected speech heard at the same time which can hinder the language acquisition, or failing to provide the necessary 'lexis' input for language acquisition because they lack the pedagogical skills necessary to consolidate the acquisition process and give it a specific language learning slant. Care must be taken in the entire process not to violate the child's original language system. Attempts to force-teach a different version of the mother tongue or another language at too early an age and to foster it to the exclusion of the one normally used by the learner can create resentment and confusion and may lead to a breakdown in communication. This does not exclude the introduction of another language in parallel with the first, or for part of the time, when the child is ready. It is not infrequent in this way to acquire two languages early on. We may refer to this process as 'enhanced *acquisition*' in order to distinguish it from the substitution of another '*language learning*' system taught separately without a deliberate reference to the first language.

The teaching methods and approaches chosen play an important role in convincing new users of the need to learn another language, and may go as far as positively to advocate the advantages of bilingualism, with the realization that increased and varied input can help to develop the personality of the learner. That children develop and learn best when taught through the medium of their mother tongue or with reference to it was mentioned earlier (see Bullock 1975; Saville and Troike, 1971; UNESCO, 1953). We have commented that such practice not only reinforces conceptual learning but compensates for apparent cultural deprivation assuring, according to Hawkins (1984), all dialects an equal social recognition and acceptance. Of course, when meeting later-learned languages the child or adolescent is confronted with two language media and may prefer to choose one, or use both to reinforce each other, or use them independently, although some 'interference' does ensue.

Of the two classical methods of education in a multilingual context known as the immersion and submersion methods, host governments' education policies prefer the second. Including ethnic minority pupils in majority classes (submersion), which is the regular pattern in schooling, does not require the provision of separate classes for the minority (immersion). In submersion classes minority group pupils learn the new national language, which is their second, sometimes even their third language, without deliberate reference to their own mother tongue which may remain intact but little used except where it is introduced in 'bilingual' sessions, for which there is not always the opportunity, with the majority language. These may take the form of, for example, translations or a singing contest, or a conversational or festive occasion at home. The learner's sensitivity and respect tend to be neglected in this approach, neither is use made of the possible positive, enriching or reinforcing impact of the two languages that we referred to earlier. Immersion provision introduces different languages in separate classes, the language used being selected according to community needs and regulations and the wishes and language knowledge of the pupil. It usually reflects the preferred or the imposed ultimate destinations of the migrants and their desire to recognize their separate identity within the plural multicultural composition of the host country. This method is also often chosen by non-immigrants who wish to acquire another language or to perfect their performance in their own territorial language, for example French in the Canadian Eest (Cummins, 1984). In such classes there is a limited, controlled, opportunity to use the original first or mother tongue as a learning aid by introducing it in lessons on occasion. Lambert and Tucker (1972) in their comments on the immersion method also discuss the teaching of so-called heritage languages (Cummins, 1982), mother tongues of the usually numerically smaller linguistic minorities, a measure which does much to preserve them.

Since the growing interdependence of sovereign states, with their multinational and multilingual economic links, requires active tuition in other languages to improve communication, some governments allow for part of the time allocated to mother tongue tuition to be given over to learning a modern foreign language, the two languages, if brought in contact, mutually reinforcing each other. The Dutch policy of the earliest possible learning of modern foreign languages supports their introduction to achieve an improved command of language overall. The simultaneous exposure to two language media may lead to full bilingualism, experienced by many in a spontaneous way early on and reinforced later in schooling, although bilingualism has to be qualified in that the users' pronunciation may not be equally good in both their languages and there may be interference. This may, however, be put to good use when training for jobs such as translating. The actual learning mechanism can be observed at work when more progress is made by the learner in one medium than in the other. Sachs (1976) quotes the learning experience of children acquiring Hungarian and Serbo-Croat simultaneously. She notes that 'grammatical realizations in the form of suffixes' are acquired earlier than the realization of prefixes, with implications for the faster learning of languages with a developed case endings system rather than those using prepositions to express these relations. A case of 'Russian made easy ?'

The role of the instructor

Teachers' explicit support of the universal language learning elements that all humans share is crucial. This tends to be ignored when learning languages in isolation from each other. With the aim to acquire skills quickly, the need is less likely to arise. However, the present-day reality of the multilingual classroom positively encourages the mutual linguistic reinforcement which is provided by stimulating and creating an interest in the plurilinguistic situation. In this light, bidialectism and bilingualism may be seen to be an advantage by reconciling the contribution made by early language acquisition and learning with that of the impact of later formal teaching on human language development. This acknowledges that language, through lexis and morphology, helps to stimulate cognition, while the pronunciation of new words stimulates the motor apparatus of speech; both practices putting linguistic interference to good use (Tulasiewicz, 1989). The general tenet of this was accepted by the Judge Joiner ruling which, in 1979, encouraged 'Black English' in Ann Arbor classrooms since it was deemed to help black pupils to achieve Standard American. Educating prospective teachers of both mother tongue and modern foreign languages in joint classes was advocated by the report of the Kingman Inquiry (DES, 1988).

The sequence in which languages are encountered can lead to different results in terms of learners' language proficiency. Language schooling which *follows* a period of mother tongue acquisition, whether received at home or in similar informal conditions, can offer a more systematic teaching approach with reference made to the language proficiency already achieved in a process which can be described as more akin to 'learning a language'. The exact onset of language users becoming language learners depends on the starting age of compulsory schooling. The Clahsen (1992) 'developmental' theory of language acquisition would suggest that lexical input by the 'instructor' (parent or teacher) facilitates the expansion of the language acquired early to the full language command possessed by the mature user. 'Shifting' the 'universal grammar', which is expressed in the medium of the language targeted for conceptual expansion, in a direction which will enable it to assume the new and more advanced functions is a situation in which the 'instructor' plays a facilitating role on behalf of the 'pupil'. The inverted commas indicate that this process may already have started in the home being an addition to the innate language acquisition mechanisms such as those which 'specialize' in the perception of sounds or the acquisition and 'ordering' of regularities heard by the language learner which function without direct intervention. The process of language development as a whole, therefore, is not haphazardly acquired but deliberately learned.

Mother tongue and foreign language in the tuition process

Both groups, national (first) and second, or foreign, language learners, share the same task, that of acquiring a vehicle of communication. However, the former, expected to conform with the standard which is the everyday medium of communication in their society at all times, are under greater pressure than the latter who have only to learn the other (foreign) language for when they themselves experience the need to use it. That is only on those occasions when they have to communicate with those who may also wish to, or have to, use that language. Insistence on 'correct' language in the school mitigates against this freedom to dispose with language, while second language learners, out of school, are in a position more like that of mother tongue users, the second language increasingly assumed to be becoming their regular medium of communication. In the case of second and foreign languages the problem is linked with the amount of 'new language' that has to be learned by the new user compared with the amount of language already known by native first language users. Apart from prestige reasons, learning motivation is affected by accessibility of the other language , a point to consider when advocating the learning of the less widely used mother tongues. Thus Welsh may be the preferred language of a Welshman but his opportunity to speak equally widely on all topics in the Welsh medium is restricted because there may not be the speaking partners available in all the areas where in theory communication is believed to be possible. In order to overcome the legacy of the language of cultural domination several newly 'surfacing' countries in Central and Eastern Europe have used their resources to open up such opportunities. As a result of this pressure, Russian has largely disappeared as the second language in the region.

Tuition in the 'mother tongues' of minorities in the schools of nation states was not as a rule provided in regular classes, the aim of schooling being to promote what was understood as national homogeneity and cohesion through the official language and literature. This policy has always been resented by the minorities, such as the Slovenes in Austria and the Hungarians in Slovakia as well as many others in Europe but it did not lead to major friction, acknowledged by international observers, until the rapid increase of immigration and ethnic cleansing after World War Two became identified with the re-emergence of a more extreme nationalism in Europe coinciding with demands for the implementation of human rights and equal opportunities legislation. In some countries the smaller territorial languages and the languages of immigrants declined with the firm installation of the major national languages as the teaching medium and their growing acceptance by all inhabitants. This was what had been happening in the case of Czech as against Slovak until the breakup of Czechoslovakia. Assimilationist and 'melting pot' policies, the acceptance or rejection of the foreign reality and their impact are widely discussed and just as widely criticized by politicians and sociolinguists alike. This criticism may be accompanied by a variety of pupil grouping policies in mother tongue and modern foreign language teaching, some of which are discussed in this chapter: immersion, submersion, homogeneous and mixed groups, for example. Several of the volumes published in the *Multilingual Matters* series are case studies of language pluralism and outline teaching approaches in a number of countries. Acceptance of the role that education in and through the 'mother tongue' plays in the child's development, suggested by the findings of psychologists such as Carroll (1986), is particularly noticeable in a number of recent language education policy reports and is not unconnected with the more socio-linguistic inspired and politically motivated intercultural persuasion of governments and education authority advisors.

The teaching of immigrants' home languages and mother tongues was originally intended to make it possible for their children to resume schooling in their own countries after their return, an option considered especially important in the case of strong immigrant communities. This policy has meanwhile been overtaken by immigrants' failure, for political and economic reasons, to return 'home', coupled with their increased economic mobility in the host countries. This has put a new gloss on the priority given to learning the host country's language by immigrants as their second language, an option at first available on a selective basis only (Skutnabb Kangas, 1981). Rethinking the role of the first, mother tongue language in this process and in helping literacy generally, as well as the improved command of a second language by immigrants in particular, have led to changes in the provision for language teaching and the use of more stimulating teaching methods, developed in several countries. Various schemes are now available in most European countries, some of them funded by the host governments with the support of the European Union and the Council of Europe.

It is widely accepted meanwhile, that all languages are capable of expressing everything that concerns their language community; this applies also to the speech of the physically disabled and the socially disadvantaged (Edwards, 1979). It holds until such time as the language communities start importing material and spiritual goods from a culture which is alien to them. Concepts expressed in one language may not directly be expressed in another and this has tended to restrict many non-Western, 'borrowing', languages to be used as the medium of instruction up to elementary level only. It is particularly after that stage that a major input of non-indigenous cultural and scientific elements is beginning to find its way into the curriculum for which the 'donor' language is used. Problems arise when entire disciplines which require a concise specialist language for ideas which are unknown in the native languages are introduced into schooling and have to be resolved either through the linguistic resources available in the receiving vernacular or, if that is difficult, by the adoption of the donor language as the teaching medium in their areas. This happens especially in teaching abstract and scientific concepts, such as expressions of quantity, for which new technical or sociological terms are required. If the receiving language does not possess them they have first to be 'translated' into it using *calques* and other newly coined phrases which according to Poth (1980) 'follow the genius' of that language. Tapping the linguistic resources of the borrowing language may result in ideas being expressed in a different way to that intended by the donor language which produce alternative, less direct ways of teaching them for which Poth gives interesting examples. A more direct route is for the ex-colonial powers to impose their own language as the medium for forming and learning the different concepts and terms for which their language then becomes the only teaching medium.

In either case the indigenous users who have to learn the new medium for this purpose may be disadvantaged by the adjustments they have to make. This is compounded by the fact that actual decisions concerning the use of non-indigenous languages in education, either as a school subject in their own right or as a teaching aid, are frequently made not so much on linguistic grounds, but for socio-economic and political considerations which determine the content of the curriculum and the place of 'second' and modern foreign languages in it. The implications of these policies for the structures assumed by both the donor and the receiving languages require research.

If mother tongue education in some countries has been more successful than in others, assuming that there are common targets aimed at, such as spelling or the ability to paraphrase or précis, which can be measured, then this is due to more efficient teaching methods their introduction determined by the socio-political climate in which the teaching takes place. National languages have to be numerically, and especially politically, secure to be accepted as the vehicle for providing the efficient medium for delivering the curriculum. It is a matter of policy whether to acknowledge and encourage the other 'mother tongues' for this purpose or to abandon them in favour of using the majority language. Belorussians may find most of their higher education conducted through the medium of Russian; the two languages are similar, the political system favours close collaboration with the fifteen times stronger partner who enjoys an international reputation, including that of original scientific output, which can easily be 'translated' into Belorussian. There is no evidence of pupils being disadvantaged as a result since Russian is widely used and understood in Belarus. The process will be different when dealing with languages whose structures or vocabulary are not so similar to the donor language as in the above case in terms of philosophical or political concepts, or indeed purely linguistic concepts such as verbal tense or aspect. This is avoided when translations of concepts and lexis can overtly use common intellectual terminology.

A different, more nationalistic, policy is being pursued by the numerically smaller Baltic republics determined to cleanse their languages of Russian elements where possible and adapt older language material to render the new concepts. Welsh may be the language of some higher education in the Principality but this is a status not enjoyed by the numerically bigger and related Breton. Where the targeted national language is not seen as linked with the mother tongues of all the users of dialects and other language variants there can arise a conflict of priorities over methods and resources, often the result of language preferences by users of dialects who being in control of funding may press for their introduction. This has been happening in Croatia with the relegation of the common Serbo-Croat *shtokavian* dialect in favour of the Croat *Kaikavian*. The introduction of tuition in regional dialects may reinforce the use of that 'mother tongue' dialect and lessen the motivation for learning the official, that is, the 'national', dialect variety mother tongue. The preferences are decided by socio-economic and political considerations, with an admixture of sentimental attachment, and can affect major as well as minor languages at various stages of their development. We note that in the Netherlands it is possible to receive compulsory education through the medium of a language other than Dutch.

THE CONTEXTS OF SOME LANGUAGE TEACHING APPROACHES

The precise approaches to mother tongue and modern foreign language teaching methods in general (for example rote learning) and in specific attainment target detail (for example the teaching of reading) differ in the various countries referred to with different teaching strategies adopted. The practice of whole class teaching or group learning will depend on classroom organization policies and will also apply to teaching other subjects like mathematics. On the other hand methods employed for teaching discrete parts of the language syllabus, such as reading, will vary not only from country to country, depending on the specific 'genius' of the teaching medium, the average length of its words, the correlation between pronunciation and spelling or the syllabic structure of the language, but they may also vary from school to school in accordance with teachers' views of the learning of reading.

There are two basic contexts to language teaching. Teaching the mother tongue is conducted in the mother tongue itself. This accords with nation-state policies with regard to the role of the mother tongue as a core subject of the curriculum in human development generally and with special reference to the language development of future citizens. Competence includes mastering the language skills and the study of texts chosen for delivering much of the humanities side of pupils' education. Teaching a modern foreign language, on the other hand, can be conducted with a minimum or a maximum reference to the pupil's mother tongue in the classroom. Knowledge of a foreign language while also acknowledged as contributing to human development serves to enable pupils to communicate, more often than not, in another language used by those who had studied it as their mother tongue. The syllabus while mainly emphasizing language skills also includes some 'background' cultural knowledge. Most pupils studying two languages acquire an unequal knowledge of two language systems, compounded by the fact that the foreign language is seen by many as superfluous since it is possible to satisfy most, if not all, of one's communication needs in one's mother tongue. Foreign language policies thus distinguish between learning in order to be able to communicate, while the more advanced cultural and linguistic goods of the other language are studied by few. Although foreign language programmes and achievement in the schools of some countries, especially Germany, can be very ambitious, traditionally the resulting command of the communicating medium after leaving school is unequal. What for one pupil is the mother tongue is a foreign language for the other, making meaningful communication difficult.

A language education across the two media is not common. However, the fact that in today's multilingual classrooms of a single country one pupil's mother tongue can be another's foreign language, is one major reason why the foreign language may have to be used to help out in mother tongue lessons and conversely, why some mother tongue elements may find their way into foreign language classes. Language classes in pupils' second language, assuming mother tongue maintenance or not, religious languages, languages for jobs or other purposes, may occupy a distinctive position in the education system – some of the arrangements for the teaching of which have been outlined. It is important to remember that they are affected by the multilingual composition of most classrooms.

The second major reason, more closely identified as 'linguistic' in favour of considering all language teaching as but two different branches of the same tree, are the findings concerning language acquisition and learning and the links between mother tongue and foreign language education. It has been recognized, increasingly more often, that improving that learning contact could be an important part of what has been called a language education conducted in both mother tongue and modern foreign language lessons. This allows for the fact that the mother tongue is taught through the medium of the mother tongue itself but that in foreign language lessons the pupils' mother tongue is referred to and vice versa use is made of the foreign language in mother tongue classes. These are distinct from lessons in the literature of pupils' mother tongues (Skutnabb Kangas, 1982).

Those accepting the two arguments would regard much traditional language teaching activity as mere skill training, relying on repetition and memory rather than language education, in a process in which the pupils' cognitive and emotional faculties fail to be fully engaged. The concluding, third part of this book, is a critical account of a Language Awareness approach which concerns itself with the function of language education in language classrooms.

A survey of approaches to language teaching methods, such as that by Richards and Rodgers (1995) to name but one, reveals that there is a large variety. However, it is possible to distinguish between a 'mother tongue = single language' approach and one which is more of a 'comparative approach which presents pupils with two linguistic systems and a tool to find their way through them'. Particularly the second approach enables language education to look beyond the surface structure and into the nature of language. Language education is the realization by users that being in command of a language does not consist of the language skills alone but is an understanding of the importance of language for their entire existence. Here the main role is played by users' first language, usually called their mother tongue. Language education, however, consists of constructing a bridge to users of other mother tongues that would enable language users everywhere to learn about the nature of language and the unique role played by language in their lives.

Language proficiency is about empowerment (Fairclough, 1989), a sovereign command of a language system or systems, in terms of language skills and of understanding language. Governments leaning towards a more authoritarian approach to policies usually prefer methods of language teaching that will provide a compliantly literate population to methods that put too much power into the hands of the learners. The differences and controversies on the teaching of the mother tongue in the various countries discussed, more loudly in some than in others, are often assumed to centre on this fact. The situation is not different in modern foreign language teaching. Much of it, too, concentrates on the language skills while neglecting the political and socio-historical backgrounds of the countries whose languages are studied.

Such issues also relate to the process of language planning which takes place in all countries. In his *Cambridge Encyclopedia of Language* Crystal (1987) provides a list of some of the linguistic issues that are the topic of debate, such as:

the place of minority languages, the role of an academy in safeguarding standards, the influence of the media on usage, the value of spelling reform, the avoidance of sexist language, the modernization of religious language, the need for plain English, stylistic standards in publishing, and the maintenance of oracy and literacy levels in school.

Clearly in language planning there are political agendas to be addressed. What Cox (1995) has described as 'the battle for the English curriculum' was instanced when English became the most bitterly contested subject within the emerging National Curriculum in England and Wales. There are also what might be described as current linguistic agendas. For example in both England and the United States there has been much emphasis in recent years on the issue of sexism and language. Politically this may be ascribed to the women's movement but it is also undeniably linked with the linguistic fact that in English there is a closer association between grammatical gender and biological sex than, for example, in French. In French usage it is still acceptable to write, *Madame, le Directeur*, as well as *la Directrice*, but, in recent English usage, the term 'Chairman' has been replaced by 'Chair', because the suffix '-man' is felt by many to carry sexist overtones. The same objection is raised to the usage of 'Chairwoman'. Examples from other European languages could be quoted to support this phenomenon. German *Schulleiter(in)* becomes 'Head' in English but could be accommodated in other European languages in a way similar to German. In Polish the equivalent is *kierownik (niczka) szkoły*. It could be that in those countries feminism has attached itself primarily to issues other than those of language with which it has been concerned in the United States and England (Spender, 1980), although the 'genius' of the English language to use metaphors drawn from concrete experience rather than abstractions, somewhat less prominent in other languages, may have something to do with it as well.

The political issues associated with the methods advocated for the teaching of the mother tongue then are closely linked with attitudes towards authority. Sociologists such as Durkheim and Bernstein have written of two kinds of relationship, which can be termed 'positional', where authority derives from the specific role played by the person in authority, and 'personal' where authority derives from a relationship between the two parties which may be negotiable. Attitudes towards most of the basic controversies on the teaching approaches of the mother tongue will depend upon the acceptance of the positional or personal persuasion (Grace, 1978). The specific detailed methods have to take account of both: the linguistic 'genius' and the political contexts of the language lessons.

Perhaps the most universal of these controversies is that concerned with the desirability of teaching the formal structure of the language, usually in the form of a grammar. No one would deny the value of the study of grammar as a branch of linguistic science, as a university discipline for example, but there remains considerable discussion of the value of teaching 'traditional' grammar to first language users in school. Most linguists would deny that there is much merit in this but the common-sense view, as so often, is at odds with this opinion. In England, successive committees of inquiry have been established by governments to make recommendations on the teaching of the mother tongue in the expectation that they would recommend a return to formal grammar teaching in schools. However, as long ago as 1965, Wilkinson in a survey of research into the teaching of grammar in schools showed that there was absolutely no evidence that it improved language performance in the case of native users of the language. To be sure, the Kingman Report (DES, 1988) advocated grammar discussions in lessons akin to the sort of 'grammar in use' comments referred to earlier in this chapter, though not the return to uncontextualized Latinate grammar. There is no room for this emphasis in a largely uninflected language such as English. In French, where grammar and orthography are closely related, there might appear to be more justification for the formal teaching of morphology and spelling and this is reflected in the weight given to it in the official French curriculum. However, grammar also includes consideration of syntax and style which in English depend on a number of elusive factors such as word order or the use of identical structures to serve as both nouns and verbs, which second-language learners may find difficult. In such cases presenting pupils with alternative texts may help to point out the difference in meaning.

A second major controversy in the teaching of the mother tongue is the relative weight to be accorded to literacy (reading and writing) as opposed to oracy (speaking and listening). The latter term was first coined by Wilkinson and was quickly taken up by many other educationalists. Traditionally, language instruction has been mainly concerned with the written forms of the language, which seem more easily codified and therefore lend themselves to classroom teaching. There is more to correct and to award marks for, and it is upon the written forms of language that government policies are usually focused. Thus proficiency in the mother tongue in the school context will usually be correlated with proficiency in reading and writing it, notwithstanding the fact that users of the language universally speak and listen far more than they read and write.

Politicians frequently express concern over the level of literacy in spite of the fact that such levels remain remarkably constant over the years. It is expected that such views will be taken into account by teachers in their school work. This has led to periodic discussions about how reading should be taught and may also be seen in terms of an opposition between positional and personal practices. The former tends towards a model of teaching reading that relies upon alphabetic and phonetic methods, building up words and sentences from their fundamental units, the phoneme upwards as it were; the latter tends to use the holistic approach with a focus from the beginning in the extraction of meaning from the text, deriving largely from the work of Goodman (1970) and his conception of reading as a 'psycho-linguistic guessing game'. The former approach will tend to rely upon texts specifically prepared for the classroom ('basal readers'); the latter will exploit the pleasure of 'real books' as early as possible. The former approach is more easily controllable and more likely, as a consequence, to be approved by authorities responsible for the mother tongue syllabus.

Chapter 5

Mother Tongues in a Wider Context

LANGUAGES IN CONTACT: GENERAL OBSERVATIONS

Some languages are achieving a dominant position in the political, socio-economic and cultural spheres faster than others: this is an undoubted fact. The conditions for this are to be found in the greater or lesser international roles played at different times by the different countries where their languages are used, ultimately placing the relevant languages in the undisputed position of a *lingua franca*. The influences exercised in this process by those users of the language who are in a position to exercise them are primarily of a political, social and cultural nature. The resulting linguistic predominance is secondary. This also applies to views which perceive the emerging dominant language as a more suitable linguistic medium to exercise the role of world language. English is not any 'easier' as a language system, even though certain of its grammatical features may be less complex – for example the indicator of noun plurals – than they are in French. Even so, the advantages of having one language to use as the unrivalled medium for facilitating international communication are obvious. What is less often discussed is the socio-political and cultural impact of the pre-eminent world language on the other languages, a situation of interest in Europe with its large number of what might be styled as equally 'developed' languages, each associated with a middle-ranking world power.

Another important inquiry linked with world language status is how the role played by the *lingua franca* on the wider stage affects the character of the *lingua franca* itself, considering the variety of people using it as their 'mother tongue', as their second or as their modern foreign language and their opportunities for doing so. The existence of this phenomenon can be observed in a variety of regional and international contexts. The position of Russian within the former Soviet Union and its satellite countries can be described as regional, as can the role of French and English in their former empires. If the linguistic penetration in the case of the Soviet-dominated region did not assume the same proportions everywhere as that in parts of Africa or Asia in the cases of French and English, then this is due to the different perception of the political roles played by the colonial powers in their areas of influence and their duration. The economic size and ethnic composition of such regions as well as the language policies pursued by their governments contribute to determining the character and the role of the language used with its reaching the ultimate stage of 'world language'. This is the situation in which English has advanced to a bigger role as a world language than French, Spanish or indeed Russian. It is also a situation which has brought forth more regional varieties of English than of French and Spanish, considering the insistence on the 'purity' of French and the social and educational class of people who use it as their medium of communication; the usually prestigious character of that communication restricting somehow though not stopping altogether the spread of 'alternative' dialects. This has implications for learning the standard *lingua franca* and for the development of suitable teaching methods of it as the world language in mother tongue as well as in second and modern foreign language education.

English is affected by all these developments. However, in mainland Europe the position of the many other mother tongues and national languages receives more attention because of the political and economic restructuring of the continent as a partnership of equals and the influence exerted by the users of the many languages found there than it does in England itself. It is safe to assume that, regardless of the British political stance towards Europe, English, the 'official' language of the United Kingdom, is likely to remain the principal European medium of communication. The questions thus arising – how does 'native' language competence differ from that of second or modern foreign language users, and to what extent is the language quality used the same in each of these situations? There are, after all, not only the dialectal differences exhibited by the different groups of language users, the amount and type of vocabulary at their disposal, but, in the case of second language users, also the impact of their 'symbolic language' which may affect the form assumed by their 'instrumental language', for example Indian English. Questions of fluency and performance, however, are relative if the different uses to which a world or regional language is subjected are taken into account. Co-existence with other languages suggests that there might be benefit in comparing the language teaching methods of the *lingua franca* in the different functions in which it is to be used with the teaching of the other languages. To begin with a more developed methodology of teaching the *lingua franca* as a second language or a modern foreign language would be available.

Language interference

Language contacts result in mutual interpenetration, borrowings made and losses suffered, the languages having to adapt to the presence of new or the absence of old elements. All language systems are subject to change, the lexical system being the most liable. The character and role of all mother tongues and dialects are affected by the force of the impact of other languages and dialects in contact with them, the *lingua franca* being in no way exempt. This is the effect of the international use made of the language. However, it is the position, and what can be described as the inner strength, the 'genius' of the languages affected, which co-determine the actual extent of the change. This has to do with the structure of the borrowing language itself, its openness to influence, the receptiveness to change of its users, as much as the force of the impact exercised by the influencing world languages. Thus, the linguistic factors, those to do with the structure of the language, as much as the socio-political strength of its users, have contributed to the emergence of more powerful and less powerful languages, resulting in languages which have experienced a greater or a lesser change in their structures. After the intermediate stages of bilingualism and diglossia the ultimate change is language disappearance. In the British Isles, this phenomenon has led to the virtual extinction of Cornish and the precarious position of Irish Gaelic. As against that, on the world scale, it has led, though not until after World War Two to the preeminent position of English as the global *lingua franca*.

Language loss in one region may be compensated by language revival elsewhere, as is seen when comparing the dimensions of the 'official' language revival in Spain with that in France. In the former Yugoslavia 'new' languages have become accepted, a development also observed in parts of Asia. As a result of this process some languages have emerged more changed than others. In a process that has been in existence for much longer than its recorded history, the English spoken and written a thousand years ago compared with the language of today strikes the observer as more radically different than the comparable versions of Icelandic, which over the centuries has retained many more of its early Germanic lexical and morphological features. This has enabled it to use its own words and compounds instead of foreign borrowings for terms such as 'theatre', 'telephone' and many others for which English and other languages have relied more extensively on Latin or Greek lexical imports. To be sure over time, such languages as Icelandic have remained more isolated than others, with the cultural influences on them weaker or different.

It is common to refer to language change, although it is the language users who determine the character and the extent of change, having through their various activities put their language in a position from which it can or cannot affect other languages or be affected by them. In this sense most languages may be said to have exerted some influence over their neighbours at some time, a process in which language size alone need not determine the extent of change. It is the combination of the number with socio-political, cultural and economic positions of the users, who make up the nation state of which the language is the national or regional medium, that is responsible for the extent of language loss or language revival. A smaller nation may affect a numerically larger but economically weaker one; an élite social class may influence it at one period, only to be influenced by mass developments at another.

This can be seen in the different linguistic impacts of different areas of development. The changes in English reflect the wide French influence on its social and political vocabulary in the Middle English period. By contrast, present-day French is much more likely to be affected by English in the technological and entertainment spheres. Indeed, all the neighbours of these two languages have exerted some influence on each other, ranging from the lexical contribution of some few Scottish Gaelic words to English to a large-scale inundation of German by French, and vice versa. Languages which are not unduly 'deflected' by foreign influences turn out to be 'stronger' and 'richer' than those unable to process the input from their language neighbours, seen in the large amount of continuing lexical borrowings and their ready acceptance of English contributing to its growth. Polish, spoken by far fewer people than Russian, has influenced the Russian 'cultural' vocabulary more than Russian has Polish. However, the vocabulary of languages within the sphere of influence of the former Soviet Union was greatly affected by Russian in the immediate post-World War Two period, as seen in the lexical additions to the German of the former German Democratic Republic by the dominant Russian political and cultural imports (Tulasiewicz, 1985). To a lesser extent, morphology and syntax were also affected by these developments. In such a case, however, it is always the 'stronger' language which exerts the influence, because it takes longer for morphological changes to become established in the language. Changes may disappear once the donor language has ceased its influence.

While the lexical system is likely to be most affected by influences from borrowing, some vocabulary changes turn out to be more short-lived than changes in the pronunciation caused by the introduction into the language of new sounds with the new borrowings. In German, for example, French nasal sounds are still present and continue to be mispronounced by many users. *Bassin*, in colloquial German, distorts the French pronunciation [ɛ̃] into [ɛŋ], although many older terms borrowed in the Middle Ages which contained this phoneme have disappeared from current use. The appearance in German of the unusual combination of stop and sibilant [*tsh*] from Polish and Russian has been particularly marked recently.

While a number of systematic sound shifts – the origins of which go back thousands of years – were responsible for the emergence of new dialects of a language family or individual language groups, so that modern German differs from modern English in respect of a fixed number of phonetic changes, such as the pronunciation [*ts*] for [*t*], exemplified by *Zaun* and English 'town', modern vocabulary influences have not achieved change on such a scale. However, they have been responsible for the appearance of new phonemes in most European languages. The English phoneme [*dzh*] or its preferred German voiceless variant [*tsh*] not found in an initial position in English is now firmly established in German in words like *Manager*, which in Polish retains the native voiced [*dzh*] but is responsible for the introduction of a new vowel competing with the regular Polish [*e*] to render the English pronunciation of the [*ə*]. It is customary to measure such changes in terms of additions to the vocabulary rather than pronunciation, although there has been a change in both.

It is, therefore, possible to speak of the presence of individual Anglo-French (*Franglais*) or Anglo-German words in the borrowing language, but there is no immediate prospect of a new language or dialect group arising as a result of the borrowings made. Those could only be achieved by a massive influx of foreign words and a consistent and prolonged sound shift. On the morphological side we may quote the example of the nominal ending -*nik*, as in 'sputnik', borrowed from Russian, which has proved productive in Anglo-American words like 'beatnik' and 'refusenik' and goes back to Slavonic influences, also found in Yiddish. 'Beatnik' and 'sputnik' will probably disappear soon from current use, other such words will take their place – with American-Yiddish a good agent. 'Apparatchik' is hardly used in spoken English but will remain in the written language to refer to the agent of a Communist 'apparat' or someone acting like one.

In the eleventh to thirteenth centuries, the courtly era influenced most European languages. The vocabulary of the donor languages responsible, French and Flemish in the widest sense, registered the new life styles and values, which originally had come to Western Europe from Italy. In some cases this vocabulary is still to be found though often with changed meanings as in the current terminology with words associated with 'courtly behaviour' or 'honour'. In modern times migrations and international trade have been responsible for vocabulary borrowings in a large number of domains. The influence of third and developing world vocabulary has increased with the large variety of foreign foods and dishes imported in a process which has exchanged the importation of 'tandoori' for the exportation of 'hamburger'. Foods and dishes are probably the largest single source of foreign words known by the ordinary European mother tongue users, while the vocabulary of business and commerce has penetrated African and Asian languages. In this respect the way the borrowing language deals with the importations, for example by distorting their spelling and omitting the German upper case in the first letter of nouns (for instance in the Audi motor car advertisement '*vorsprung durch technik*'), can be compared with the complete acceptance or rejection of the borrowed objects themselves.

This means that the borrowings may be direct, such as 'pizza', adopted by English and Polish with no change in the word itself or in its pronunciation. In the case of inflected languages the spelling may be adapted, as in Polish *szosa* from the French *chaussée*, the original word still surviving in German *Chaussee*, having adopted the German upper case spelling convention for nouns. In Polish it was included in the feminine declension system analogous to Polish feminine words. Word *calques* may be formed which disguise foreign origins, such as the adaptation of German *Hof* to denote both a 'yard', its original meaning as in *Schulhof* (school playground), and a royal or nobleman's 'court' in imitation of French usage in the eleventh century. English uses the two terms 'yard' and 'court' which have different word family origins – Germanic and Romance respectively. In Middle English and later both variants can be found as in 'courtyard'. German seems to manage with one word (*Hof*), as does French. The language itself may create further: the adjective *höflich* (courteous) is an example of the creation of a new word with existing German linguistic resources, in this instance it is the suffix -*lich*, analogous to French.

Such English words as 'beef' and 'pork', borrowed from their French originals, provide evidence of a different semantic change – a narrowing of the meaning to 'animal flesh' occurring after the borrowing since the original words referred to both the animal and its meat. Examples of a morphological change in some of these words have appeared in recent years. French *bifteck* shows the reverse borrowing process (English into French) of the original *bœuf* and the equivalent of 'beefsteak' with a French spelling returning to France. It has retained the original French *bœuf* which in English has been cut off, resulting in the abbreviated 'steak', denoting a cut of meat, not implied by the French borrowing since the English predilection for monosyllabic words was not followed by French. Other examples of morphological change are not difficult to find; for example, German verb endings in '*ieren*' from the French (*ir/er*) also added to non-French words, like *spazieren* (to walk), already equipped with the German infinitive suffix: '*en*'. Russian went further with the extra (*ir*) syllable in: '*registrirovat*' or '*telegrafirovat*'. Spanish syntax has been affected to a lesser extent by English than often claimed, as shown in the case of new ways of using Spanish passive constructions which rely on developing existing Spanish constructions and not on copying English ones (Pountain, 1994).

All such influences provide evidence of different degrees of penetration of the cultural products imported. In the above examples the change was caused by socio-political and cultural events such as the Norman invasion, the restructuring of English society resulting from this, and the cultural influence of the influx of English or French inventions on other languages. There are other sources of influence. Individuals' or trade names may also contribute; for example the words 'hoover' and 'biro' are found in a number of European languages. Linguistic purists may readily reject such words for which native equivalents exist, such as in German, *Staubsauger* and *Kugelschreiber*, or in English 'vacuum cleaner' and 'ball-point pen'. While Polish may use *odkurzacz* alongside 'hoover' (or indeed the older *luks* in some dialects) the word *długopis* maintains its independence from 'biro'. Russian *karandash* for pencil betrays its French trade-mark origins. The fact of the openness of the lexical system to all kinds of borrowings has made finding examples a relatively easy task. Indeed, much has been written about this phenomenon by David Crystal, Stephen Ullman and others.

Part of the current linguistic situation in Europe can be summed up as the impact of an all-pervasive transatlantic culture, with its language, English, poised to fill the vacuum created by the collapse of communist culture as well as to penetrate political and cultural spheres in the languages of areas which had not experienced the Russian post-World War Two dominance. American political supremacy and the widespread commercial success of its cultural products have left an imprint on the vocabulary of all European languages, affecting their pronunciation to some extent. The weaker impact of morphology has been responsible for the lesser acceptance of English monosyllabic words.

The impact on language users

It is possible to pick up pronunciation patterns or vocabulary from neighbours, especially by those who have lived outside their own language area for a long time. Canadian-Ukrainian has not kept pace with recent language developments in the Ukraine in terms of vocabulary or indeed pronunciation. Factors such as the predominance of a particular dialect used by a large group of immigrants can play a decisive part. Their original dialect is still frequently heard in the speech of the *Sudetendeutsche* expelled more than 50 years ago. Users are themselves often unaware of the changes until they are confronted by the 'official' version of their 'mother tongue', changes in which follow the 'genius' of the language, for instance in the French example of *bifteck* or the double verbal endings in German or Russian.

The linguistic penetration process which can affect the structure of the language, as in the examples given, is of course accompanied by a shift in customs, values and attitudes of language users who accept some or all of the new importations. It is certainly arguable that *Franglais* is not just the existence of isolated English words in French but the acceptance of a whole range of goods and practices which may result in the dislodgement of the original French goods and practices together with the words which symbolized them. In protecting the purity of the French language, members of the *académie* are indirectly indicating their attitude to the cultural and social importations.

The implications of language change as socio-political and socio-cultural change have been recognized and the change resisted, on occasion in more radical ways. Attempts to cleanse German of French and English and even Latin elements, were made with the active support of the government and the ruling often extreme nationalist political parties and fiercely resisted by the opposition. The introduction or withdrawal of lexical change by decree is easy – the public use of words can be banned. However, individual users can still decide whether to accept or reject them. German has *Telephon*, *Telefon* and *Fernsprecher* between which individual users may choose, where Dutch uses *Telefoon* only; in French business letters *telecopieur* can be found instead of 'telefax' or 'fax'. Fashion becomes an important determiner of such matters, especially in the world of popular entertainment. The Anglo-American 'pop' itself is widely accepted helped no doubt by the fact that the adjective 'popular' can be found in most European languages and it is easily understood by both those in favour of the fashion and by its opponents.

Imported terms and expressions may fill the surface gap in the 'instrumental language', introducing a new tool or concept, for example 'computer', or using an older coined word like the German term *Katalysator* for a new product to fit existing car exhausts. The subsequent fate of terms such as these later in the language may, however, be determined by their 'symbolic' features, likely to affect the instrumental language; accepting a new word because of its similarity to existing elements, for example, or rejecting it. Users' preference for certain sounds and word structure symmetry may be the decisive factor, for example, as in the refusal by the French to use *mercatique* (marketing) although *informatique* has been fully integrated into the language.

The process may result in metaphors and other linguistic creations. As an illustration we may quote the following case of the choice of a given name. The Romanian name *dracul* (devil) was given by its owner to an English marmalade tomcat whom the owner did not wish to call by the English word 'devil'. The reason, it was discovered, was that the English word possessed a deeper, more real religious connotation for him which was absent in his much less fluent, more 'surface' Romanian. The owner, a non-Romanian, had spent several years in

Romania as a youth and associated the young cat's exuberant behaviour with practices mildly 'diabolical'. The Romanian name, in a language which was not his mother tongue and in which he felt more detached, enabled him to register this wish in a more playful way.

The national language or mother tongue can play an important part as the 'official' guardian or protector of that part of sovereignty which can be expressed in words. 'Home' languages perform the same service on a local scale. This accounts for the tenacity with which users hang on to their dialects. The language may be capable of withstanding the foreign impact by 'refusing access' to new developments; on the other hand, the borrowing language has the capacity to heal the wounds inflicted when 'alien' elements have become integrated and are no longer felt to be importations. For example the Russian *pyesa* is an importation of the French *pièce* to denote a theatrical play, the French form of the word having disappeared under the impact of its integration into the Russian declension pattern. The lasting cultural influence is also obvious since the new, more sophistically constructed theatrical pieces, invariably called *pyesy*, replaced the more homely performances (*spyektakle*) not executed on a formal stage. Probably few ordinary Russians would readily think of either term as an alien element in their language. Similarly, German *tanzen* replaced the original German dancing steps expressed by *steppen*. The courtly French dancing style for which *danser* was the acceptable word has meanwhile completely taken over the entire dancing area. An examination of the borrowings actually made, their meanings and their provenance, is a good indicator of the degree of successful cultural penetration. A world language such as English used by people living in a variety of cultural environments will have acquired a larger amount of borrowings than a language not used so widely. It will also have exported more vocabulary. 'Curry' has been tasted and its spelling is known by more schoolchildren in England than it has in Germany.

In recent years the influence of world languages has accelerated. The impact of the most powerful of these languages, English, disseminated by the (Anglo-American) world media, film, television and computer, is being felt by many of the smaller and not so small mother tongues in Europe. The potential conflict resulting from this has drawn attention to the relative 'strength' and 'weakness' of the different national and ethnic communities alongside their languages expressed by their ability to resist by curtailing the import of cultural goods, for example in France. Discussions of language change as part of language education, both mother tongue and foreign, which include the topic of users' 'openness' to change and the agents and agencies responsible for it, enable learners to see language study not just as a medium for efficient communication but also to recognize language as a powerful marker of ethnic and political identity. On the other hand, the frequently expressed fear of the inclusion of foreign elements fails to appreciate the undoubted enrichment of the target language achieved by these imports.

EXAMPLES OF LANGUAGE IMPACT

The basic problems of language status and parity of esteem, coupled with the users' attitudes and the 'genius' of the language affected, can lead to acceptance or rejection usually modified by official intervention acting in favour of one or the other. Pressure group intervention to preserve the original language often identifies the agents responsible for language change as both users of the language and the language planners. In addition to catching up with the religious and economic views of voters, politicians may seek to influence them by letting themselves be identified by a dialect or their knowledge of a regional mother tongue. Even so, de Valera's preference for an independent Irish language rather than political freedom as declared in his choice 'between political freedom without the language, and the language without political freedom . . .' (quoted by Dwyer, 1980) did not do much to arrest the decline of Irish Gaelic.

The impact of Information Technology (IT)

In addition to the worldwide spread of American English as the language of international business and diplomacy, the impact of the new technologies and the need for rapid international communication using these technologies have contributed to creating a new, distinctive, variety of English, American English, on an unprecedentedly large scale. Because the Internet uses English as its international *lingua franca*, it means that not only English and American but also Japanese and Chinese business and commercial users use English to communicate internationally.

The point was well put in a paragraph in the Report of the Kingman Inquiry (DES, 1988):

> Round the city of Caxton, the electronic suburbs are rising. To the language of books is added the language of television and radio, the elliptical demotic of the telephone, the processed codes of the computer. As the shapes of literacy multiply, so our dependence on language increases. But if language motivates change, it is itself changed. *To understand the principles on which that change takes place should be denied to no one.* [authors' emphasis]

These changes are far from superficial but affect the meaning of words and their various uses. Writing elsewhere about the implications of information technology for Language Awareness programmes, Adams (1996) noted how much language is itself being changed by the new technologies and how metaphors drawn from the older technologies are used to talk about this change so that words like 'book' and 'typeface' have been recruited into a context which endows them with an extended meaning. As yet, there is no metalanguage in which to describe the language of computers: we fall back on metaphors drawn from the more familiar world of print ('fonts'), low-level technology ('cut and paste') and the world of the study ('windows', 'desk top' and 'waste paper basket'). There are dangers here in that the technology does not behave in any real sense like conventional print forms; we fool ourselves if we really believe that we are putting something away in a waste paper basket or opening a foolscap file when sitting at a computer. Because the giants in the hardware and software fields (IBM, Apple, Microsoft) are American, this means that a new variety of English is rapidly developing, although the word 'trash' does appear as 'waste [paper] basket' in computers meant for the English purchaser. In Europe, German and French technology especially has managed to translate or encourage *calques* for many of the terms, so that the computer menu looks German or French. Even so many of the American terms or uses remain, such as '[Print or file] *manager*' on a German computer.

A comparison of some computer terms found in German with their English equivalents illustrates the penetration of American English and the weaker resistance of German compared with French. The equivalent French terminology shows a somewhat lesser penetration in that language probably due to the insistence on the 'purity' of French by the academicians responsible.

An interesting term is that of 'mouse', an American acronym which includes the words '*m*ovement *o*peration (*s*ystem)' as its integral components. The German equivalent *Maus* puts the term alongside the popular acceptance of 'mouse' in English, not as an acronym which is even more distant in German but as a device which resembles the small rodent. New users of the technology may be helped to handle their 'mouse' by being reminded that 'the mouse has its tail at the back'. This advice may fit a German situation more easily than a French one with *souris*. Most German computer terms are in English: *Cursor*, *Laser*, *E-Mail*, including *Computer* itself distinguished only by the capital letter 'C' and not the 'K' found in 'Latin' words like *Konferenz* or *Kongress*. Only the most general of words which have an existence outside computers have been translated or *calqued*, for example: 'delete' (*löschen*), 'menu' (*Menü*), 'insert' (*einfügen*), 'save' (*speichern*). *Soundkarte* is an interesting hybrid which shows the dominant term (sound) in its original English. 'Desktop' is *Bildschirmoberfläche*, *Bus-Fahrten*, literally 'bus trips', itself an interesting metaphor, is used as an equivalent to the English command 'switch to' to enable switching between different programs. The distinctly French *ordinateur* is unique to that language and culture, since elsewhere in the world computers are generally known by that term. Using *souris* for 'mouse' is clear, but what is one to make of the Spanish *ratón* (rat) for the same device?

In English, this language variety is currently marked by the use of the metaphors mentioned above and by an increasing importation of American idioms and spellings, such as a 'bug in the program'. One reaction is not to allow the new technologies to creep up unannounced. We owe it to the next generation of pupils to make them aware of how language is changing and being changed by the technologies they increasingly take for granted. A critical awareness of the language of IT is an important part of the field of language awareness.

Nowhere can this be seen more clearly than in the relatively new communication field of electronic mailing, especially as this becomes more familiar and accessible through the universality of the Internet. Most beginning users of this medium model its use on the more familiar field of the written medium: the letter, the memo, the report. As experience and confidence grows, this quickly changes and the realization dawns that electronic 'mail' (another metaphor) has features that are in some ways much more akin to speech than to written forms. Electronic mail text is not always composed in complete written sentences; users are tolerant of 'errors' of spelling, style and syntax not admissible in a conventional printed text. Characteristically, they talk of 'chat mode' and the language used tends to be much more informal than would be that of a written form. In writing electronically, most users are more likely to write ('say'), 'Hi! Brian', something that they would be unlikely to do in writing even the most informal of letters. Users have even begun to develop a whole new language to express emotion in electronic mail – something that the technology does not naturally lend itself to – in the form of the 'smiley', forms which are themselves leading to the development of a set of new conventions known as 'netiquette'. Some examples of these, which are now universally understood by net users and have even developed into a dictionary of their own, are the following:

:-)	happiness
:-!	foot in mouth
(:-%	anger
:-X	don't say a word

The thrust of the argument is that one should no longer limit one's interest in language to the 'word' alone. It has to be extended to encompass all manner of communication, which in essence means all forms of symbolization not exclusively conventional vocal symbols. Just as electronic communication has as much in common with speech as with written language, so too it has much in common with other iconic forms of communication. If recent speculation is right in suggesting that much of the origins of human language can be attributed to its being the equivalent to 'grooming' behaviour in the higher primates (Dunbar, 1996), electronic communication may be bringing us closer to our roots: the period of dominance by the written (and printed) form may be seen as a historical accident and the walls of the cities of Caxton may already be on the point of tumbling down.

The impact of language planning

Of the many ways in which a development affecting language comes about, language policy or language planning is an example of deliberate language change. As the instrument of communication, language is subject to formal and informal steps taken by different categories of users and their influence in deciding on the best way in which language can serve its intended purposes. The languages of education and administration are the most likely to be affected by formal policies, since the private use of language is difficult to police, except insofar as the use of languages in school playgrounds or in church may be forbidden or restricted, as happened in the past to Polish at the hand of the Russians and to Welsh at English hands.

Language policy operates on macro and micro levels. The former is concerned with such matters as language planning, consolidation of an official language together with the release of funding necessary to achieve this, the eradication of illiteracy, the introduction of a school language syllabus, and the exclusion or inclusion of regional minority or immigrant languages from compulsory schooling. Here the governments of most nation states pursue a policy of assimilation, recognizing teaching the standard variety of the 'official' mother tongue language as one of the main core subjects of the compulsory school curriculum. The need for foreign language skills is increasingly being debated, with implications for which languages to choose and their status as languages of regional or world communication. In this area too, language planning is involved although the term is most frequently applied to the policies regulating the use of regional mother tongues. At the micro level, policy concerns such things as setting pupils' standards of achievement, the introduction of spelling reforms or the extent of access to information technology. In France, some of these matters are within the jurisdiction of the *Académie*, with public opinion consulted in a variety of ways, mainly indirectly, which has led to the abandonment of some of the more extraordinary spelling reform proposals and the introduction of substitutes for words in *franglais*. Particularly disliked is 'walkman'. Its French equivalent, *le balladeur*, shows no generation gap since the latter is equally disliked by the young who are most likely to use the device. French insistence on preserving the French character of the language is documented in Muller (1985).

The German publishing house, *Duden*, which fulfils a similar function to the French *Académie*, though lacking the status and prestige with regard to language policy decisions, has been concerned, together with a committee of ministers and experts from the Federal Republic as well as from Austria and Switzerland, to simplify German spelling. The members of this committee, unlike the French *'Immortels'*, have the status of civil servants and are probably unknown to the general public. Their proposals are also published and subject to criticism by the public although in a way perhaps less formal and more similar to British practice. The proposal to spell *Ritmus* for *Rhythmus* was rejected as outrageous as quickly as similar French proposals, such as the abolition of the circumflex and the doubling of the consonant (*l*) in certain classes of verbs. German *Filosofie* was considered too revolutionary in breaking its ties with Greek origins. A simplification of rules for using the comma has been welcomed as has the virtual disappearance of the German *ß* in favour of *ss* (*weiß* becomes *weiss*; *daß* becomes *dass*). However, the proposal to spell logically *Betttuch* instead of *Bettuch* and *Programmmanager* for *Programmanager* leads to an accumulation of the same consonant.

Spelling reforms approved in principle by the governments concerned have met with strong opposition from writers and publishers, who see the reprinting of books that this action would require as too costly. Lexical changes on the other hand have the habit of appearing more unobtrusively. A number of earlier borrowings, such as 'Off the rails', has a German equivalent – *entgleisen* – but this is used in the literal sense only. 'Hit the buffers' has no metaphorical equivalent, being rendered by one verb – *aufprellen*. Both examples show that a language may resist converting a literal borrowing into metaphorical usage, another example of the foreclosure of its system to aspects of openness considered to be going too far. This is another example of the different way language alone manages its metaphors already referred to in more detail in the previous chapter. Time is the one dimension with which to measure language change. In time the 'symbolic language', with its elements of idioms from religious and cult practices for example, has a part to play in penetrating the instrumental medium of language used for communication. This is demonstrated particularly strongly in the figurative medium. The English phrase 'having a heavy cross to bear' will be found replicated with minor variations in other languages used in Christian societies but will not be readily understood in most other parts of the world.

Many of the language policies resulting in change mentioned earlier actually occurred, within a surprisingly short period of time, after a war or a civil war. Normally changes of such order take centuries to come about, during which period events accumulate to become manifest at an opportune time. Political upheavals in history, foreign occupation coupled with cultural dominance, can be identified as the causes whose impact affects the language used, which may, once the territory has been liberated, attempt to rid itself of features perceived to be alien to the 'genius' of the language. The various alphabetical and spelling reforms, the lexical and phonological differences, are a characteristic part of the different influences which speed up the process of growing apart in terms of their users' perceived political and social world views.

In the period of nation state formation in Europe, the language adopted by the newly established countries was frequently in the news. After World War One, the role of the national language as the official language of the state figured prominently in the drafts of several state constitutions. Where the mother tongue is identified with the written form of the national language, it has enjoyed a particularly privileged 'official' status, providing a clear indicator of distinctiveness and featuring as a national symbol. This process was repeated in the somewhat unexpected resurgence of nationalism after World War Two. In the Federal Republic, German as the 'official language' was enshrined in the 1949 constitution *Grundgesetz*. A similar sequence of events happened after the break up of the USSR, especially in the case of the constitutions of the liberated Baltic republics. In France, the second article of the 1992 constitution, revised just before the referendum on the Maastricht Treaty, is an especially strong example of identifying the French language, together with the *tricolor* and the *Marseillaise*, as an integral part of the Republic.

A new distinctive form of the language can be adopted by a newly constituted state, the government of which may be anxious to mark its independence. Croatian is now the name of the official language of the Republic of Croatia, with editors and compilers of dictionaries, some published by state publishing houses, busy determining the differences between it and Serbian. This is because many linguists continue to use the term Serbo-Croat which links both the Serbian and Croatian dialects of the language now politically decreed to be separate. Bosnian, virtually another Serbian dialect, is also beginning to be recognized as an independent language. It contains more Turkish elements, but, unlike Serbian, uses the Latin alphabet. The decreed use of the Latin and Cyrillic alphabets at different times of the country's history by Romanian, especially the official language variety of what is the present-day Republic of Moldova, is another example of language planning.

The policy of the central government of Spain after the Act of Autonomy in 1978 encouraging the separate development of the regions may, contrary to some views, be interpreted as a deliberate policy to keep the Kingdom of Spain together. There are insufficient distinctive linguistic markers in some 'languages', such as Murcian, virtually indistinguishable from Castilian, to make them stand on their own as a distinct national language so removing an important plank from the structure of an envisaged autonomous existence. Only established languages, such as Catalan, supported by the strong economic and historical base of the region, can together guarantee a measure of independence, other regions being forced to abandon radical policies aiming for greater independence and finding refuge in Castilian. In his comments on the Act of Autonomy for Galicia, Wardhaugh (1987) thought the measures taken to revive it could be 'largely irrelevant to the future of the Galician language'.

In the case of the French sovereignty over the Tuscan dialect speaking island of Corsica, however, language changes imposed by war and long-term foreign occupation may no longer be attributed to war, as may enforced language extermination caused by the persecution of Jews or the conversion of Indians. Current language changes, including language loss, are likely to be caused by the impact of migrations and the cultural and economic force of superpowers, which may be kept in check by some sovereign states such as France, which has a large number of committees for the protection and preservation of the French language, a situation not replicated in Germany. Their existence alone is not a guarantee of their success.

There has to be a measurable quantity and quality of distinctive cultural features to justify the self-contained national existence of a linguistic territory in order to keep pace with the political measures working in the direction of independence. However, the interference of 'symbolic' linguistic together with socio-political, economic and psychological factors is a feature which will continue even if the original mother tongue and national state have been 'lost'. This can be seen in the unmistakable distinctiveness of Irish English, Silesian Polish/German and other ethnic groupings. Cultural distinctiveness can, after all, also be expressed in ways other than language, while the continued existence of a language, for instance Cornish, as a 'museum exhibit' is another possibility.

The impact of language loss

The statement that languages in contact are also 'languages in conflict' takes account of the fact that each language asserts its dominant role in its existing territory, resisting the encroachments of other languages which may lead to the displacement of the original language used (Wardhaugh, 1987). This has been illustrated by a number of recent 'local' sociolinguistic studies, in the wake of national revival which has affected all of Europe, such as those by Haugen (1972), Allworth (1980) and Trudgill (1983, 1984a, 1984b). Large-scale migrations have demonstrated the problems of language loss and language maintenance caused by multilingualism, prompting rather unrealistic efforts to limit its impact by curbing or indeed eliminating migration altogether. Multilingualism, which is the result of 'holding on to one's mother tongue', or indeed of the study and use of other languages, is only slowly being accepted as an enrichment, either in terms of improving communication or leading to ethnic tolerance. For example, the growth of language through lexical input has met resistance not only from acknowledged xenophobes but also from allegedly impartial individuals arguing for retaining 'correct' and 'standard' versions of their language. Also, the priorities of efficient communication using a simple language medium available to all are difficult to set against the merits of a complex and creative diversity of language whose only value is measured in terms of tolerance in intercultural relations. Private preferences for linguistic purity can easily get confused and mixed up with political power struggles taking decades to resolve, as in the case of the German-speaking territory of Southern Tyrol. Some Russians regard Belorussian as an inferior dialect of the Russian language. Language can be just as easily a disuniting as a uniting factor in human relations.

Political independence alone may not guarantee the preservation of linguistic purity nor the prevention of language loss. National language policies address issues of status, parity, standardization, purity and change, all with a cumulative effect, since, except in the process of a detached study of a language, it is impossible to keep the discrete language elements separate from each other. Everyday language users do not recognize boundaries created by linguists or politicians for the purpose of identifying a particular dialect or aspect of language such as its lexis to establish its distinction, nor are they necessarily in favour of standardizing the language. They like to decide on what they use themselves and stay with that.

Indeed, language purity, expressed in terms of a 'standard', can be achieved most easily when the language is learned as a subject at school, requiring pupils to observe the regularity of the 'home medium' as compared with the vagaries of lexical or phonetic elements, often regarded as 'incorrect', brought in under the impact of the encroaching 'other' languages and dialects. Governmental intervention to provide protection against language disappearance and individual language loss and change, may, as seen in the example of Ireland, not be powerful enough when pitted against personal language choice (Riagáin, 1977 and Trudgill, 1984b).

Supranational political and economic units have their own multilingual intercultural policies. In some cases, diversity may be encouraged; in others, the desire to preserve the unity of existing political structures and to facilitate communication overrides such considerations. Both are difficult to operate, since at their extreme ends they may be mutually exclusive. This may be offset by the intervention of sovereign governments, coming out in support of minor regional languages, of which current policies in Europe provide many examples. Insisting on established linguistic rights is a powerful and emotional issue exacerbated by new claimants demanding their newly discovered rights for their own languages. Contacts with users of other languages resulting in the exchange of linguistic 'goods' may create mutual awareness, but may also turn out to achieve the very opposite, such as leading to the ban on individual foreign words. In Europe, *linguistic persecution* is no longer seen as a problem. However, language status, which, as indicated, is linked with the status of its users, has a decisive role in the process of language change (Skutnabb Kangas, 1981; Cummins and Swain, 1986; Skutnabb Kangas and Cummins, 1988). The language selected as the medium of a liturgy, as seen in the example of the Belorussian Orthodox Church, can affect the choice and language status of educational and cultural domains, with the language of the church responsible for activating the 'symbolic factor', which in turn can affect the character of the 'instrumental language'. The policy regarding the role of a *lingua franca*, which is the 'property' of more than one government, is not an easy one officially to formulate by one of the governments involved and, except in such cases as the American 'English Only' movement, it is avoided, although penetration and influence continue in private.

A language loss must be accompanied by the availability of a new medium of communication which will take its place. The exact dimensions of the changes necessary to achieve this cannot be measured accurately or objectively. Even total loss is never 'total'; language loss only refers to its loss as a spoken medium, since it may survive as an object of study. Teaching provision of a new medium may be resisted, although there are limits beyond which resistance is an impractical option. Most language users have to conform, with many finding themselves willing to do so, with the alternative medium close at hand in the form of the majority or influential language. The personal loss of language is not infrequent, inevitably leading to the acceptance of the new medium in which to operate or create further. On ethic grounds it might be questioned whether well-placed cultures, such as that of the white settlers in Canada, have the right to go to the rescue of native cultures which, though not their own, they see as threatened and deserving of preservation. In the case of the Cree language in Alberta, the few original users left are reconciled to its disappearance (McNeill & Griffith, in preparation).

The impact of bilingualism

Most mother tongue users may be loosely described as bilingual or, more accurately bidialectal. They are so partially, at least, being conversant with two different language media. For most, the different dialects and languages are acquired early and used throughout a lifetime. Two languages can be acquired in the home with two parents speaking different languages to the child. In the case of a non-home foreign language, the more usual pattern is for the child deliberately to start learning it in the formal context of schooling. There is rarely a perfect fit between the two languages, even for 'natural', or early, language acquisition, because several areas of communication, for example 'child language' or 'professional language', depending on the time and type of bilingual exposure, may remain totally unused in one of the languages acquired. Even so, it is not infrequent to find individuals who can communicate bilingually (and bidialectally) on many topics and use their capacity easily to 'switch codes'.

Those likely to be exposed to an often involuntary bilingualism are immigrants or, more correctly, the children of immigrants once they have been made to start their formal schooling in their future new (second) language medium. Unlike the more freely chosen immersion education given in a foreign language medium or the mother tongue, submersion can be a traumatic experience, although most users at some stage have to put it behind them and will be able to operate in both languages. The ease with which they can do it depends on such factors as motivation and language availability. These language users are exposed to a form of language awareness, when they themselves experience linguistic interference or, in a more formal way, when they arrive at understanding the nature of the two parallel systems.

'Interference' from one or the other of their different languages is a frequent feature of bilingualism, with users experiencing it particularly frequently in pronunciation or in the intrusion of such lexical items as particles (Weinreich, 1953). 'He's a clever young man, isn't it?', uses the French construction *n'est ce pas*, or German *nicht wahr*, rather than the English, 'Isn't he?' Bilingualism involves the ability to formulate and test language rules, as in the examples just given, which need not be a deliberate process. However, it can be used to help in the process of second language learning.

The advantages of bilingualism are claimed to be improved language skills and language knowledge. Both enhance the facility actively to use more than one language medium and the potential to use other languages, the ability, that is, to use one's knowledge and linguistic intuition the more easily to acquire another medium. The committed advocates of bilingualism (Baker, 1993; Dodson, 1972 and 1985) see bilingualism as developing the user's cognitive and psycho-motor faculties. There is no agreement about what came first: bilingualism or the intelligence to become bilingual. However, according to recent studies made in bilingual environments, especially in Canada, there is no doubt that bilingualism can stimulate linguistic development, at least. Theroux (1984), who thought bilinguals were 'inexact' in their language usage, had to deal with language users whose repertoire was unexpectedly wide.

Language acquisition and language learning processes distinguish between 'transitional' bilingualism and 'substitution' bilingualism. In the first case the mother tongue is used for a limited time in schooling to help learners obtain an education in their host country's language and to improve their general educational development, a strategy widely advocated by some. Maintenance of the learner's mother tongue may further try to ensure that both languages can be expected to continue to be used. The mother tongue will not be discarded while the new language is acquired. An awareness of language, which can be useful when learning a language, will occur if the process is properly handled (Cummins, 1982 and 1984). In 'substitution bilingualism' the new (second, L2) language takes over from the original (first, L1) mother tongue. This is usually the result of a deliberate policy fully to assimilate. Teaching policy varies, but the intended result is that ethnic groups assimilate to the host countries' language and culture in which case their bilingualism represents little more than a 'symbolic' or 'associated' language with only traces of users' first language found in their second language. As a result language awareness is not made explicit. To some extent this process probably affects all non-native (second) mother tongue users. Depending on the circumstances, however, groups who insist on full first language maintenance, the mother tongue, can be more or less successful in their endeavours (Tulasiewicz, 1994).

There are complex reasons leading to language maintenance or language rejection and assimilation. Governments faced with an immigration problem have an array of policies to encourage or discourage bilingualism. The criticism of the 1968 US Bilingual Education Act was that it had no clear vision as to why bilingual education was to be made available and whose responsibility it would be to teach it (Gans, 1979). On the whole, the 'transitional' model is the likely norm, where the objective is to encourage bilingualism as part of a general improvement of modern foreign language skills. There are those, of course, who set out to learn another (second) language to replace their (first) mother tongue to make full use of it in their work or to flaunt it to demonstrate their new ethnicity. Skutnabb Kangas (1981, 1982), one of the linguists most committed to the cause of bilingualism, analyses the mixed advantages and disadvantages that are associated with the different social and educational forms of bilingualism and their impact on users.

Under ideal conditions, bilingualism can be 'environmentally friendly' – a claim made for opening up for users a whole new language environment and endowing them with a linguistic flexibility which enables them to make further use of it. In Chapter 2 we showed how artistic creativity in one's second medium is well attested. In the circumstances described by Leopold (1971), the two languages are 'acquired' simultaneously in early childhood. Educational and emotional problems are more likely to occur in the more formal context of schooling. These are long-lasting adjustment problems and language dysfunctions, for instance, poor perception of one's 'mother tongue', or indeed of the second or foreign language which accompany the social choices faced by learners. They have been the subject of extensive literature: Skutnabb Kangas (1981), Skutnabb Kangas and Cummins (1988) and Edwards (1977) to name but three. In the European Union, the social problems of bilingualism have probably been the object of more attention than the psychological impact on language development.

The above comment was needed to provide an objective evaluation of the often very optimistic comments made about 'language enrichment' and ease of communication, particularly in the case of languages which are extensively used in a wider context. To achieve bilingualism in all contexts and registers is not easy; partial bilingualism, the possession of some language skills, can, depending on circumstances, be very useful in users' professional lives. Language Awareness, as a by-product of bilingualism, may lead to linguistic tolerance and more harmonious interethnic relations, a topic only beginning to be explored in intercultural education (Jago, 1998). Some forms of bilingualism, especially those associated with language preservation, may be linked less with tolerance than with chauvinism as noted by Gellner (1964).

Politicians and business interests, who promote improved and extended language education and unreservedly advocate the usefulness of bilingualism, take little account of the difference between 'acquired' and 'learned' bilingualism. Policies which see the second language as another school subject take insufficient notice of the traumatic effects of language loss and language maintenance. Encouraging bilingualism without considering the nature of its impact ignores the fact that another language is another way of life. Not all would regard this as an unmixed blessing.

The problems of learning to become bilingual and the choice of methods are as many as there are methods in language teaching. Acquiring another language medium by a child learning English in an English home, or French in a French home, are bound to be different from those of learning English in a French home, or vice versa. The difficulty is that these cannot easily be calculated in any detail, since the learners, after entering their mother tongue or second language worlds, may have become indistinguishable except to skilled or indeed prejudiced observers. A complete linguistic failure, while in all likelihood immediately recognized, cannot trace all the circumstances that have led to failure. It is certainly possible that a multiple input can activate in children the ability to use more than one language, however, the exact amount is impossible to determine. Although the costs of a multilingual policy in governing the European Union, for example interpreting and translating, can be calculated (Coulmas, 1991), the social and educational costing of individual bilingualism has not been attempted. An article in *Language Awareness* (Henry, 1995) is critical of the supposed financial advantages of learning another language, though this is not a view that is supported by the Confederation of British Industry.

Language policies in the European Union emphasize the need to learn foreign languages. One of the main results of the European Dimension, as defined in the European Community Resolution of May 1987, has been to draw attention to the socio-political and economic need for bilingualism and multilingualism as ways to improve international communication. This development has also been supported by language teachers and psycho-linguists (Dodson, 1985; Hagege, 1987). It is necessary to distinguish between what may be regarded as commercially useful bilingualism, actively supported by the European Union and the Council of Europe, and the recognition of the support it provides in educational development. That happens when the first language may be jettisoned after full mastery in the majority communication language (second language) has been acquired (Edwards, 1985). This policy is more likely to be used in the case of minor languages, since political priorities favour the teaching of the major languages of communication or at least of the national languages of member states of the European Union. Some commentators have warned against the danger of regarding the minor languages as inferior (Alatis, 1970).

There are vastly more teaching methods available for use in the study of a recognized *lingua franca* as second language (L2), especially English, than for the study by foreigners of some of the smaller languages. Indeed Teaching English as a Foreign (or Second) language (TEFL and TESOL) has become a major industry. One of the tests of the efficacy of its teaching methods is to check on what account is taken of language interference as a result of penetration. Sadly, the impact of a method on first language, mother tongue, maintenance as opposed to 'correctness' is hardly likely to be considered.

SOME PROBLEMS OF WORLD LANGUAGE STATUS

More than anything else the rapid political and economic growth of a small number of superpowers on the world stage has driven home the need for easy communication in a shrinking world. In this development the superpowers have emerged as cultural superpowers also, their languages assuming a role which extends far beyond their original territories. The speed and extent of the spread of English and American English has been felt more widely than previous hegemonies, such as those of Latin or Greek. Much of this process is due to the activities of Europeans, with the worldwide growth of superlanguages until recently confined to European languages, whose users have been the strongest stake-holders in the unequal distribution of resources.

The status achieved by the world language has been responsible for the revaluation of priorities in economic, cultural and moral terms, expressed in those languages. The values accepted are probably those represented by the nations whose mother tongues play the dominant communicative roles. This has an impact on the users of all the languages affected, the dominant as well as the dominated. The values disseminated through the world languages then meet with general, if not always willing, acceptance. Assessing the moral issues surrounding the transmission of those values through the world language media is outside the concern of this chapter; it must be stressed, however, that language changes in both the donor and borrowing languages caused by the impact of the world languages are not only of linguistic interest. They are important for the impact these languages have on both world language and minor language users. World language does not mean that everyone in the world will use it or will have equal fluency in it. These considerations merit more extensive treatment than has been given them.

While the political and economic factors for English to have assumed *lingua franca* status have been well rehearsed, of the 145 countries trading in international commerce there is no country which does not use English, the question why it is English that should have assumed that role also requires a more closely linguistic answer. English, the strongest contender for world language status, cannot be seen as an exclusively distinguishing mark for a nation in the same way as, for example, German. As the language spoken by many different nationalities, as their mother tongue or first language or alternative, second mother tongue, English is not the exclusive mark of Englishness as is the case with languages spoken by fewer people in a more confined territory. However, size alone cannot be accepted as the only criterion, since there are smaller languages which have successfully aspired to dominant status within their regions, such as Spanish or German. Despite their use of English, Northern Ireland and

Scotland are distinctly separate entities in respect of their using different variants of the English language. They are, of course, also characterized by their political and cultural links with the English Crown and the Protestant Church. There is further the distinction that exists in the different Irish dialects of the north and of the south. If the English language did not succeed in changing the Scots into English in the United Kingdom, it is hardly surprising that it is necessary to accept the existence of very different 'Englishes' spoken by non-English native users not just in Great Britain, but even more so in the more distant parts of the English-speaking world. It is all these variants of English which *together* account for its status as a world language. They also have implications for the status of English as a *lingua franca*. The total number of mother tongue speakers of German in their much more compact home territory is higher than the corresponding number of users of English in the British Isles (Ammon, 1991). However, this is not matched by the number of users of German as their first language worldwide compared with the significantly higher number of users of varieties of English worldwide. Taking numbers alone, French has less claim to world language status compared with Spanish; however, the number of countries in which French is the official medium is greater than the corresponding number of countries in which German or Spanish are so used (Ammon, 1989).

It is the very diversity of English which makes the problem of a standard a very difficult one to settle. The publicity given to the need to maintain a distinctively British English 'standard' may be seen as an unnecessary attempt to make political capital out of the distinctiveness provided by that variety of the language. Since there can be no single standard for all the different 'Englishes' worldwide taken separately, though there is an Australian standard as there is a Welsh English one, the existence of different standards for the one world language has implications for its millions of users. Even the notion of a standard variant of English as the *lingua franca* must allow for the large number of variations in pronunciation and lexis. It could of course be argued that the standard to be adopted should be American English because of the political and media power that lies behind it. On the other hand, in view of the existence of a large number of distinctively different dialects of English throughout the English-speaking world – for example, Australian and South African English as well as American (which itself has many varieties) – one might ask whether English *qua* 'world language' might not more properly be regarded as a number of different though related languages rather than as a single entity. This in turn is complicated still further by the populations in each of the dialects who use English differently, either because they have acquired it as a second language, as in many parts of Africa and Asia, or because they have adopted it as an equivalent first language to their mother tongue, as, for example, in much of the Indian subcontinent and many individuals scattered elsewhere. They may also have learned it as a foreign language. It is these factors, additional to that of number, which must be considered together when thinking of English as a world language and which give rise to the need for devising efficient methods of teaching it in widely differing circumstances. In Europe, English mother tongue as used in the United Kingdom may be compared with mother tongue Italian in Italy, but its world language status has implications for Europe which go far beyond those of Italian.

Early in the existence of the United States, Americans made a strong attempt to distance themselves in language terms from the British by creating American English or American. This practice was not followed in the majority of ex-French territories where the 'pure' French medium was in the hands of those who wanted to make full use of it to demonstrate their cultural (French) superiority to the other inhabitants. The emphasis on 'pure' French may satisfy a linguistic solution for the imposition of a 'standard', but this fails to take account of the language needs of the socio-political and cultural realities of the nature of the territories settled either in terms of population density of the original inhabitants or their stage of development *vis à vis* that of the newcomers. It is the political reality and the economic vitality of a territory as a whole that play a role that has to be considered alongside the linguistic differences such as those between dialects.

Language used as a mark of separateness by nationalists is one of the factors at work behind the American 'English Only' policy (Baron, 1992). Acceding to the demands for a privileged position for American English would discourage both the teaching and the commercial use of other languages. This policy, while welcomed by some as a unifying factor helping to strengthen the economic position of America, is seen by its opponents as dictated by fear and racism and doomed to fail to achieve its objectives. It will impoverish those unable or unwilling to abandon their mother tongues by denying them access to education and jobs, while unable to stop the private use of minority languages.

Language planning policies by governments do not necessarily reflect the wishes of the users, whose own priorities lie in their personal economic prosperity rather than the satisfaction of political motives. Preferences for 'assimilation' rather than maintaining one's original ethnic identity may not coincide with government plans. A telling comment is that Galicians regard the Galician standard as *hablar mal* when compared with Castilian, the use of the latter being designated as *parlar bien* (Green, 1994). In the former Yugoslavia one of the authors (Tulasiewicz) was rebuked for not being able to speak a 'human' language which for the peasant informer meant Serbian. The cultural impact of language change initiated by smaller groups of speakers may get hijacked and blown wide open by political and economic interests. Dialect variants of related languages, like southern German *Oberdeutsch*, may be seen as distinguishing marks of users but it was the reality of the political rise of Prussia over Austria which gave the impetus to the supremacy of the central German dialects over the southern ones. As in the case of the English in England, the language itself played a secondary role to the political one.

The need for languages, especially those aspiring to world or international language status, to develop a pluralistic policy distinguishing between the different domains of language, public and private, commercial and creative, which requires appropriate study methods, is one which has been debated in Europe. This is also a way for some languages to justify their continuing existence by specializing. However, assuming that these factors are of equal worth fails to distinguish between the more personal priorities of language maintenance and the socio-political ones for ease of communication. A chauvinistic attitude to national language should have no place in determining language policies. However, the lesser incentive for users of English, of whatever variety, to learn another language leaves a gap in their anglophone education which should be filled by language study based on linguistic sensitivity, enabling 'mother tongue' users better to understand those whose language or dialects are different.

CONCLUSION

During the French Revolution a uniform form of French was encouraged by the Jacobins who believed that the existence of different dialects divided people, while the use of the same dialect gave the best chance to achieve equal social and economic progress. This change in policy happened in 1792, after the initial encouragement, for different ideological reasons, of linguistic diversity and autonomy, immediately after the outbreak of the French Revolution in

1789. A similar policy was also pursued by Lenin who, while broadly in favour of protecting and encouraging local languages in the Russian Empire and the Soviet Union, went on to regard Russian as the common language of the proletariat fighting for its rights, reconciling national differences.

This brings the discussion back to the need for a *lingua franca* for international communication placing a concern with foreign or second language learning on a par with that of mother tongue maintenance. A mother tongue will be preserved as long as it is loved as well as widely used. Learning a foreign language is not normally undertaken unless that language is to be used. For professional linguists to advocate linguistic diversity is to take no account of the realities, such as the problems of codifying languages and finding fellow users, if they are to be used for communication.

Interestingly enough, the well-meaning, if misguided, attempts to impose equality through language manipulation of the French Jacobins has seen a recent revival in England in the thinking of conservatively minded socio-linguists such as Honey (1983) and Marenbon (1994) and is firmly embedded in the latest version of National Curriculum English (DfE, 1995).

A world language such as English has the best and the worst of both worlds. If taken as an entity, it may be thought to be less of a distinguishing mark of ethnicity but is more likely to endure compared with other mother tongues because of its size. It is also the carrier of the economic and cultural values associated with its users. Its ownership lays a responsibility on its users to respect other smaller languages, endowing the language with a linguistic sensitivity which may, despite some critics, manifest itself as in the case of English in the ready acceptance of 'alien' elements, which may enable it to become an even more efficient instrument of international communication.

Chapter 6

Language Policies in the European Union

A CLASH OF PRIORITIES?

The need to reconcile the cultural and linguistic diversity of Europe with that of making Europeans aware of their common heritage and their everyday necessity to communicate easily and efficiently with one another in the peaceful pursuit of economic and social objectives presents problems. The history of the continent has been a mixed one of wars and trade, persecution and fraud alternating with artistic and technological achievements and social policies which most can readily identify as European. Over the years Latin, French and English have all functioned as European *linguae francae*, with English meanwhile assuming an unassailably dominant position as the world language of international communication. In socio-economic, if not yet in political terms, the European Union of fifteen member states, with the accession of a number of central and eastern European states set to expand further, no longer the (West) European Economic Community of ten years ago, is being acknowledged as a single unit. The recognition of common responsibilities: economic – to ensure the prosperity of the populations; social – to offer them a healthy as well as a secure existence including the fullest protection of human rights; global – preserving the peace and maintaining the environment to which political concerns are being added, requires a system of communication that will enable the fullest understanding of measures taken on behalf of all citizens of Europe. This is particularly necessary in view of the real possibility of international misunderstandings and the arousal of national suspicions.

The potential clash between the introduction of a single language of communication and the acceptance of diversity is one which other socio-economic units, like the North Atlantic Free Trade Agreement (NAFTA), have had to confront to a much lesser degree. Respecting the linguistic diversity of NAFTA, which of course does exist, seems to be much less of a problem than is the case with the European Union. To take account of the diversity and turn it into an asset is a challenge Europeans must be prepared to face.

The implications of professional and social mobility in the Single Europe have confirmed the need for a European language policy. Not surprisingly with fifteen sovereign members of the Union this still awaits comprehensive implementation. Mother tongues are required not only for intranational communication, which has accelerated with the growth of the demand for information, but also for international links. Efficient teaching of the mother tongue has become a task of national and cultural as well as international economic and social priority. Teaching modern foreign languages has been recognized as an important component of the education of all children. Attempts to revive artificial languages, like Esperanto, have not been particularly successful, while the development of 'communicative languages' intended for specific purposes, such as Airspeak, devised in Cambridge by Edward Johnson, have achieved success within their particular spheres of operation only. Airspeak and similar 'languages' have an English base to which many non-English speakers have to adjust first, requiring knowledge of a language which they do not possess. Working for an integrated Europe is a political priority accepted by some, while social and economic development would be regarded as more urgent by others. Both are probably accepted as more important than appeals to a common past; a fact only half-recognized by early European reports such as that of Henri Janne in 1957 and some of the more historical elements of the European Dimension in school curricula (Adams, 1993; Adams & Tulasiewicz, 1995; Tulasiewicz, 1993).

The concept of a permanent multilingualism in Europe, which allocates each language a distinctive contributory role in the whole communicative process as outlined by Haarmann (1991), distinguishes between world languages, with English as the main contender for use throughout Europe; regional languages with a currency beyond one nation state, possibly Russian or German in eastern Europe; national languages with a state-wide currency at least, the mother tongues that constitute the principal concern of this book; and second and official languages which many would require in addition to enable them to function in the bureaucracies of Europe. Private and home languages have a legitimate role to play which often goes unrecognized.

The more liberal language, and language education, policies pursued by individual member states and regional political units have diminished the need to 'resist' the crudest forms of 'linguistic imperialism'. However, there remains the need to demonstrate and delimit the existence of separate minor languages. This is not to preserve them as museum pieces but to use them to devise language strategies which would ensure the full comprehension of the documentation usually produced in the major languages and the opportunity to present their own case by the often forgotten many million users of the 'smaller' languages (Koch, 1991). There is, otherwise, the danger that their views will not be heard, what with their concepts neglected and their comprehension of things taken for granted since they are often unable to articulate them in the major languages. The users of these languages find it difficult, in turn, to understand users of the small language. Nowhere is this more apparent than in international meetings where the official, that is, major, languages make the running while contributions in the smaller languages, even if admitted, are not heard out for lack of time, are often misunderstood and generally regarded as irritating interventions by those not in fluent command of the major tongues or too slow to catch the attention of the audience.

The languages affected by European Union interventions are, in the first instance, the official languages of member states, which for the most part, according to the Brussels Resolution of 1977 are the national mother tongues. As regards the regional minority languages, such as Irish Gaelic or Galician, the European Bureau for the Lesser Used Languages located in Dublin has been more active on behalf of the latter languages than in respect of the languages of non-European immigrants. The use of their languages, such as Arabic or Urdu, has to be negotiated for the purpose of education or for admissibility in official transactions.

The languages of the member states of the European Union enjoy a particularly protected position in governmental transactions, in second and foreign language education, though probably less so in business, through the provisions of the LINGUA Programme. All European Union sponsored initiatives involve languages and require the participation of at least three national groups to prevent domination by a major language. However, the LINGUA Action Horizontal Measures are exclusively identified with enhanced communication and improved mobility within the EU and the European Economic Area. They concentrate on linguistic competence with attention given to the acquisition of skills in the less widely used languages, though not to what we have called Language Awareness teaching approaches. The various 'Actions' defined within this and other European educational co-operation programmes are available to teachers, their pupils and administrators.

The Council of Europe, not a governmental organization, with its distinguished record in matters affecting human rights has been particularly influential in generating an interest in languages and cultures. The impact of population movements with the associated problems of provision of schooling and employment often compounded by prejudice, affect not only those immigrants who leave their usually poorer countries in search of work or asylum, but also, though to a lesser extent, the international civil servants, professionals and business people who also may have to use the official languages, but who may spend only a limited period of time in another European country.

Article 128 of the Maastricht Treaty proclaims Europe's diverse heritage. Except in the case of certain legal, economic and health measures and social security, the European Union is in favour of diversity. This applies also to language diversity supported by the Arfé Resolution C 287/106 (1981), which aimed at reconciling minority with national interests, and the establishment of the European Bureau for Lesser Used Languages in 1983. These institutions protect the minor languages, mother tongues and national, by giving them a forum in government and trade. However, under the provisions of article 126 of the Maastricht Treaty the governments of member states have the final say in the drafting and implementation of laws and regulations relating to education. That is why the policy of Europeanization has to be set against the fact of the continuing heterogeneity of a multilingual and multicultural Europe. Some policies were interpreted by the governments of member states as protecting their national languages against other national languages, rather than to foster the minority languages used in their regional territories. The French government had initially understood this as a policy of not supporting the smaller regional languages of France. The Arfé Resolution adopted by the European Parliament on 16 October 1981 called for a charter for regional language rights, such as allowing the use of Breton in a court of law. However, it could not be ratified and implemented because of the principles of sovereignty and subsidiarity which give member states the right to opt out of some legislation. The Charter for Regional and Minority Language Rights, proposed by the Council of Europe, was not ratified by the French and British governments when it was first presented in October 1992.

There is provision for the teaching of modern foreign languages in Europe, in terms of school level (primary or secondary), the curricular time given over to them, and the resources invested. This provision, however, is unequally distributed. Compared with the United Kingdom there is considerable difference not only as regards the more generous provision available in Spain, with her extensive programme of regional as well as foreign language teaching, or in France, where all EU languages are available at the primary level within a group of schools in a geographical area, but also as between England and Scotland. In Scotland, unlike England, a modern foreign language is a part of the regular primary school curriculum.

LANGUAGE AND IDENTITY REVISITED

The distinction between language as an instrument of communication and a mark of identity is important, even though difficult to make: language characterizes the user in the very process of its being used as an instrument of communication. The language transmits information, the messages themselves containing elements of the user's identity. However, the dominant language imposes its symbolic elements and conceptualization which prevents the dominated identities of the smaller languages from being fully expressed. This is the reason why the different ways of 'thinking', are difficult to comprehend by many and become more so the more abstract discourse becomes. Though language competence alone may not determine the quality of language performance it does help to give it direction. Good translations which rely on linguistic competence as well as knowledge of the subject matter are difficult to achieve and only rarely are they fully adequate. In terms of the European dimension in education language competence must include an acquaintance with the various institutions of the country whose language is being used.

Modern foreign language teaching, which should never be too far away from the considerations of mother-tongue teaching, must take account of users' need to recognize the linguistic skills of translation and interpretation, a priority emphasized by Roche (1991). In foreign, indeed second language study, especially at the level of beginners, these skills are rarely practised; with all the available time given over to the development of communicative proficiency in the medium selected. This fails to recognize that translation and interpretation, a language education input which includes references made to the learner's mother tongue, can help to firm up the process of learning another language. This intelligence was recognized by Steiner (1975) when he spoke of 'interpreting' with reference to the 'same' language used by different individuals, a comment which fully acknowledges the inadequacy of so many translations.

Both the European Union and the Council of Europe have been recommending the implementation of an intensive programme of collaboration and co-operation at all levels and for all types of transactions. This requires an improved and intensified knowledge of foreign languages recognized by the European Commission's Green Paper of September 1993. There is scope here for an examination of attitudes to languages other than one's mother tongue in general, and to language teaching methods and approaches in particular. Language support schemes require governments of member states to organize and help finance the tuition of immigrants' mother tongues, but the outcomes of such programmes are often unequal because the inputs are unequal as a consequence of conflict with policies which define the status of particular languages. The multicultural (and *ipso facto* multilingual) classrooms of Europe are excellent examples of a situation which taxes both material and attitudinal resources, because of the need to reconcile unity with diversity, a situation replicated at work as well as in leisure activities. The costing of all such measures is enormous (Coulmas, 1991) and, to be sure, not all governments of member states are agreed that such measures merit priority funding.

The problems posed by diversity: those of language sovereignty and language comprehension, do not look as if they will be speedily resolved. This is despite new approaches to teaching and the creation of new attitudes to language in general. Bilingualism has to pass the test of commercial usefulness before it will be recognized for its educational, helping children's language development, and communicative, integrating with Europe, advantages. Language Awareness, as an approach, is not sufficiently established as yet to be recognized for its contribution to reconciling the diversity of linguistic interests in Europe. There is an urgent need to pool together all existing resources and expertise in every aspect of language education.

Part II

The Mother Tongues of Europe:
Nine Case Studies

Figure 1: The states of Europe

Figure 2: Some linguistic minority areas of Europe

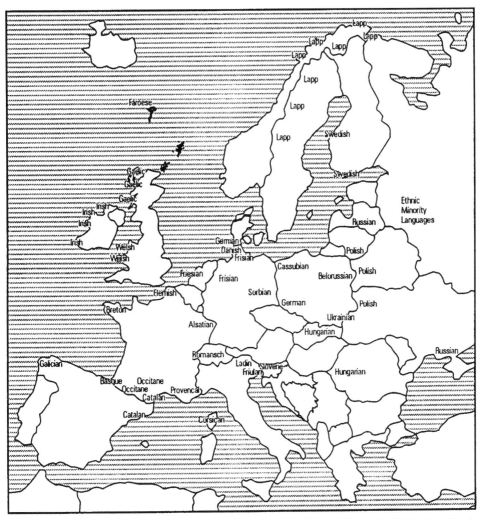

Introduction

The thirteen authors of the nine case studies appearing in Part II have addressed the topic of teaching the mother tongue in their respective countries by defining the mother tongues used and exploring their teaching within the context of the respective school systems. They have critically assessed the curricular policies existing in their countries and their impact on the details of the mother tongue syllabuses in force. By identifying and developing those elements which are of particular concern in their countries and highlighting them as they consider appropriate they have, taken together, produced a stimulating debate on the variety of issues which confront mother tongue education. These include such topics as the teaching of a standard language; the specific language education components which constitute a mother tongue syllabus; the assessment of mother tongue competency inasmuch as this can be achieved; and the mutual interference of rival language systems. Such topics as Language Awareness, which made an entry on to the school arena in Britain in the 1980s, are also to be found in the schools of other countries and the place allocated to them in syllabuses is discussed. Because of the different emphasis given by authors to particular items, in some case controversial, their accounts of priorities and innovations in mother tongue teaching, together with the constraints and pressures imposed upon them from various directions, enable their chapters to be read as more than a chronological and itemized collection of discrete facts.

In today's increasingly multilingual European classrooms there are the more recently identified problems of what is the mother tongue of a country and what is its role *via à vis* the other mother tongues used in relation to their users' personal development. In some countries there is the accepted challenge of providing regional mother tongue education for their territorial minorities and to cater for the often conflicting needs of immigrants' language maintenance or their cultural assimilation. Although these factors are present in all the countries represented in this Part, different authors having chosen to concentrate on particular features, such as the position of immigrant or territorial minorities, and so depending on where the priorities lie, a richer and more varied critical account of mother tongue education and its problems emerges.

Since it would be beyond the scope of a single volume to give meaningful accounts of the teaching of more than a few mother tongues, the authors of this Part were chosen to represent the four European major language groups in both large and small countries with more than one mother tongue of different provenance to be found. The chapters illustrate different problems, attempted solutions and policies to deal with linguistic plurality. In five cases (Denmark, France, Germany, Russia and Spain) this has been accomplished in a single chapter; in the cases of the United Kingdom and Poland, two separate chapters deal with what in the national context are the major (English and Polish) and the minor (Welsh and Belorussian) mother tongues respectively. This helps to emphasize the phenomenon of national identity in a multicultural Europe. Omissions, especially the fate of the demotic in Greece, are due to unforeseen circumstances which arose in the course of the compilation of this Part.

Chapter 7

Teaching the Mother Tongue in England

Robert Protherough

HISTORICAL INTRODUCTION: ENGLISH AND 'ENGLISH'

Significant tensions underlie our use of the word 'English'. Whereas Latin, Greek and, particularly from the seventeenth century onwards, French were nouns that referred both to a language and to a corresponding subject for study, the same is not true of English. For centuries that word signified the language itself (and such usage is considerably older than that of 'England' for the country), but the first recorded use of 'English' as a *subject* for school study was not until 1889. Mother-tongue learning has gone on for as long as the language has existed; what we know as the subject 'English' has been studied for little less than a century.

The learning of the mother tongue in England has been socially and politically controversial from the very beginning. There has been no general consensus for over five hundred years about who should be taught what, or how, or why. For much of that time, few people of power or influence thought the topic of any importance. Although for the Tudors, English was the language of the nation ('the King's English' in Shakespeare's *Merry Wives of Windsor*), Latin remained the universal language of learning and French the language of politics and culture. From the Middle Ages onwards 'grammar' meant essentially Latin grammar and 'Latinum' had come to mean language in general, while French was the language of the schoolroom until the second half of the fourteenth century (Lawson and Silver, 1973). Any education in the mother tongue was for the very earliest stages, or for those unsuited to receiving the education of a gentleman (which, of course, included women). The first Tudor treatises on education, for example Elyot's *The Governour* (1531) and Ascham's *Schoolmaster* (1570), although written in English, assumed that what was to be taught was 'the ready way to the Latin Tongue'.

Consequently, instruction in the mother tongue developed to meet the needs of two groups of people. The first consisted of the upwardly mobile but unlettered, or the devout who wished to read the Bible for themselves. A time of commercial expansion demanded apprentices who could read and write English, and their educational needs were met by teach-yourself textbooks or unqualified teachers, 'such men and women of trades (as Taylors, Weavers, Shopkeepers, Seamsters, and such other) as have undertaken the charge of teaching others', wrote

Edmund Coote in his preface to *The English Schoole-Maister* (1596). (For fuller details of this expansion of literacy, see the classic study by Wright, 1935.)

The other group with distinct English-learning requirements consisted of the large number of middle-class Protestants driven by persecution out of France, Spain and Flanders, eventually amounting to nearly 10 per cent of the total population (Howatt, 1984). For social and educational reasons, these immigrants were anxious to accommodate themselves as rapidly as possible to the language of their chosen country, and many aids were produced to help them towards their adopted tongue (Howatt, 1984). There is evidence of interesting and forward-looking cross-fertilization between the texts aimed at these two kinds of learners: the native speakers and those for whom English was a foreign language.

Richard Mulcaster, headmaster of Merchant Taylors' (1561–86) and later St Paul's (1596–1608), was perhaps the first significant figure to insist that learning to read and write in English should be the basis for all education: We should learn:

> . . . to read first that which we speak first, to take most care over that which we use most, and [begin] our studies where we have the best chance of good progress owing to our natural familiarity with our ordinary language, as spoken by those around us in the affairs of every-day life.
>
> (Oliphant, 1903)

Mulcaster also asserted the importance of properly qualified teachers for this task, acknowledging with regret that 'good scholars will not abase themselves' to teaching the mother tongue, which is therefore 'left to the lowest and the worst' (Oliphant, 1903). His words seemed to have little effect. Until well into the nineteenth century a rigid two-tier system existed. Basic instruction in reading and writing was given in homes, dame schools, charity institutions, elementary schools and mechanics' institutes by unqualified amateurs. It was assumed (often incorrectly) at secondary school and university levels that students would already have attained any necessary competence in their own language:

> The ancient universities, public schools and grammar schools ignored English throughout the nineteenth century. This neglect was partly because of confidence in the superior humanism of the classics, and partly because of the vernacular's association with working-class education.
>
> (Mathieson, 1975)

Indeed, it was not until the second half of the nineteenth century that a Professor of Poetry at Oxford chose to lecture in English rather than in Latin.

Not only was the vernacular rated lowly, but there also seems to have been no notion that it might form an organic field of study. Discussing the 'chaotic material' offered mother-tongue learners over the centuries, Ian Michael has pointed out that punctuation was sometimes taught as part of grammar, sometimes as an aspect of composition, and at other times as part of elocution:

> Some spelling books contain grammars and some grammars contain spelling. Skill in finding words is exercised in logics as well as in rhetorics and books on composition. The analysis of judgement of literary style may be part of anthologies, handbooks of elocution, composition or rhetoric.
>
> (Michael, 1979)

As late as 1900, the Board of Education's Schedules for each age group show Reading, Writing and English as separate subjects, possibly handled by different teachers. What was called English simply consisted of grammatical knowledge. In the school curriculum of the time, the activities were broken down even further into periods devoted to 'recitation', 'spelling', 'handwriting', and so on. It was clearly thought a revolutionary proposal when Alice Zimmern suggested in 1900 that all these activities might be integrated:

Give all the English in a class to one teacher; let him add together the hours now given to reading, grammar, composition, recitation, and literature, and redistribute them at his own discretion according as need may arise.

(Zimmern, 1900)

Only in 1904 was there any significant political acknowledgement of English as a subject. In that year, the Code of Regulations of the Board of Education required all state secondary schools to include English Language and Literature in their courses, thus perpetuating a division in the subject that has remained to the present.

THE EMERGING MOTHER TONGUE CURRICULUM

The learning of most subjects begins with school, is completely in the hands of its teachers and goes on within a ready-made curricular framework. None of this, however, is true of English. Children bring to school a wealth of experience of talk (and in some cases of reading and writing), they learn language from parents, friends, the media and teachers of other subjects, and there has been a notorious lack of agreement about what the subject matter of English should be. It is 'the least subject-like of subjects, the least susceptible to definition' (Rosen, 1981).

As a late arrival on the curricular scene, English came to define itself gradually and empirically through the pioneering activities of a few. For example, the methods of relating reading and writing that had been practised in the education of girls came to be more widely recommended in the official Board of Education report of 1910, *The Teaching of English in Secondary Schools*. Many years before Oxford and Cambridge offered degrees in English Literature, ways of teaching and learning the subject had evolved through the work of local committees that organized programmes of literary studies for women and working people, offered by sympathetic university lecturers (Dixon, 1991). The Oxford and Cambridge Universities Local Examinations also arranged a system for examining a range of subjects which included English, at ages below 16 and below 18, which consisted of dictations, grammar questions and parsing, as well as history of English and literature.

The short history of English as a subject is largely the story of successive attempts by different groups at particular moments to shape ideas about how the mother tongue is to be learned and taught. The 1910 report was careful to deny any potentially 'harmful' intention to frame a syllabus or to prescribe in detail the methods which teachers should employ. The authors acknowledged that 'English is the last subject to which a teacher should be bound by hard and fast rules'. That awareness of ideological and methodological variety and a consequent reluctance to prescribe 'official' courses of study came to be tacitly accepted until the 1980s. As has been said of the similar situation in the United States, 'English had become a "prescribed" study in schools and colleges . . . but this did not make the nature of what was prescribed precisely clear' (Graff, 1987).

What the 1910 Report did achieve was the proposition of a set of enlightened principles. Among these were the suggestions that literature and composition are 'organically interrelated', that children should be encouraged to talk to one another in class, that English should be studied as a living language without too much attention to grammar, that literature must be based on 'first hand study', that Shakespeare plays should be read through rapidly and practically without comment, that surface errors in writing are less important than failings of style and structure, that revision of writing should be encouraged, and that teachers must not allow themselves to be dominated by the supposed requirements of external examinations. The authors of the Report would be alarmed to know that, more than eighty years later, there is still the need to struggle to uphold some of their principles.

The most significant attempt to outline a national policy for the mother tongue was the publication of the Newbolt Report, *The Teaching of English in England*, in 1921 (Board of Education, 1921). That report brought together what had previously been separated in several senses. First, it made bold claims for English as the central element that gave the whole curriculum coherence, the 'foundation of all the rest.' Second, it united all mother-tongue activities within English 'taught as a fine art'. Third, it saw English as bringing together practical, emotional and spiritual aims: higher standards of literacy, concern for self-expression, literature as a means of moral and social improvement, and a concern for children's related linguistic, emotional and moral growth, 'the full development of mind and character' (Board of Education, 1921, para: 57). Fourth, there was the suggestion that this subject could be socially unifying. Through a shared experience of English, the social class divisions of the country might be healed and a 'national culture' be established.

Significantly, George Sampson's *English for the English*, published in the same year, had as its sub-title 'A chapter of national education' (Sampson, 1921). After the trauma of World War One, this newly framed subject was invested with the patriotic resonance of 'Englishness', defined through the powers of the language and supremely through the heritage of literature. The committee could hardly have foreseen that debates and divisions lasting to the present day would centre on their interconnected definitions of English culture, of the literary heritage, and of the teaching and learning of English.

As society changes, the list of what might be considered 'English' skills has had continually to expand to include, for example, answering the telephone, using a keyboard, the critical viewing of television and film 'texts', composing on a word processor, communicating using e-mail and exploring the Internet. A comparison of Ordinary Level or General Certificate of Secondary Education examination syllabuses between 1970 and 1995 shows how demands have increased, particularly as coursework has been added to formal examinations. 'Composition' in a single mode has been replaced by writing for different functions and audiences, including revising and editing; 'comprehending' unseen passages by a range of responses to whole texts and in practical criticism. Talking and listening, once totally ignored, have become an integral part of the assessment. It is difficult to realize now that fewer than thirty years separate the coinage of the term 'oracy', when Andrew Wilkinson wrote passionately about the 'shameful neglect' of spoken English (Wilkinson, 1965, 1990), and its acceptance as an essential element of the National Curriculum. Such additions have inevitably involved changes in the ways that English teachers work, as well as in the content of their lessons. What is sometimes called the 'new' English of the 1960s, associated with the growth of comprehensive schools and mixed-ability teaching in a time of economic expansion, was concerned to establish a curriculum and methodology that would be appropriate for the whole school population. It therefore widened conventional views of topics like literacy, texts and literature, response, classroom drama, the writing process, language development and interaction. It also involved increased use of group work, greater valuing of students' own experiences, a richer variety of materials, more concern for learning processes than for finished 'products', working for real purposes and audiences. This 'expansion of the English curriculum' was celebrated in books like *New Directions in English Teaching* (Adams, 1982). By contrast, as a result of New Right shifts in the social and cultural order, recent curricular statements have become progressively more narrowly instrumental and prescriptive (Green, 1995).

In 1975 the theme of the Bullock Report, published by the Department for Education and

Science (DES), was that: 'Language competence grows incrementally, through an interaction of writing, talk, reading and experience, and the best teaching deliberately influences the nature and quality of this growth' (DES, 1975). Less than 10 years later, the references to incremental growth, to children's experience, to quality and to good teaching practice got whittled away. The pamphlet produced by Her Majesty's Inspectorate (HMI), *English from 5 to 16* (DES, 1984), defined the aims of English teaching simply in terms of 'achieving competence in the many and varied uses of our language', worked out questionably in terms of what 'most children should be able to do' at different ages. The debate over this pamphlet prepared the way for the Cox working group, which was set up by the Secretary of State for Education to recommend programmes of study and 'attainment targets' for English. Ironically, he and the Prime Minister very much disliked the group's report, which seemed to them unacceptably 'progressive', as has been entertainingly described by Professor Cox himself (Cox, 1991). Their report claimed (surely unexceptionally) that:

> The overriding aim of the English curriculum is to enable all pupils to develop to the full their ability to use and understand English. Since language can be both spoken and written, this means the fullest possible development of capabilities in speaking and listening, reading and writing.
>
> (DES, 1989, 2.13)

In the 1995 version of the curriculum, published by the renamed Department for Education (DfE), this has become:

> English should develop pupils' abilities to communicate effectively in speech and writing and to listen with understanding. It should also enable them to be enthusiastic, responsive and knowledgeable readers.
>
> (DfE, 1995)

The role of language here has been reduced to mechanical skills of communicating rather than seeing English as all those human processes of knowing, perceiving and becoming that are carried on through language. Little is added by those question-begging evaluative terms (effectively, enthusiastic, responsive, knowledgeable).

It could, perhaps, be held that the emphasis on developing the interrelated language modes has remained constant over the years, but any consensus disappears as soon as discussion shifts to the way in which those agreed aims are to be achieved in practice. Clusters of views tend to be expressed in competing metaphors, like growth, heritage, skills, standards, cultural literacy. Arguments about how children should speak and write, what they should read, or what knowledge of language they should have, are really arguments about how education should shape young people's views of the world. Controlling English is seen as one way of controlling society. Professor Cox has rightly said that:

> '. . . a National Curriculum in English is intimately involved with questions about our national identity, indeed with the whole future ethos of British society. The teaching of English . . . affects the individual and social identity of us all.'
>
> (Cox, 1990)

Some may have believed that the proposed National Curriculum would result in something fixed and definitive. This was not to be; instead the process has simply demonstrated the lack of agreement. Within five years, three irreconcilable versions of the English Orders have been promulgated and four committees or working parties have been charged with drafting or revising these documents without ever reaching consensus. The 'revised' Order of 1993 was far more than a revision of Cox's; it was actually grounded in a more reductionist philosophy and embodied different views of what talking, reading and writing actually mean. It is quite plain, therefore, that even if there may be agreement about the principle of establishing a written curriculum for English, such a text will have to be tentative, continually changing and evolving, and will have to be adapted to meet the particular needs of different schools and teachers.

TEACHERS OF THE MOTHER TONGUE

Because of the long tradition of domestic and unqualified teaching of the mother tongue, it is hardly surprising that, before this century, there were 'very few teachers who could be called or would have called themselves teachers of English' (Ball, 1982). Uncertainty about what such people should be like or how they should be prepared was universal until about 1930, and some would say has continued to the present day. At first the absence of degree courses in the subject inevitably resulted in a lack of academically qualified teachers. In 1921, the Newbolt Report was anxious to reject the common argument that 'any master or mistress can teach English', but the persistence of the idea has been shown in the fact that a fifth of all English teaching has remained in the hands of staff with no qualifications in the subject beyond their own experience (DES, 1975; HMI, 1979).

If for centuries those who taught the mother tongue were despised by classicists and others, they have had ample revenge since. The Newbolt Report offered them a seductively important role as the élite of the profession, concerned not simply with teaching a subject but with the total personal and social development of students and with the health of society. From that time onwards, English teachers have traditionally viewed their role as concerned with changing lives rather than with simply imparting knowledge. Effective English teachers today still see themselves as 'different' from teachers of other subjects. In a recent survey (Protherough and Atkinson, 1991), the majority of those asked believed that they worked in the classroom in ways distinct from others, marked by a particular relationship both with their subject and their students. Four out of five thought that qualities of personality and attitude should be the dominant criteria in selecting entrants to the profession. In direct contrast to government policy, they were overwhelmingly in favour of extended post-graduate training ('more theory and more practice', said one) and concerned for a fruitful (if vaguely defined) 'partnership' between schools and higher education that would help to produce reflective practitioners. However, it is significant that their initial studies were seen as less important to their own development than the influence of other English teachers. This fact, together with the high ranking they gave to professional associations, suggests the importance they attach to a co-operative learning community and a sense of group solidarity.

Until the 1980s, this largely self-regulating community had assimilated new topics and new approaches over time. Change was driven by factors like the influx of 'new' English graduates into schools, the growth of English departments, the increasing theorizing of English teaching, the foundation of the National Association for the Teaching of English (NATE) in 1963, the impetus of the Anglo-American Dartmouth Seminar in 1966 and the Bullock Report in 1975. However, from the beginning, uncertainty about the subject and its pedagogy meant that major differences of view were represented within the English-teaching community. A number of researchers have pointed to the different paradigms that operate, often within departments (Barnes, 1984; Grace, 1978; Hodgson, 1975). The report of the Cox working group identified five broad but not mutually exclusive models of English teaching, characterized simply as 'personal growth' (concerned predominantly with the individual's development), 'cross-curricular' (focusing on the language demands of all subjects), 'adult needs' (preparing for life beyond school), 'cultural heritage' (emphasizing the significance of the literary tradition) and 'cultural analysis' (concerned with critical understanding of both culture and society). Although several surveys have suggested that of these five 'personal growth' is dominant in teachers' thinking, it is also clear that many of them manage to hold contrasting views (like 'literary heritage' and 'cultural analysis') simultaneously. Indeed, in Goodwyn's study the great majority felt that all five models could contribute to their practice in different circumstances (Goodwyn, 1992; Peel and Hargreaves, 1995; Protherough and Atkinson, 1991).

What teachers said they valued for themselves was the 'freedom', 'variety', 'range' and 'diversity' of work in English. However, that cherished individualism and the failure (or lack of concern) to achieve professional consensus about policy have been accompanied by a wider failure to convince those outside the profession. This was made manifest when reactions to the HMI document *English for Ages 5 to 16* (DES, 1989) were analysed. Only a quarter of the responses from schools and colleges approved even slightly of the recommendations, but three-quarters of the letters from the public (some of whom had not actually read the document) were unreserved in their approval. Politicians were quick to cite such instances in order to claim that there was such widespread public concern over the teaching of English that its direction could not be left to those in schools. It was this that opened the way for more direct political intervention, accompanied by sustained populist denigration of 'educationists', 'experts', 'intellectuals', 'research' and 'professionals' (repeatedly voiced by Secretaries of State for Education, Kenneth Baker, John Patten and Prime Minister John Major, among others). The deliberate shift of power into the hands of quangos whose role and membership were both dictated by the government has been particularly opposed by teachers of English. It is not surprising, therefore, that when asked what the most urgent problems were that faced English teachers, their most frequent response was to mention 'imposed' models and tasks and 'interference' with teachers' autonomy (Protherough and Atkinson, 1991, Chapter 9). The sense that 'political and administrative considerations have been allowed to dominate educational and professional ones' runs through the chapters by different hands that are gathered in a recent book on English in the National Curriculum (Protherough and King, 1995), and through the opinions of one of those involved, Professor Brian Cox (Cox, 1995). The resultant ideological clash has led to disputes over such topics as the place of drama and media studies, knowledge about language, the significance of information technology, the definition of literacy and the literary 'heritage', the teaching of reading, approved kinds of talking, and the relationship between teacher assessment and standard tests. What this conflict has meant for some key areas of mother-tongue teaching can be very briefly illustrated in the following sections of this chapter which address the issues discussed in the preparation of the English curriculum.

WHAT SORT OF KNOWLEDGE ABOUT THE MOTHER TONGUE?

'We need to question just what it means to *know* about language', as Ron Carter has said (Carter, 1990) and to distinguish between cognitive, experiential and intuitive forms of knowing. All depends on how such knowledge is defined (Mittins, 1991).

The HMI subject paper of 1984 suggested a narrowly mechanistic aim: 'to teach pupils *about* language, so that they achieve a working knowledge of its structure' (DES, 1984, 1.6). The paper advanced three justifications for this proposal. First, it suggested that language knowledge improves language use ('Learning about language is necessary as a means to increasing one's ability to use it'). What research evidence we have hardly supports this view, and it may well be that the converse is true: that becoming more skilled in language creates an interest in how it works. Second, it suggested that knowledge of grammatical terminology is necessary for understanding and correcting mistakes. ('Many pupils are taught nothing at all about how language works as a system, and consequently do not understand the nature of their mistakes or how to put them right.') This is equally dubious, and the paper admits that 'the least able at using language are the least likely to understand the terminology'. The third suggestion was that knowledge about language is 'interesting'. This is more plausible, but hardly applies to the report's proposal that knowledge should be of the parts of speech, of terms like 'subject' and 'object' and 'a vocabulary for discussing stylistic effects'. It was hardly surprising that this section 'prompted a good deal of disagreement' within the profession and that the only clear trend was 'a widespread and vigorous rejection of grammatical analysis and of teaching the terminology listed in the objectives' (DES, 1985a, para 39).

The Kingman Committee was set up by the Secretary of State in 1987 to propose a model of the English language that might provide a basis for teaching and teacher-training. However, its rejection of 'old-fashioned grammar teaching and learning by rote' and its insistence on the role of English teachers to 'ensure their pupils develop as human beings as well as communicators' (DES,1988) proved as unpopular with traditionally minded politicians as Cox's report. How controversial the issue became has been demonstrated by the way in which the government established an expensively funded national project, *Language in the National Curriculum* (LINC), to provide teachers with ideas and materials based on the Kingman Report, but then refused to permit the publication of its report because of disagreements about what was proposed. This decision was hailed by the *Sunday Times* (23 June 1991) under the headline 'Ministers veto "wacky" grammar teaching guide'.

From the start, the LINC teacher-led project took a much wider view than the HMI document of the kinds of knowledge that would be appropriate in schools. The development of materials was grounded in a view that language structures the way in which we see ourselves and the world, and that knowledge about it can help pupils 'to understand, practise and question the forms of language which currently . . . hold sway in our society' (White, 1990). The first principle of the project was that: 'There can be no return to formalist, decontextualized classroom analysis of language, nor to the deficiency pedagogies on which such teaching is founded' (Carter, 1990). It deliberately avoided the first part of the Kingman model, dealing with the forms of the English language, and instead concentrated on expanding those sections dealing with language development and variation.

In explaining the government's decision not to publish the LINC materials, Tim Eggar, the then Minister, complained that 'fashionable' concerns had dominated the essentials. Apparently, unexceptionable phrases to which he objected include 'Language should be explored in real, purposeful situations' and 'there are intimate relations between language and social power'. Such topics, he said, are 'a distraction from the main task of teaching children to write, spell and punctuate correctly', 'Our central concern must be the business of teaching children how to use their language *correctly*' (Eggar, 1991). The arguments in his short piece neatly encapsulate the conflicting attitudes in society towards mother-tongue learning, and his stress on correctness (something that can be neatly tested) requires further consideration.

How significant is correctness?

Tim Eggar's views are clearly shared by many others outside the schools. Employers complain about graduates' 'poor communication skills' (*Guardian*, 11 November 1993), university tutors are said by the Queen's English Society to believe that two-thirds of their students are shaky on grammar and that one-fifth cannot spell accurately (*Guardian*, 13 July 1992), and the Joint Matriculation Board's examiners' reports at A level complain that 'standards of written expression continue to fall', mentioning 'idiosyncratic' spelling and 'poor' grammar (*Times Educational Supplement*, 28 February, 1992). A reader in genetics claims, on the basis of a very unscientific enquiry, that 'most [university] students have obvious deficiencies in spelling, word-choice, grammar and punctuation. Asking what can be done, he concludes:

> We need pressure to improve English teaching in schools, with a closely specified National Curriculum stating that schools must explicitly teach and test spelling, grammar and punctuation, showing pupils how such knowledge makes their English clearer.

(Lamb, 1995)

This assertion glides over a whole series of suppressed questions. Who are included in that opening 'We'? Is there any likelihood that a 'closely specified' curriculum of this kind will enable teachers to 'improve English teaching'? What evidence from past experience or research is there that explicit teaching and testing of grammar has any beneficial effect on pupils' language use?

Historically, little or no attention to correctness and grammatical precision was paid before the eighteenth century. From that time it became increasingly asserted that the mother tongue should be learned by rote, like Latin, and by 1800 'grammarians gave their approval to fifty-six different systems of parts of speech' (Michael, 1970). Such gathering of linguistic 'prejudices, taboos and prescriptions' based on 'illogical concepts of language and usage' had a lasting effect and can still be found 'earnestly and convincingly taught in schools'. The author of one major study (Leonard, 1962) concludes that 'the potential harm is enormous . . . Notable examples are the usual small, meaningless distinctions of parts of speech . . . the false "logical rules" of case and concord, and the absurd purisms in wording which are the staple of much English teaching.' Certainly up to 1920, the stress in mother-tongue learning was overwhelmingly on correctness of usage. Exposition, exercises and tests all 'served to impose and maintain the dominance of the patterns, structures and conventions of Standard English and received pronunciation' (Ball, 1984). Examining the books used in schools at this period, David Shayer remarks that 'the type of grammar work done in schools before 1920 was, frankly, nasty' and 'composition was almost entirely absorbed by grammar work' (Shayer, 1972). There is little to suggest that students gained any benefits from this obsession with grammatical conventions.

Those who pride themselves on the accuracy of their own language have always tended to see its 'rules' as an important part of a threatened social order and to view surface errors as some kind of moral weakness. Significantly, pupils themselves have internalized the view that correctness is all-important, without apparently achieving it. When young children describe what they have to do in order to write well, their comments emphasize the avoidance of 'mistakes' (Czerniewska, 1992; Thornton, 1986). Asked what they saw as the most important qualities in writing, 15-year-olds predominantly mentioned 'the correct management of surface features such as spelling, neatness and punctuation', whereas assessors found appropriateness, style and interest considerably more significant. Contrary to popular opinion, the Assessment of Performance Unit survey, which was set up after the publication of the Bullock Report to monitor standards, concluded that 'schools are not failing to instruct pupils in the need for control over so-called "basic skills", nor are pupils failing to heed such lessons' (White, 1986).

Despite this, the various National Curriculum documents, relating to English (especially the 1993 version) hold fast to the prescriptive myth that there is some absolute correctness to be achieved in language use. Claims for Standard English were bolstered by the argument that 'Standard English is characterized by the correct use of vocabulary and grammar'.

'Standard' English and 'standards'

The notion of some 'standard' form of English has long had a seductive appeal. Concerned by the variations in the English of his time compared with the fixed nature of a dead language like Latin, Mulcaster was among the first to propose steps (an English dictionary, an agreed grammar and consistent spelling) that might regularize the mother tongue. Dreams that there might be some normative, fixed system, from which individual usage varies to a greater or lesser extent, have persisted to the present day.

According to the Kingman Report, Standard English is what we call the non-localized form of 'the language which we have in common . . . on which we all draw and to which we all contribute' even though 'all of us can have only partial access to it' (DES, 1988). It should not be contentious to say that all children have a right to acquire this language, so defined. Problems come when, by analogy with other uses of the word 'standard', people use the term to suggest that Standard English is some 'accepted or approved example against which others are judged or measured' or 'a level of excellence', and thus that it has an inherently higher value than other dialects. Unlike standard measures of length, weight or area, what is considered Standard English varies with time and linguists disagree about how it should be defined. There is no clear gap between Standard and non-standard English, and there are differing degrees of standardization. Crucially, as Cox remarked, Standard English is not necessarily good English.

Any uncertainty about the term is ignored in the general requirements of the 1995 National Curriculum for English, which say that: 'In order to participate confidently in public, cultural and working life, pupils need to be able to speak, write and read standard English fluently and accurately' (DfE, 1995). What follows does little to define this 'standard' with any precision. The clauses are either vague and possibly inaccurate (Standard English is 'distinguished by its vocabulary, and by rules and conventions of grammar, spelling and punctuation'), or obvious (contrasting the 'spontaneity' of speech with 'often carefully crafted' writing'), or negative ('spoken Standard English is not the same as Received Pronunciation'). The National Curriculum Council 'pursued several definitions' of Spoken Standard English without reaching the agreement that is assumed by the Attainment Targets (John Johnson in Protherough and King, 1995). In Speaking and Listening, pupils are said to be 'beginning to be aware' of Standard English at level 3, using 'appropriately some of the features' of its vocabulary and grammar at level 4, using it 'in formal situations' at level 5, are 'fluent' in such use at level 6, and 'confident' at levels 7 and 8. (For a fuller description of the National Curriculum with its Attainment Targets and Levels of Attainment see Appendix page 85.)

'Standard' and 'standards' are intriguingly interlinked. From the time of the Greeks, linguistic standards have tended to be set by reference to a standard established by writers of the past and linguistic change is perceived as some kind of corruption or degeneration. Many are convinced – like Prince Charles – that nowadays people 'can't speak properly, can't write properly and can't punctuate' because 'English is taught so bloody badly' (*The Times*, 28 February 1992). However, the cries of falling standards ('You can't write proper' and 'Save the Queen's English', say the headlines) and the allegations that 'English is badly taught and .

. . used to be taught better' (Marenbon, 1987) have been common for even longer than English has existed as a separate school subject. Early this century it was confidently asserted that public schoolboys, with all the advantages of a classical training, left school at 18 or 19 'able hardly to write a coherent sentence, with no knowledge of punctuation, no vocabulary, no power of expression' (Mais, 1914; Peers, 1914). Over seventy years ago the Newbolt Report said of employers that 'All complained, often bitterly, of defects in spelling, punctuation, vocabulary, and sentence-structure' (Board of Education, 1921, para 137).

It has to be added that most of those concerned about 'standards' in general and of school-children in particular, assume that assessing the quality of language use is easier and more reliable than it is. Estimates depend on what precisely is being judged, by whom, how and in what context, by what criteria and for what purpose. As I have argued in detail elsewhere (Goodwyn, 1995) there are at least six reasons for being cautious. First, estimates of ability are inevitably subjective: different markers disagree and the same marker rates a piece differently on different occasions. Second, the term 'language ability' is not the simple unitary concept that some examiners and politicians would like to pretend, but a convenient blanket phrase for a complex of separate interlocking abilities. Third, the criteria used for assessing ability are shifting and culturally determined. Fourth, estimates of ability are heavily influenced by the purpose for which the operation is being carried out: diagnosing the needs of an individual, monitoring the success of a teaching programme, measuring one group against another, or illustrating an ideological point. Fifth, there is no consensus over what 'good' talking, writing or reading looks like in any absolute sense. Finally, language use is heavily, indeed dominantly, influenced by its topic, purpose, audience and situation. The first version of the National Curriculum for English summed this up in the words 'Language competence is dependent on the task: children will show different ability on tasks of different kinds' (DES, 1989, para 17.25). Politicians need to be disabused of the notions that 'simple pencil and paper tests' prove anything, or that unqualified comparisons over time can be established.

ENGLISHNESS AND OTHER CULTURES

Whose mother tongue? For whom are 'English' curricula and policies intended to be applicable and who is excluded? The social and political assumptions underlying such questions have often been left unexpressed, as though language learning and teaching are value-free activities that do not transmit beliefs and assumptions along with the language.

In the nineteenth century, the emerging nation-states of Europe saw their identity as being shaped by and simultaneously expressed in a national language, a national literature and a national school system. The previously quoted Newbolt Report linked these three elements in explaining its view of English as the essential basis for 'a general and national education' (Board of Education, 1921, para 11). After the trauma of war, national unity would come about by making English literature the central core of the curriculum. Indeed one crucial passage argues that English literature shows us both what being English is like historically and what being human is like in other cultures:

> All great literature has in it two elements, the contemporary and the eternal. On the one hand, Shakespeare and Pope can tell us what Englishmen were like at the beginning of the seventeenth and the beginning of the eighteenth centuries. On the other hand they tell us what all men are like in all countries and at all times.
>
> (Board of Education, 1921, para 195)

Such a claim comes dangerously close to implying that awareness of other languages and cultures is of no real importance. Acceptance of the idea that our schools should foster 'a national cultural identity' (recently proposed in the speeches of the chief executive of the Schools Curriculum and Assessment Authority) can suggest a monocultural view that both undervalues the learning of other languages and has a damaging effect on the identity and self-esteem of children from ethnic minorities.

For years it was tacitly assumed that English schools were homogeneous language groups, and some teachers believed that mainstream English lessons should not be concerned with those native speakers of other languages or others seen as somehow incapable of following a 'normal' English programme. Nowadays language diversity is more widely acknowledged. The *Linguistic Minorities Project* of the 1980s revealed, for example, that speakers of minority languages, including Greek and Turkish, accounted for nearly a third of the school population in Haringey, and that more than a third of the children in inner London were 'non-Anglo' British (Reid, 1990). Rosen and Burgess found that 55 different languages were spoken in schools in the London area (Rosen and Burgess, 1980). Such schools contain children who are bilingual and multilingual, others who are in the 'interlanguage' stage of adaptation, some who switch flexibly in and out of dialects and creoles, and some who as yet have little English, as can be seen from the report of the *Mother Tongue Project* (Tansley, 1986). Provision for supporting pupils having problems with English was made through what was known as Section 11 funding to enable help to be given in the classroom frequently alongside the regular classroom teacher. Although, by law, the actual language of instruction has always to be English the support teacher could use the pupil's own language to assist in explanations.

Over time, there has been a shift from seeing English instruction as a major mode for 'integrating immigrants' into an English-speaking community towards views of a multicultural, multilingual society in which English should provide a linguistic and cultural centre. The Swann Report, entitled *Education for All*, published in 1985, criticized any policy for minority ethnic groups that saw them as a 'problem' or 'disadvantaged', and said that pupils should 'come to appreciate the positive aspects of living in a linguistically diverse society' (DES, 1985b). However, the compromises of the committee have failed to satisfy either those who believe that pluralism is a disguised form of cultural domination and that tolerance is unattainable in a racist society or those who feel that everyone should be assimilated into 'British' culture and ways of life. Professor Parekh has sensitively teased out the tensions implicit in the committee's terms of reference and in interplay of different groups within it (Parekh, 1989). In summing up responses to *Education for All*, Verma concludes that the essentially monocultural British education system has failed: 'It fails to concern itself with the preparation of all individuals to function in a society composed of varied races, cultures, social norms, values and life-styles, each different but interdependent (Verma, 1989).

Arguing that all education can be seen as multicultural by nature, concerned with creating a common means of communication for those who participate in it, Professor Brumfit has suggested that: 'its function should be to enable . . . those who happen to be living in Britain at any given moment to interact together most productively for the development of the highest form of civilization of which they are capable' (Brumfit *et al.*, 1985).

But what precisely is that common means, and how is it to be created? What is the status of the pupils' first language for them, for their families, for their language communities and for their teachers? When the Cox Report claimed that competence in English is 'sensitive to the knowledge of other languages which many children have' (DES, 1988, para 3.7), how did it envisage that sensitivity as being realized?

Two contrasting ideals have been promoted. The first urges full bilingual programmes, in which the mother tongue is taught alongside English as a medium of instruction, but this has rarely been attempted because of the expense, the variety of languages and the educational problems involved. For whatever reasons, the Swann Report opposed any form of bilingual education or mother-tongue teaching in schools. The second and conflicting ideal of promoting a common English culture can be seen as an oppressive kind of 'cultural imperialism' if it implies ignoring or downgrading other cultures (as in the 'Official English' movement in the United States). If the goal is to be Standard English for all, in line with the new regulations in England and Wales, then what is to be the place of non-English dialects and creoles? The National Curriculum documents offer no real guidance about how the language needs of bilingual pupils might best be met. Professor Carter summed up these interlocking issues neatly in his inaugural address at Nottingham:

> A view of one standard English with a single set of rules accords with a monolingual, monocultural version of society intent on preserving an existing order in which everyone can be drilled into knowing their place. A view which recognises Englishes as well as English and which stresses variable rules accords with a multilingual, culturally diverse view of society. Most teachers occupy a middle ground between these two positions.
>
> (Carter, 1993)

APPENDIX

The structure of the National Curriculum in England and Wales

The National Curriculum applies to pupils of compulsory school age in maintained schools. It is organized on the basis of four *key stages* which are broadly as follows:

	Pupils' ages	Year groups
Key Stage 1	5–7	1–2
Key Stage 2	7–11	3–6
Key Stage 3	11–14	7–9
Key Stage 4	14–16	10–11

For each key stage, *programmes* of study set out what pupils should be taught and *attainment targets* set out the expected standards of their performance. These standards of performance are set out in eight *level descriptions* of increasing difficulty. For English the attainment targets are defined in terms of: Speaking and Listening, Reading and Writing.

Figure 3: The regional languages of the British Isles

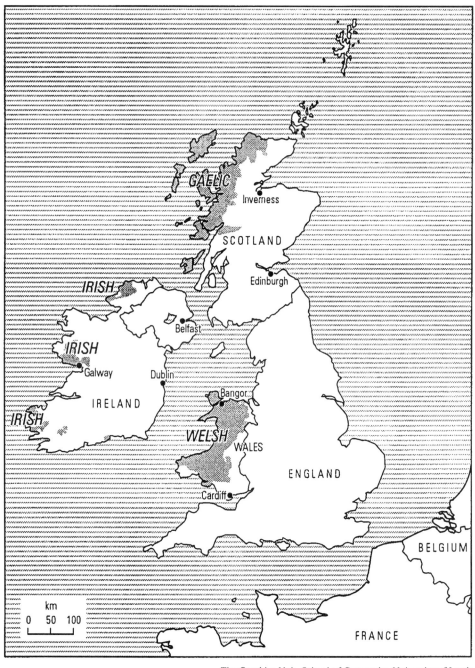

The Graphics Unit, School of Geography, University of Leeds

Chapter 8

Teaching Welsh and English in Wales

Mary Rose Peate, Nikolas Coupland and Peter Garrett

The Welsh language is very old. It evolved from the Celtic branch of the Indo-European family of languages as did the related languages spoken in the British Isles: Cornish, Irish, Scots Gaelic and Manx, as well as Breton spoken in western France, to which it is particularly close. All of these languages, once spoken widely in Europe, have been declining in the number of their speakers until recently but are now undergoing revival. The 1991 census gave the figure for Welsh speakers as 508,098, representing a total of 18.7 per cent of the population of the Principality (Welsh Language Board, 1995). All of these speakers are bilingual, the last monoglot Welsh speaker probably having died in the 1960s.

THE CURRENT SITUATION AS A RESULT OF THE NATIONAL CURRICULUM

The majority language in Wales is British English, and that is the medium of instruction in most of the primary and secondary schools in the state education system. However, around one in five of the people of Wales also speak Welsh (Aitchison and Carter, 1994). Large numbers of these speakers have Welsh, rather than English, as both their mother tongue and their preferred language, but many are learners, who have made a conscious choice of Welsh as their preferred language, as is implied by the term 'revival'.

Wales is a very diverse country, both geographically and culturally. Many of the natural Welsh-speaking areas (Raybould, 1995), such as Gwynedd in the north-west and Dyfed in the south-west, are predominately rural and relatively depopulated. In these areas, the usual medium of education is Welsh, and in some cases English may not be used or taught during the two years of Key Stage 1, that is pupils aged five and six. However, in all cases if English has not been used before, it is introduced by age seven, at the latest. English is therefore an additional 'core' subject in the National Curriculum, which applies in Wales as in England, alongside the teaching medium (which may be Welsh). In schools where the teaching medium is Welsh, the core subjects are then four in number: Welsh, English, Mathematics and Science. The total curriculum in all primary schools in Wales has eleven subjects, because, in English-medium schools in Wales, unlike similar schools in England, Welsh is taught as an additional foundation subject, though not a core subject.

Ysgolion Cymraeg (designated Welsh schools) are increasingly being established in the Anglicized areas. Children attending these primary and secondary *Ysgolion Cymraeg* are educated through the medium of Welsh, because that is their parents' preferred language, although it may not be the mother tongue of the parents or the child. Children are expected to attend a Welsh-medium playgroup before starting such a school. As a result, they do not usually come into the system after the age of five, and they need to have parents prepared to make an explicit commitment to support the choice of language from the outset. The system was devised to sustain the Welsh language by meeting the needs of children who do not live in the 'natural Welsh-speaking' areas, but whose parents want them to be fluent in the two main languages of Wales. Pupils may in fact be learning Welsh as their second language but the Programme of Study which they follow is that for *Cymraeg* (Welsh as a first language). The expectation is that they will become totally fluent. They are likely to have teachers who are fluent Welsh speakers. Their school experience is designed to mirror that of children in the 'natural Welsh-speaking' areas, but their out-of-school experiences may be very different.

When the National Curriculum was first implemented, it explicitly stated that all children in Wales were entitled to be taught Welsh, either at the core of the National Curriculum, or as a foundation subject. This was intended to prepare them to live a fully participating life in societally bilingual Wales. However, the statutory requirement for schools to provide Welsh as a second language in Key Stage 4 (that is, for children aged fourteen to sixteen) has now been suspended until 1999 (DfE, 1994).

Prior to the reorganization of the Welsh counties in 1996, almost all children of all ages in Gwynedd and Dyfed were taught both languages, and used them in their everyday lives, as is still the case. The declared aim of the education policy of Gwynedd, in particular, is to enable the children in their care to become fully bilingual by the age of eleven in order to benefit from Welsh-medium secondary education. There are very few children in Gwynedd who know no Welsh at all. Children who come into the counties of Gwynedd and Dyfed after the infant stage are offered induction courses in Welsh, in specialist centres, for about one term. Their education continues by means of a mix of Welsh and English instruction, depending on what the schools which they attend perceive their linguistic needs to be. They may be taught *Cymraeg fel ail iaith* (Welsh as a Second Language) by teachers who will be fluent in Welsh.

About one-tenth of the entire population of Wales live in and around the city of Cardiff. It was primarily in order to maintain the momentum of the Welsh language revival among children living in these Anglicized areas, the south-east, north-east and rural Mid-Wales, that the Programmes of Study (A and B) for Welsh as a Second Language were developed. The teachers who teach these programmes may well be learners themselves. Indeed, Raybould (1995) says bluntly, 'Most of the teachers that are teaching that course . . . don't speak Welsh themselves'. The relatively slow pace of acquisition required allows as much for teacher needs as for the needs of those being taught. All local education authorities in the Anglicized areas have induction and support systems in place for teachers at all levels who teach Welsh. Support materials – books, videos and computer software – are also widely available. Their production is subsidized by central government through the Welsh Office. Welsh language teaching materials of all kinds are heavily subsidized in the same way, because the smallness of the market would otherwise make their publication uneconomic.

Some degree of extra commitment is demanded of primary school teachers in Wales, not merely because they have to teach Welsh as well as English, but because they have to teach an extra subject in the legally mandatory National Curriculum. There needs to be considerable residual goodwill towards the national language (as Welsh is often called in Wales in order to distinguish it from English) because primary school heads and staff are accepting extra work and responsibility without extra tangible reward.

The Curriculum *Cymreig* (Welsh in the cultural rather than the linguistic sense) recognizes that Wales is culturally distinct from England. There are separate Orders for several subjects of the National Curriculum, including English. The first page of the 1995 revised Orders for English states, under the code-switching heading, 'The Curriculum *Cymreig*', which is itself two parts English to one part Welsh:

> In Wales, pupils should be given opportunities, where appropriate, in their study of English to develop and apply their knowledge and understanding of the cultural, economic, environmental, historical and linguistic characteristics of Wales.

The corresponding instruction on the first page of the Orders for Welsh reads as follows:

> Pupils should be given opportunities, where appropriate, in their study of Welsh to develop and apply their knowledge and understanding of the cultural, economic, environmental, historical and linguistic characteristics of Wales.
>
> (Welsh Office, 1995, 1)

Since Welsh is only taught in Wales, there is no need for the introductory phrase, 'In Wales'. Similarly, Irish is only taught in Northern Ireland, and Gaelic only taught in Scotland; however, neither of these other British languages is given such a privileged provision as is Welsh. These three, together with English, are the only languages which are required to be taught in the primary stage of education. There are other bilingual nations in Europe, so the recognition of the place of Welsh in the life of the Welsh nation is not by any means a narrowly focused, romantic, backward-looking flight from the realities of life in Britain as part of late-twentieth-century Europe. In fact it is monolingual England which is unusual, in having no second language provision in the primary years of schooling.

The 1991 Census Report for South Glamorgan showed that 6.4 per cent of the population of Cardiff, aged three and over, are returned as 'Welsh-speaking'. For the first time in Wales, there was a question posed in the 1991 Census about ethnic origin, and 6.2 per cent of the population of Cardiff returned themselves as having ethnic origins other than White. Most children from such families will have some knowledge of English, but not all. They are almost certain to be studying through the medium of English, since very few attend the *Ysgolion Cymraeg*, and, although English may in fact be their second language, there is no recognition in the National Curriculum of English as a Second Language, as there is for Welsh.

Not only are there two Programmes of Study for Welsh as a Second Language, but in the case of those studying Welsh as though it were their first language the need for awareness of 'varied linguistic backgrounds' of pupils is made explicit. It is stated that it is only 'for some [that] Welsh is a natural medium of communication on a personal and social level'. Contrast this requirement of language awareness laid on teachers in their task of fostering the language development of the child with the case of the Orders for English, which insist on the need to teach Standard English from the very outset. As pointed out by Peate (1995), Standard English is a new dialect for many English-speaking children, and there are those for whom it is a new language. Raybould stresses the need of children not only to feel confident that they can understand teachers and peers but also that they are readily understood by them:

> The important thing to consider is that there is not a single teacher working in a Welsh-medium situation who isn't bilingual. They are all fluent in English . . . So there is no child in any school in Wales that comes from an English-speaking background that cannot be understood when they want to make a point showing understanding.
>
> (Raybould, 1995)

Raybould celebrates the official entitlement under the National Curriculum of all children in Wales to be taught Welsh, at least as a foundation subject. His paper was written before the apparent victory of the three secondary schools in Gwent who seem to have succeeded in their attempt to resist introducing Welsh into the curriculum until 1999. He states emphatically that the crucial difference between the situation with Welsh in Wales and with other non-English language groups is not merely that those whose mother tongue is Welsh can be taught their mother tongue and can also be taught through the medium of that language, but that those whose mother tongue is not the medium of education are equally considered. However, this is only true if that mother tongue is English. English-speaking parents can be sure that their children will be understood when using their mother tongue. Unfortunately, those who have other mother tongues, those who speak one of the other languages of Wales (Peate, 1996a), including non-English immigrants, are in the same difficult position with regard to making themselves understood in English, as they would be in England.

Section 11 funding, supplied directly to local education authorities by the Home Office, has traditionally been used in England since the middle 1960s to support the learning of English by children who do not have it as their first language. This provision has barely penetrated into Wales. South Glamorgan received some limited funding in the late 1980s and early 1990s. Gwent and West Glamorgan have been allocated a small share of this in the last two or three years, which makes the situation in Cardiff rather more strained. The whole of the Section 11 system, across Britain, is being dismantled. This is in tune with the complete absence of any consideration of the linguistic needs of ethnic minority, refugee and non-English European migrant workers' children in the National Curriculum. Money is now being made available from the Department of Environment for English language support schemes. This provision does not apply to Wales. In this limited sense of financial provision, therefore, it cannot be denied that children from ethnic minorities are less well provided for in Wales than in England.

THE HISTORY OF THE USE AND TEACHING OF WELSH AND ENGLISH

Official recognition of the fact that there are children at school in Wales, whether indigenous or not, who may need to be taught English in the primary stage as a second language is relatively recent, and the right to teach and learn the Welsh language has only been achieved as a result of considerable struggle by committed individuals, and even personal suffering.

The Welsh language became the language of common use, acquired informally by the mass of people, in about the eighth century. It would not have been formally taught. By the Middle Welsh period (approximately 1150–1400) a standard form of Welsh was taught to the bards, but this was because they were especially trained to 'guard' the form and content of the language, as well as the history and, to some extent, the laws of the nation, under the patronage of the princes and the nobles (Lewis, 1987). The language of the bards appears to have contained many archaic forms and to have been substantially the same wherever in Wales it was heard. The common people spoke then, as they do today, in a variety of dialects, and there is no evidence of any one standard form, apart from the literary Welsh of the bardic tradition.

It is much more difficult to put even an approximate date on the earliest use of English in Wales, even by the nobility and rulers. Durkacz (1983), among others, dates the more widespread use of English in Wales, inaugurating the process of shifting from Welsh to English, to the Act of Union of 1536. This Act is sometimes referred to as the Act of Annexation

(Edwards 1991) because it is seen as representing an attempt to integrate Wales into the English state and to proscribe Welsh, by laying down that no person who could not use English should hold public office. This appears to have been because the use of the Welsh language was seen as a seed-bed for sedition, since it was secret from the English. Yet, when Henry Tudor (a nobleman of Welsh descent) acceded to the throne of England in 1485 after the Battle of Bosworth, as Henry VII, he was hailed in Wales as the *mab darogan* (promised son). He would restore the fortunes of the Welsh nation which had declined since the defeat of Llywelyn by Edward I in 1282 and the putting down of the revolt by Owain Glyndwr at the beginning of the fifteenth century. It might seem that the great mass of the people were not affected by the ruling of the Act of Union 1536, because they were unlikely to be in a position to hold public office whatever language they used, but they were obliged to keep the law. If they broke any of the laws, they were tried, and had to defend themselves, in English. Since people who were neither learned nor politically powerful continued to use Welsh rather than English in their family and community life, they could be seen as being by this means debarred from just and equitable treatment under the law.

THE ROLE OF RELIGION IN EDUCATION AND THE SURVIVAL OF WELSH

The language of religion in Britain until the Reformation was Latin, and such education as was available, for the very few, was in Latin, both in the universities and in the schools. In Wales, there were a very few private grammar schools established in the Tudor period and later, but these were modelled entirely on the English system and afforded no time or status to either the Welsh language or culture. There were no schools for the secular education of the mass of the people until the day schools were set up in the nineteenth century. Most of these early day schools were funded by the Anglican Church. The University of Wales was not established until the end of the nineteenth century.

One of the main convictions of the Protestant Reformers in the sixteenth century had been that they had a duty to take the Bible out of Latin and out of the hands of the priests and give it to the people to read for themselves. The common people of Wales neither spoke nor read English, and so William Morgan was given the task of translating the whole of the Bible into Welsh. His translation was published in 1588. It drew heavily on the language of the bards. This and subsequent Welsh Bibles consolidated a written standard Welsh, called by the common people 'literary' or 'book' Welsh. Preaching in Welsh also led to the development of an oral standard, which was largely restricted to the domain of religion. The result was a state of diglossia (Jones, 1987), an effective separation of the Welsh language into distinct high and low varieties, which people colloquially distinguished as 'book Welsh' (based on the written language) and 'our Welsh' (the local dialect – *Cymraeg llafer*, or 'spoken Welsh'):

> The language of the Welsh Bible was markedly different from spoken Welsh, and over the centuries the difference widened as the spoken language evolved. Yet despite the archaisms (which became more marked in the revised edition of 1620) the Bible provided an exalted model of correct and majestic Welsh.
>
> (Davies, 1993)

At first, the provision of the Welsh Bible and of services in Welsh may have succeeded in reconciling the peasantry of Wales to Anglican orthodoxy, but by the late seventeenth century some sectarian groups considered the authority of the Bible to be above that of the Church. In terms of the reading of Welsh, the desire to read the Scriptures made adult literacy a very strong popular movement. In 1731, an Anglican clergyman, Griffith Jones, Vicar of Llandowror, began to establish what he called 'circulating schools' throughout Wales to teach both adults and children to read the Bible and the Prayer Book in Welsh, as well as to listen to it. By 1761, when he died, 3,325 schools were being attended by about 250,000 people, over half the entire population of Wales.

The Welsh language was both subject and medium of instruction in the circulating schools, which stayed in one place never more than a matter of months. The aim was not education for its own sake, but the saving of souls. Neither writing nor arithmetic were taught. The aim was not principally to teach the people to express themselves in their own dialect of Welsh, and risk giving them ideas above their station, but to teach them to understand the elevated language in which they were being instructed and taught how they should live.

This kind of induction of speakers of the low variety into the forms of the high variety is the classic diglossic pattern of organization (Ferguson, 1959). 'It is by no means the design of this spiritual kind of charity', Cavenagh (1930) quotes from the Rules of the Welsh Circulating Schools 1745, 'to make them gentlemen, but Christians and heirs of eternal life'. The Sunday schools, established in the early nineteenth century by Thomas Charles of Bala, also taught adults as well as children. They taught reading, but not writing, and focused their endeavours on using the Welsh language to make the people good Christians rather than the English language to make them gentlemen. Jenkins (1908) quotes Charles himself writing in 1807: 'The continued progress of the Sunday schools is very great . . . I can hardly ask them a question in divinity but they will give me a proper answer and repeat texts the most suitable to prove it.' This shows that the Sunday school scholars, when speaking to a sympathetic interlocutor such as Thomas Charles, could manage both 'book Welsh' and 'our Welsh'.

In short, the Bible and the Sunday schools had become an important motivation for the development of a Welsh-speaking religious life. This found its culmination in the Methodist movement of the eighteenth century. The achievements of Methodism, and Nonconformity as a whole, often referred to jointly as 'the chapel' (Edwards, 1991), in theology, hymnology and Bible studies remain an important part of the identity of many Welsh people today. Edwards also asserts that the absence of significant social class variation in the Welsh language can perhaps in part be explained by the fact that access to the chapel, unlike the Anglican Church, was not determined on the basis of social class. However, only the middle class and the respectable poor were welcomed as members of chapel congregations, while those who were richer or poorer than this wide central band were not represented. Nor were outsiders, such as the Irish, who came to both north and south Wales in the late 1840s in large numbers, fleeing from the Famine and seeking work. The Irish remained almost exclusively Roman Catholic. They built their own churches and their own schools. The only language used in either was English, since the Irish language had been even more effectively stigmatized than Welsh.

THE COMING OF THE DAY SCHOOLS AND THE TEACHING OF ENGLISH

The positive attitude towards the use of Welsh in the Circulating and Sunday schools stands in stark contrast to that of the day schools, which came into existence partly as a consequence of industrialization and partly in response to the rise in population. The Industrial Revolution caused the creation of great urban centres where none had been before, just as in England, but the language used in them was, at first, mainly Welsh: 'Alone among Celtic languages, Welsh has had a considerable degree of success in becoming an urban tongue' (Davies, 1993).

In 1770, there were about 489,000 people in Wales, almost all of whom spoke mainly or only Welsh. By the time of the first census in 1801, the population had risen to 587,000, more than three-quarters of whom were still monoglot Welsh. In 1851, the population was 1,163,000, of whom 115,000 had been born in England and 20,000 in Ireland. About 800,000 were Welsh-speaking, so they greatly outnumbered the non-Welsh-speaking people, and were thus able to linguistically absorb them. 33 per cent of the total population in 1851 lived in Glamorgan and Monmouthshire. By 1911 this proportion had almost doubled to 63 per cent (Evans, 1989).

The 1847 Report of the Commission of Inquiry into the State of Education in Wales, known today as the Blue Books, stated that Welsh was only spoken by the labouring classes and not by the middle or upper classes, that no written material was published or read in Welsh other than the Bible, and that the population was almost completely illiterate in English (Peate, 1996b). This is in contrast to Commissioner Lingen's report in Volume I of the Blue Books that the levels of literacy in Welsh were surprisingly high. Presumably, this report was based on hearing people read Welsh aloud in his presence, since he does not seem to have been aware that literacy in terms of the writing of Welsh was scarcely taught at all, although reading certainly was. He may have assumed that the writing of Welsh was being taught, because in England it was customary to teach both literacy skills at the same time:

> The Welsh peasantry are better able to read and write in their own language than the same classes in England . . . They learn to read in Sunday-schools . . . The people have not been accustomed to think much upon any but religious topics. The great want is good secular education.
>
> (Lingen, 1847)

This good secular education was to be conducted solely in English. The day schools which were inspected (and therefore already in existence) in 1847 were being nominally conducted in English and it is evident that the Welsh Not (a device for marking out for punishment any children caught talking Welsh in school) was in use, because it is mentioned and deplored. The children were not being taught to use English; they were simply being punished, both by beating and by fines, for failing to use it and for using Welsh, their mother tongue, instead. This situation appears to have come about because the parents would only pay for teaching which was conducted in English. However, efficient teaching of English was difficult to obtain because the great majority of the teachers were not only totally untrained but themselves spoke only a very little English which, like their unfortunate pupils, they had picked up as they went along. Most poor children had no education at all outside the home and Sunday school. Fewer than one in five children under fifteen in Wales attended day school; many of the schools were kept open for only six out of the twelve months; school attendance was frequently not for more than one or two years. It appears that in Wales as late as the middle of the nineteenth century the general use and effective teaching of English had hardly begun.

DIALECTS, ACCENTS, DIGLOSSIA: LANGUAGE DISTRIBUTION AND SOCIAL CLASS IN WELSH

The Welsh language has no generally accepted 'standard accent' comparable to Received Pronunciation in British English, and dialect forms are officially unstigmatized. However, it is interesting to note that members of each of the major dialect continua can often be heard informally describing the speech forms of the other group by using pejorative terms, and even name tags such as 'Gogs, Cardis and Hwntws' (Evans, 1989). Fluent speakers tend to elide parts of words and even parts of phrases. The National Curriculum definition of Standard spoken Welsh is perhaps worth quoting in full. It may reflect some light on the ongoing Standard English debate:

> Standard spoken Welsh might be described as a neater form of everyday spoken Welsh. In the everyday spoken language there is a tendency to abbreviate and glide over words, and to take key parts of the sentence for granted. The occasional English word or idiom is used in an informal situation. In more formal situations, on the other hand, an effort is made to articulate words and sentences fully; more care is taken to select Welsh words and use structures stored in the subconscious mind through the influence of reading or listening to others speaking more formally. Speech is slower and expression more self-conscious. This does not mean uniformity. There is room within standard spoken Welsh for accents, vocabulary and sentence structures from different parts of the country . . . Having learnt what everyday language and Standard Welsh are, it is equally important to know when to move from one register to the other. Standard Welsh gives pupils a formal register and a mode of speaking and writing which will be understood by literate Welsh-speakers throughout Wales, and is the key to a large body of creative and discursive literature.
>
> (Welsh Office, 1995)

The term 'register' is relatively uncommon in discussions about varieties of Welsh, omnipresent though it is in pronouncements about the teaching of English. There is one thought-provoking paper from 1982 by Ceinwen Thomas on the subject, entitled 'Registers in Welsh'. She identifies Wales as suffering a situation of 'out-diglossia' in two languages, because many of those domains of use which otherwise would have been transacted in Standard Welsh (*yr iaith safonol*, otherwise 'literary Welsh') have been appropriated by Standard English.

The reference to 'different parts of the country' is perhaps an allusion to the generally accepted opinion that there are two major dialect continua in Wales – the northern and the southern – with an extensive transition area where northern and southern forms overlap. Alan Thomas (1973) refers to three rather than two speech-areas – northern, southern and midland. Northern and southern are relatively homogeneous and easy to distinguish; but the midland speech-areas 'tend either to be associated' in terms of description 'with one or other of [the northern or southern] areas or to be distinguished by intensive internal variation'. Of the Welsh of *Sir Drefaldwyn* (Montgomeryshire) Griffiths (1981) writes: '*mae I iaith Sir Drefladwyn ei chymeriad a'i thiethi pendant ei hun*' (Montgomeryshire Welsh has its own peculiar features). The highest concentration of Welsh speakers in the midland areas is still in South Gwynedd and North Powys, the old counties of Merioneth and Montgomeryshire.

The language planning exercises of the 1960s, culminating in the launch of *Cymraeg Byw* (Living Welsh), attempted to construct a single standard for spoken Welsh where historically none had existed. Ceinwen Thomas (1982), in contrast, regards standard Welsh as having gone underground for social and political reasons, not as having never existed. According to her view, a dialect speaker's sense of speaking dialect, 'our Welsh', depends on that speaker's native speaker intuition of the standard form of the language. *Cymraeg Byw*, and the various forms of 'Welsh for learners' descended from it, claim to incorporate forms from all dialects, but the dialect of south-west Wales predominates.

In recent years, the notion of *y Fro Gymraeg* (the Welsh heartland), which corresponds to Raybould's 'natural Welsh-speaking' areas has increasingly been discussed. Before 1981, Dyfed (south-west Wales) was seen as part of the heartland area, but since 1981, although the Welsh-speaking area of Gwynedd has remained largely intact, that of Dyfed has not only shrunk but become fragmented (Williams, 1982). Despite this, or possibly because of it, southern variants, particularly those of south-west Wales, are heavily represented in the modern Standard Welsh which is recommended in the DfE and Welsh Office 1995 document just quoted as being the customary register of 'literate Welsh-speakers'. People in Gwynedd, who are overwhelmingly literate in Welsh, do not use this 'modern Standard Welsh' except when conversing with those who only know that variety and cannot follow the variety spoken in North Wales. They characteristically use Welsh because it is their language, not because they have been taught a formal register in which to impress people with their erudition.

Literary Welsh, as traditionally understood, is not local; it is simply the standard form used in writing. Local Welsh has only been written in comparatively recent times, certainly not before the second half of this century. People who would naturally have spoken Welsh in face-to-face communication tended to write in English because they had never been taught to use the written variety of Welsh. Snatches of Welsh appear in nineteenth-century letters which have been published, but characteristically alternate with English in a code-switching style, when the recipient can be assumed also to be bilingual. *Llythyrau Ceiriog* (Hughes, 1906), the letters of the poet John Ceiriog Hughes, are very touching in this way, expressing a love of the Welsh language through English phrases:

> Names of places, when got together, would be valuable;
> and to explain prehistoric events and things, nothing
> else has been left us in the shape of linguistic fossils.
> You see I am getting very learned; but instead of
> getting wise before I was old, I have got old first.
> *Dim ychwaneg y tro hwn.*
> Yours very truly,
> John Ceiriog Hughes (22nd December 1885)

The idea of a Welsh heartland has attracted considerable political attention (Baker, 1985). However, Ambrose and Williams (1981) have shown that the numbers returning themselves and their children in successive censuses as speakers of the Welsh language are rising in certain sub-zones in areas of apparent decline, and that the largest absolute numbers of such speakers may be greater than in the sparsely populated heartland areas. Aitchison and Carter (1994) show that although the highest concentration of Welsh speakers may continue to be in Gwynedd, the largest number may eventually be in the populous urban south-west, where they are surrounded in their daily lives by people whose preferred and habitual language is English.

One of the linguistic questions that remains largely unanswered is whether the revived or recovered 'second-language Welsh' or 'learners' Welsh', which is learned at school rather than acquired as a mother tongue, and later only rarely used in everyday adult life conducted in English, is as full, vibrant, lively and as varied in style, register, even accent as the traditional dialectal speech of Welsh in Raybould's 'natural Welsh-speaking areas' in *y Fro Gymraeg*. The overall community of Welsh speakers is holding its own at just under the 20 per cent level of the total population. It has ceased to fall. But the great majority are very young, and in the south may rarely hear fluent adult conversation between native Welsh speakers. As Davies (1993) reminds us, 'triumphalism is not in order – not yet, at least'. Commissioner Lingen's warning from 1847 still holds good:

> Nor can an old and cherished language be taught down in schools; for so long as the children are familiar with none other, they must be educated to a considerable extent through the medium of it, even though to supersede it be the most important part of their education. Still less, out of school can the language of lessons make headway against the language of life.
>
> (Lingen, 1847)

English may not be cherished in the *Ysgolion Cymraeg*, but it is the mother tongue of most of the children, as Welsh was in Lingen's day. Welsh as the 'language of lessons' can only grow if it is also 'the language of life'.

A survey by Professors Carter and Aitchison, conducted in 1988, indicated that at least half the pupils receiving a Welsh-medium education rarely make use of the language outside school. Carter and Aitchison came to the conclusion that, among the young people of Cardiff, 'Welsh is a plant which has been growing energetically but which has not as yet produced a deep and extensive root system' (Davies, 1993).

THE RISE OF POLITICAL PROTEST ABOUT THE STATUS OF THE WELSH LANGUAGE

Much of the current political attention given to the threatened dying out of the Welsh language has been inspired by the writer J. Saunders Lewis, one of the founders of *Y Blaid* (The Party), full title *Plaid Cymru* (The Welsh Nationalist Party), in 1925. Born in Liverpool to Welsh-speaking parents, Saunders Lewis had the exile's *hiraeth* (love, longing, passion, drive-to-return) not, as is customary, to a particular locality of birth and upbringing but to Wales as an entirety, a nation, a vision, somewhere small, white and green, but splashed with the red blood of martyrdom.

Lewis was one of those who had returned from World War One to set about winning the peace. On becoming a lecturer in Welsh at the University of Wales, Aberystwyth, he was beginning to be regarded by young Welsh speakers as the father of the reborn Nationalist cause. When, in 1936, a bombing school had been set up in Llyn, despite strong local protests, Lewis and two friends had set fire to the empty buildings and been arrested. Lewis later attempted to address the Caernarfon Assizes in Welsh, and was contemptuously silenced by the judge. The Caernarfon jury refused to convict the three of arson. However, at the Old Bailey they were sent to prison for nine months. In 1938 a quarter of a million people signed a petition launched at the *Eisteddfod* (the annual Welsh cultural assembly) which sought the repeal of the language clause of the Act of Union, and demanded that Welsh be given equal status with English.

The result was the Welsh Courts Act of 1942, which gave Welsh parity with 'languages such as Greek or Arabic, which were occasionally used in courts in the south Wales ports' (Davies, 1993). Following this Act, comments Davies, 'any party or witness who considered that he would otherwise be at a disadvantage by reason of his natural language of communication being Welsh' was given the right to 'use the Welsh language', and the court became responsible for paying the interpreter who then became necessary. Welsh speakers still had no absolute right to use their language, and Welsh was hardly ever seen at that time on an official form or public notice.

On 13 February, 1962, Saunders Lewis, by then an admired poet and dramatist, made the broadcast on the BBC called *Tynged yr Iaith* (the Fate of the Language). He put the survival of the Welsh language into the hands of those who speak it, if not as a first language, then as a preferred language, a language of choice. Davies asserts that it came as a great surprise to many people that the resulting formation and subsequent activities of the *Cymdeithas yr Iaith Gymraeg* (the Welsh Language Society) were not condemned out of hand by the middle classes. However, on the other hand, some writers assert that it was and remains predominantly a middle-class movement.

This is so because in the nineteenth century, particularly after the shame which was induced by the Blue Books Report of 1847, speaking Welsh outside the domains of family, friends and religion was regarded as a mark of very low social standing. Speaking Welsh was also seen as being likely to lead to speaking English with a strong Welsh accent, an invariably stigmatized variety of English. The Welsh language was thus seen as a potential source of variation from 'the standard' of British English, which had become the new high-status language variety in Wales. As a result, the within-language diglossia of literary Welsh and the dialects had given way to a new two-language 'out-diglossia' with English as the high and Welsh as the low variety (Ceinwen Thomas, 1982). The middle-class association with the English language was certainly held by the writers of the 1927 Board of Education Report, 'Welsh in Education and Life', quoted by Davies, in which particular concern was expressed about previously rural Welsh-speaking families:

> Welsh Wales will be unable to develop a middle class because the members of that class will necessarily become Anglicized as they rise in the social scale, unless some immediate provision is made for their children in those areas in which economic conditions have forced their parents to settle.
>
> (Davies, 1993)

It was this concern for making possible the development of a Welsh-speaking middle class which had led to the recommendation in the 1927 Report that designated Welsh-medium primary schools should be set up in these urban areas to complement the natural Welsh-medium primaries in rural areas. Entry to these designated schools was at first restricted to children already fluent in Welsh, by a kind of 4+ examination, but they have increasingly taken on a pivotal role in the peaceful language revival (Raybould, 1995).

The Code for Wales issued by the Welsh Department at the Board of Education in 1907 had given some grudging recognition to the principle of bilingualism, but the 1927 Report was the first sign of official movement in this direction. Various developments within the country had gone towards creating a different climate of opinion: the cultural renaissance marked by the founding of the University of Wales, the National Library of Wales and the National *Eisteddfod*; a growing sense of national confidence witnessed by the formation of *Undeb Cymru Fydd* (The New Wales Union) and the adoption of Home Rule policies by both Liberal and Labour parties. The 1927 Report recognized for the first time the legitimacy of bilingualism in Welsh education as a national system, rather than on the basis of local need, and recommended that the mother tongue should be the sole medium of education in the early years of school, thus establishing a case for designated 'Welsh schools'.

The curiosity is that what started as 'mother-tongue' education has little by little become 'immersion' education aimed at achieving an élite bilingualism and the recovery of the lost heritage language, which was not lost to the individual but to the community, or even the nation. In Cardiff, for example, the first primary school teaching through the medium of Welsh opened in 1949 with only 18 pupils. In 1992, there were 1,400 pupils attending six Welsh-medium primaries, out of 5,208 Welsh speakers under fifteen. The number of Welsh speakers overall in the city has risen from 9,623 in 1951 to 17,236 in 1991. The majority of the Welsh-speaking migrants to Cardiff are employed in administration, education and the media. As a consequence, the rise in the number of Welsh speakers has occurred almost exclusively in the middle-class suburbs, and as a result of in-migration from *y fro Gymraeg*: 'Ever since the Anglicization of the gentry, the speaking of Welsh had been associated with low social status; its association with high status, apparent in Cardiff but also elsewhere, is a new development' (Davies, 1993).

The first Welsh-medium nursery school was established soon after World War Two in Maesteg. At the 1971 *Eisteddfod*, the Welsh Nursery School Movement (*Mudiad Ysgolion Meithrin*) was established with 70 playgroups. In 1992, there were 600 schools with 9,338 pupils, as well as 4,156 pupils in 377 mother-and-child groups (Raybould, 1993). *Merched y Wawr*, an organization for women, was set up in 1967 as a reaction to the refusal of the National Federation of Women's Institutes, which had been founded on Anglesey, to permit the use of Welsh at an official level. *Merched y Wawr* is still very active, and there are many other special interest groups. *Cymdeithas yr Iaith Gymraeg* combined with *Plaid Cymru* to press for the broadcasting of Welsh; the then solitary *Plaid* MP, Gwynfor Evans, began a fast to death unless this was granted. In November 1982, *Sianel Pedwar Cymru* (S4C – the Welsh Fourth Channel) went on air for the first time.

THE STATUS OF THE WELSH LANGUAGE SINCE 1991

There have now been two Language Acts, the very limited one of 1967, and the Welsh Language Bill of 1993. This has set up the statutory Welsh Language Board (*Bwrdd yr Iaith*) which subsumes the functions of the Committee for the Development of Welsh-medium Education (*Pwyllgor Datblygu Addysg Gymraeg* (PDAG)), which had been set up in 1987 as part of the preparing of the ground for the coming of the National Curriculum. The 1993 Bill contains no mention of the right to education through the medium of Welsh, only a require-ment for governors, in common with other public bodies, to draw up a language policy. There is some anxiety felt in Wales about how effective a purely advisory Board will be able to be, particularly in maintaining the momentum of the language revival among the young.

The 1991 census showed that 18.7 per cent of the population of Wales over three years of age claimed to have a knowledge of Welsh. A similar figure, 18 per cent, had claimed knowl-edge of Welsh in the 1981 census, among those aged three to fifteen. The Welsh-claiming proportion of the latter age group, the all-important young, in 1991 had risen to 24.9 per cent, virtually a quarter – not only in the heartland – in Wales as a whole. However, the dual factors of rural depopulation and influx of English business managerial staff, academics and retired people is substantially altering the linguistic and social makeup of what were once remote rural Welsh-speaking fastnesses. Davies sums it all up very succinctly:

> Some of the incomers were intrigued by the distinctiveness of Wales and set about learning Welsh. Others, feeling that all they had done was to move from one place to another within their country of Britain, were annoyed at any suggestion that they should be assimilated into a culture which they considered inferior. Some of the incomers were considerably perturbed at finding that they had, by moving, deprived themselves of some of their favourite television programmes. Many were parents of school-age children who reacted angrily to the discovery that lessons in the local primary school were conducted largely through the medium of Welsh. On the other hand the Welsh population, feeling under siege and fearing that the influx would squeeze them out of exist-ence, also began to voice concern. Thus the traditionally Welsh-speaking areas of Wales became areas of potential conflict.
>
> (Davies, 1993)

These modern new settlers may have moved to live where there was work, or, increasingly nowadays, where property prices are lower than in England. Not many have learned Welsh in those districts where they outnumber the original inhabitants. This is not necessarily the result of prejudice, or laziness. Davies asserts that there was an historical conviction over many cen-turies on the part of Welsh speakers that their language 'could not be learned by those not brought up to speak it'. It was this conviction that the *Cymraeg Byw* movement attempted to dispel. After all, centuries of contact with the resolutely monolingual English may well have served to reinforce this belief. It must have seemed to the 800,000 Welsh-speaking people of Wales in 1851, still 67 per cent of the steeply rising total population, that those who had not been brought up to speak Welsh could not hear or see the language which was in some senses all around them, much less learn to speak it. They were only aware of the language which they understood, English. As more and more people began to understand English, the need to understand Welsh decreased and the recruitment of 'those not brought up to speak it' into the Welsh speech community declined.

Some writers have alleged that the irresistible force of English monolingualism, by the turn of the twentieth century had encountered the immovable object of the Welsh language, and was beginning to roll it downhill. They would claim that if Welsh is not now dead, then it is dying (Adler, 1977). But there is a contrary view which is becoming more and more popular in Wales, especially among the young. That view is that Welsh people's identity as Welsh people is more central to their experience than their identity as inhabitants of Mid-Western Britain. For many, this positive Welsh identity includes pride in the continued existence of the Welsh language, but this is not a consensus view across the nation as was the nineteenth-century's domain-specific English/Welsh diglossia, with both Welsh English and the Welsh language itself being widely regarded as stigmatized variations from Standard British English. In the 1990s, there are two contrasting views:

1. Coupland (1990) and others have suggested that the monoglot speakers of Welsh English may feel proud of their identity independently of the language issue, and may feel that there is more to being Welsh than just speaking Welsh. This group is likely to have some notional Welsh Standard English as the linguistic norm rather than British English as generally understood.

2. Others have identified what may be called 'the new diglossia', with Welsh as the new High form, a reversal in the relative status of the two main languages of Wales. This view of the socio-linguistic context in present-day Wales is shared by many people; it is not restricted to Welsh people who are themselves fully bilingual; it is held by many people who speak Welsh English, do not themselves speak Welsh, but feel that the Welsh language is central to Welsh identity.

Those who hold this second view tend to argue that without the Welsh language, Welsh identity is flexible to the point of being formless. For them, the continued existence of the Welsh language is central to Welsh identity; for the first group, it is not. But the lived realities of a Welsh identity, like any other, are complex. An individual may subscribe to one view in some conversational settings and hold the opposite in others. Current research is showing the multi-dimensional nature of Welsh teachers' and pupils' attitudes to their own and others' ethnicities (Coupland *et al.*, 1994). 'Authenticity' is emerging as a highly salient dimension for the expression of attitudes to English in Wales. Although, as just asserted, for many people the warranting criterion for Welsh identity is fluency in the Welsh language, attitudes to Welsh appear to be less popular as a research topic in the 1990s than they were earlier in the century.

Baker (1992), of course, has pioneered research into attitudes towards bilingualism in Wales. There are regional factors affecting attitudes towards Welsh English, as there are towards Welsh itself. *Iaith cymysg* (mixed language), such as is common in the speech of working-class people in Bangor, is not regarded as either good English or good Welsh, as the 1995 Orders for Welsh quoted earlier make plain, but Bangor speech may still be rated as a 'truly Welsh' variety of Welsh English. These regionally based 'versions' of ethnicity deserve to be investigated more precisely in future studies.

To highlight one particular opportunity, the fascinating area of North Powys in Mid Wales cries to be considered. This is the old county of Mongomeryshire, constituted and named as part of the Statutes declaring the Act of Union. It has maintained a dynamic bilingualism for three centuries and there are established dialects, still current, of both English and Welsh. The English dialect shows some influence from Shropshire; some of the characteristic words and phrases of the Welsh dialect have been outlined by Iowerth Peate (1981a, b). That this part of North Powys is the subject of an ongoing research project aimed at identifying the Welsh of Llanfair Caereinion as a distinctive variety, if not a classical dialect, demonstrates the fact that the Welsh language continues to attract wide attention.

Chapter 9

Teaching the Mother Tongue in France

Françoise Convey

HISTORICAL BACKGROUND

Since the early nineteenth century, French education has been undergoing a continuous process of change and development, under the impact of two factors: the struggle between the State and the Catholic Church for the ideological control of French society and the attempts of successive education ministers to reform the system by means of legislation. Throughout this period, the one feature that survived was the administrative structure of state control created by Napoleon, together with the principle inherited from the French Revolution that provision for education was a duty of the State. This resulted in a highly centralized system and a uniformity which has become one of its familiar features. It also implied that any significant alteration of the educational system required a political decision by the minister or by the government of the day.

Until 1833, the state monopoly system was based upon Catholic principles, and primary education was mainly in the hands of religious teaching orders. It was the 1830 Revolution that began the process which was to lead to the removal of the Catholic Church from the school system, leading the way to the secularization process of *laïcité* in the state, in society and in education.

The school had as its primary function the objective of reducing differences between children within the perspective of national unity and unification. Already, at the start of the French Revolution in 1789, in one of his speeches to the *Etats Généraux*, Mirabeau had talked of unifying the mix of population which made up the French people. The first charter of primary education dates back to the Guizot Act (*Loi Guizot*) of 1833 (Cahm, 1972), which made local authorities or *municipalités* responsible for primary schools and *départements* for the training of primary school teachers. It also produced a circular letter to all primary schools imposing the use of the French language in the classroom. The legislation aimed to ensure that all children used French in school, and to forbid the use of regional languages in order to produce 'the school of the Republic'. A constant preoccupation of the state was to spread the use of the French language as a sign and a means of national unity. Yet, a century after the French Revolution, the problem of diversity of idioms and dialects was far from being resolved and rural communities remained in an enclosed world, isolated equally by linguistic barriers and

Figure 4: The regional languages of France

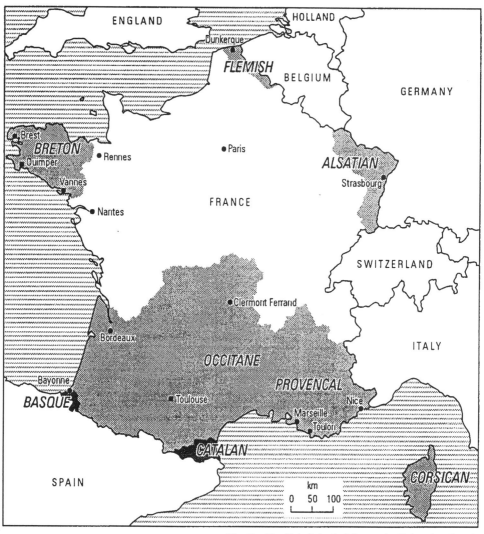

The Graphics Unit, School of Geography, University of Leeds

by difficulties in communication. In 1867, one third of the soldiers in the conscript army could not express themselves properly in French. The foundations for the present system were laid by Jules Ferry with the educational laws of 1881–82, which established the basic principles of an education system which was free, secular and compulsory (Cahm, 1972). Jules Ferry's famous letter to primary school teachers in 1883 stressed that each school had to become 'a French-speaking colony in a conquered country'; local forms of speech, whether languages, dialects or patois had to be eradicated. The school teacher (*l'instituteur*) would stand out, in a non-francophone district, like the priest (*le curé*) and sometimes the mayor (*le maire*), as the person who possessed two competencies that were rare in the village: the knowledge of French language and the ability to write it. As he was in a position to promote both, one then understands the importance attached to the role of the school teacher by central government. The action against regional languages and all forms of dialects and patois would lead eventually to their elimination in France for a century and a half, until the '*contestation*' of 1968, with the rebirth of regional cultures and the regionalist, even autonomist, movements. Under the Third Republic, it was a matter of political objective: the *Nation*, citizenship, the *Code Civil*, the army and the school were all seen as tools for the unification of the French nation which aimed to reduce all forms of diversity among French nationals, as well as being a process of integration for those people coming from elsewhere. The role imparted to the school by the political power therefore led to both the elimination of regional languages and dialects and to the integration of immigrants through a process of assimilation. As Durand-Prinborgne (1990) puts it: 'To take account of diversity would be a most deeply disruptive process.'

The defeat of France in the 1870 Franco-Prussian war had demonstrated that France was no longer the dominant power in Europe and that the balance of power had shifted to Prussia. In view of these external dangers, it was crucial for France to cement national unity. The new secular moral code was to be based, not on religion, but on the *morale laïque*, a secular moral code, which would be taught through compulsory daily classes in *Instruction Civique*, which were to serve as a substitute for religious instruction in schools. This secular moral code was strongly associated with patriotism and patriotic duty (Ozouf, 1967). The school is presented as 'the temple of the new faith' and the teachers as its ministers:

> *L'école, voilà désormais le temple de la foi des temps nouveaux. Il incombe aux instituteurs d'être les pasteurs de ce temple.*
>
> (Spuller, 1888)

In the long and passionate ideological debate of the time, education was seen as providing this unifying factor: '*la mission unificatrice de l'enseignement*' (Prost, 1968). Based upon the ideas put forward by the French Revolution in 1789, the school created by Guizot and Jules Ferry was designed to become the pivotal axis of the collective national consciousness around the concept of citizenship.

Historically, therefore, this accounts for the development of the so-called 'monster' of the highly centralized and bureaucratic *Education Nationale*. It also explains why all debates concerning education in France become so passionate and irrational. It is essential also to keep in mind another characteristic feature of the relationship of the French with their mother tongue. As far back as 1634, the Cardinal de Richelieu created the *Académie Française*, stating that its principal object was to be the perfecting of the French language, and its role was to codify the French language through the tools provided by a Dictionary, a Grammar, a Rhetoric and a Poetic. For Richelieu and Louis XIV, the *Académie* was to provide them with a language that could be used at national (or even international) level as a tool for culture and administration.

Its '*Commissions de terminologies*' have been instruments in the hands of the governments ever since. Since the *Ordonnance de Villers-Cotterêts*, signed by François I in 1539, on the use of French as the national language of the country, a number of legislative documents have been published by successive governments, particularly in recent years, most recently the *Loi Toubon* (1993) making the use of French compulsory in all official acts of social, professional and intellectual life (including the sales of goods and services, work contracts, conferences and colloquia, advertising, news and presentation of programmes on radio and television and in all public places) and making it illegal to use foreign terms at all levels of official life. All presidents and prime ministers of the Fifth Republic have signed their names on legislation concerning the French language. The European Union support for linguistic diversity has been interpreted in France as support of French in the linguistic plurality of Europe.

THE PRESENT SITUATION

Nowadays, the role of the French language and the idea of the unifying function of the school have become more complex, particularly as the heterogeneity of the school population is accompanied by linguistic and cultural differences that are linked to the presence in schools of children of foreign origin. Political and ideological factors, extraneous to education, make it crucial that education should take account of this diversity of pupils and that education should take into account the cultural identity of the pupils. It has taken France a long time to accept the development of local initiatives for the differentiated treatment of pupils, which will lead in the long term to the development of a policy aiming at the recognition and teaching of both regional languages and of '*langues et cultures d'origine*' (ELCO). This relates particularly to immigrant children or to the children born in France of immigrant parents.

Faced with the increasing linguistic and cultural diversity of its pupils in the 1970s, the French school system adopted a programme of measures aimed specifically at children of immigrant origin and at the teaching of regional languages and cultures. In the early 1980s, this policy was part of François Mitterrand's candidacy programme for the French Presidency, in his manifesto: '*110 Propositions pour la France*', leading to the education key policy document, '*Université 2000*', of Lionel Jospin. François Bayrou, the Minister for Education, under both the second *Cohabitation* Government of Edouard Balladur and after the election of Jacques Chirac as President of the Republic, continues to implement largely unchanged policies. The plan of action which has been drawn up is designed to ensure that regional languages and cultures, as well as those languages and cultures specific to children of foreign origin, have a place in the school curriculum, with both time allowed on the time-table and the provision of specialist teachers. The plan also sets up *classes d'accueil* for non-francophone children and recommends that the education authorities work together with the families and the communities of these children.

The recognition of these linguistic and cultural differences is now considered as a source of enrichment for national cohesion, based upon mutual respect. Schools are invested with a mission of integration, arising from the fear that the confrontation of cultures could turn into a confrontation between communities: the crisis in the suburbs (*les banlieues*) is perhaps symptomatic of this confrontation. The problems lie in the imprecision of the objectives, in the means of implementation and in the uncertainty of the status given to these languages and cultures within a school system faced with new requirements of efficiency.

When considering the issue of the teaching of mother tongue in French schools therefore, there are three scenarios which need to be considered:

1. The teaching of French to pupils for whom French is their mother tongue: for this, official documents (*'Programmes, Instructions et Conseils'*) are available which give very detailed information to teachers (Babin and Pierre, 1991).

2. The teaching of mother tongue to children from immigrant families, whether the first generation of recent immigrants or children of subsequent generations. This needs to be studied in context and the examples chosen will refer to the *Maghrébin*, or North African, population in France in general and to the Portuguese community in the south-west of France.

3. The teaching of a regional language in those areas where regional languages are recognized and approved, but where it may not necessarily be the pupil's mother tongue. A case study which is particularly relevant here is that of the Corsican language.

The teaching of French as a mother tongue

Primary schooling in France (*'l'école élémentaire'*) is organized into three stages (or *'cycles'*):

- *le cycle des apprentissages premiers* (the nursery school or *école maternelle*)
- *le cycle des apprentissages fondamentaux* (the first two years of compulsory schooling from the ages of six to eight)
- *le cycle des approfondissements* (the final three years of primary school).

The two most recent key documents on education policy are Lionel Jospin's *Loi d'Orientation sur l'Education* of 10 July 1989, and François Bayrou's *Nouveau Contrat pour l'école* of 1 September 1994. Priority is given in both documents to fundamental learning (*'apprentissages fondamentaux'*) in the *école élémentaire*: French language, reading, mathematics and study skills.

> The first priority is the mastery of the French language, both spoken and written; particularly in priority areas, the teaching of the French language can draw from the experience of and the methods used in teaching French as a foreign language (FLE). There is provision for a programme of continuing training for teachers.
>
> (Bayrou, 1994)

Bayrou's *Nouveau Contrat pour l'école* concludes, listing the virtues that are basic to a civilized democratic society, among which are search for truth, faith in human reason, intellectual rigour and a sense of responsibilities, respect for oneself and others, rejection of racism, and the spirit of solidarity and co-operation (Bayrou, 1994).

Official instructions (*les Instructions officielles*) applying to all schools are issued regularly by the Ministry of Education and are expressed in terms of objectives and programmes of study, published under the title of *Programmes, Instructions, Conseils* (Babin and Pierre, 1991). These constitute a document which is both simple and accessible to all and part of its role is to ensure straightforward and confident relationships between the school and the parents, who also have an essential role to play. (*Arrêté Ministériel*, 23 April 1985). If one is teaching in a French school, it is essential to refer to the *Instructions officielles*, which also define the competencies which pupils need to acquire at each stage. Whilst methods and approaches are left to the initiative and responsibility of the individual teacher (who has to take into account the diversity and the learning difficulties of the children), these programmes and instructions are compulsory in all schools (Bayrou, 1994).

The *Instructions officielles* concerning the teaching of French as mother tongue are to be found in the *Arrêté ministériel*, 23 April 1985. In these, the teaching of French as mother tongue comes under the rubric of '*Maîtrise de la langue: langage oral, lecture et production de textes à l'école maternelle et à l'école élémentaire*'. This *Arrêté ministériel* underpins the whole primary school system: the objective of the *Instructions et Programmes* is to provide a school that is active and open to the future and to enable all pupils to acquire the mastery of basic knowledge that is believed to be the best way to prevent failure at school. Success in initial learning is regarded as essential, particularly in the area of reading.

The official instructions are very detailed and specific. They state that, in the first year (*Cours préparatoire*), the objective of the teaching of the French language, as a continuation of the work done in the nursery class, is for pupils to master oral expression, the aim being to gain access to the written text (*premier degré de l'instruction*). In the second and third years (*Cours élémentaire*), the regular practice of reading and writing at a more demanding level aims to improve the quality of language, allowing the pupils to start a process of reflection. In the last two years (*Cours moyen*), pupils learn to question, answer, explain and justify; their ability to read and write should improve in quality and complexity and their enriched knowledge of language is expected to become more precise. For this purpose, it is essential that the teacher's speech should be clear, articulate and correct, providing pupils with a model. The teacher will encourage pupils to speak, to listen to their classmates and to formulate their thoughts, to extend their vocabulary and their quality of expression, particularly for those pupils for whom family and social experience is different from that to be found in the school. Specific exercises are suggested which include pronunciation exercises, as well as exercises aimed at describing situations, narrating and commenting upon events, inventing and modifying stories, tales and scenarios, or expressing feelings and emotions, arguing and using a variety of language registers.

When it comes to the teaching of reading (*la lecture*), the document states that, since reading means understanding, the teacher should discourage a mechanical or passive form of learning. The approach advocated is a 'pedagogy of activity'. The practice of, and the taste for, reading must never cease to be developed, though the choice of methods and pedagogical approaches is left primarily to the initiative and responsibility of the teacher. The text recommends that teachers should use not the so-called 'global method' of reading, which is hardly ever advocated in France, but the method of '*la combinatoire*', establishing links between letters and syllables and between written symbols and the sounds which correspond to those symbols, and of sequentialization which consists of 'splitting the words within a sequence'. But all this is only of value if it is associated with the comprehension of the ideas expressed, with an awareness of the structure of the sentence, and an understanding of the meaning of words. Since, for many children, the written form is not part of their familiar reality, it is essential at school to surround pupils with books and texts and to provide the model of a teacher who reads to them. The teacher has a responsibility to make use of all possible sources from a reading corner in the classroom to the school or local library, to the window of the bookshop, to television programmes on books, or even the reading of a television or computer screen. The teacher should also encourage an initiation to works of literary quality, read and discussed in class, including texts and materials relating to daily life. The teaching of reading has to be systematic, and involves silent reading as well as reading aloud, a competency to be practised with a clear, intelligent and expressive diction. All this implies a regular process of evaluation and a progression towards more complex forms of texts, taking account of the individual pupils' ages, development, and learning patterns. The teacher should not lose sight of the fact that all children have the ability to learn to read and must be able to do so. This may be summed up in the provision of a policy for reading: wanting to read in order to learn to read; learning to read in order to know how to read; knowing how to read in order to enjoy reading. All methods have their merits. Whatever the method used, it is essential to nurture and encourage the desire to read, the objective being to lead everyone towards wanting to read, being able to read and enjoying reading, which is seen as a process for a lifetime.

The observation of practice in a number of schools makes one aware of the extensive use of innovative teaching and learning methods, especially in those schools where the experience has been going on for some years. The approach is based on the initiation of children to the pleasure of reading, making use of game-like activities (*l'approche ludique*). '*La lecture puzzle*' is one of the most popular activities with pupils, in which the objective is to reconstruct the original version of a text from sentences which have previously been cut up with a pair of scissors and mixed up by the teacher. Other activities include *décloisonnement*, that is, regrouping the children by reading level, which allows the teacher to have two groups working on the same reading text in pairs; or through a dialogue to promote a better understanding of the text which is being read, with, for instance, the guessing of missing words. The advice given would be to read the text three times in order to assimilate it: first to look, then to understand, finally to assimilate. Silent reading accompanied by a written questionnaire to verify the understanding of the text is also often used. Dictionaries are consulted as early as the age of six. What is intended is to arrive at a situation where the children play with words and read while playing; at the reading of books, but also the reading of anything written: a process of *désacralisation*, removing the sacred aura surrounding the reading process. Comic strips and strip cartoons are always very popular with pupils and they often constitute their favourite reading. Increasing importance is given to the reading of texts of a documentary or informative nature and the encouragement of silent reading, which provides an initiation to the techniques of rapid reading so essential nowadays. The overall aim is to arouse in children a new interest for all that is written.

The use of Information Technology in the teaching of French is still very limited, although it is developing in a number of *académies*. It is often used by specialized teachers dealing with children with language-learning difficulties: those teachers take the pupils, between the ages of five and eight, for an hour each day in small groups. Some new products exist in this field, presenting the children with activities aimed at developing visual discrimination, spatial reference (*repérage*) and language exercises. Both teachers and pupils have a very positive and enthusiastic reaction to the IT approach. The children enjoy learning and have fun with learning in a friendly, relaxed atmosphere. For the pupils, a better understanding leads to a better appreciation of what they are reading – they enjoy the activity. For the teachers, it is part of a lively pedagogical programme designed so that the pupils do not end up in a situation of failure. All are provided with an equality of opportunity, without slowing down those pupils who are able to move faster, while at the same time developing their autonomy.

When it comes to writing, handwriting must be the object of constant attention from the teacher, including consistency of style, respect for the rules and quality of presentation. It also involves initiation into such other forms of writing as keyboarding skills and word processing.

The practice of written expression cannot be dissociated from the learning of reading. The nursery school develops in children the desire to write: *l'école élémentaire* induces the pupils to write in a simple manner but with confidence and freedom, as an enjoyable exercise.

The study of language and language awareness uses two methods: the development of an implicit competency, in which the pupils use a variety of the elements and structures of language, and the explicit analysis of the notions and functions that come into play in language use. All forms of written language provide a source of materials for controlling and enriching spelling, grammar and lexical knowledge.

Often, however, children arrive in the primary school without having mastered oral language. The language they use is not structured because there has been no introduction or mediation from the family, often the result of absence of communication within the family. In such cases, the only chance of success for the pupil is through schooling. This means that the teacher has to use differentiated pedagogical practices, adapted to the developmental stages, difficulties and social diversity of the children; it also implies that the child must be encouraged to play an active role in the learning process in which the pupil is always regarded as being at the centre. It is worth noting, for instance, that the French use the expression '*l'apprentissage de la lecture*', the learning, rather than teaching of reading, and that they make a distinction between speaking French fluently and merely expressing oneself in French.

The *Contrat pour l'école* includes the creation of a National Observatory for Reading (*l'Observatoire national de la lecture*), whose brief is to produce an annual report summarizing the work accomplished and the research undertaken in the field of reading. It also suggests new areas of research and provides a programme for in-service, now called continuing vocational education, since one of the points is the lack of support for teachers, particularly inexperienced ones.

All these measures have been in operation since the beginning of the 1994 school year. Particular attention is given to pupils who experience language difficulties, the aim being to enable them, at the end of primary schooling, 'to read ten pages silently without getting tired' (Bayrou in an interview in *l'Express*, 12 May 1994).

For François Bayrou, the fundamental mission entrusted to primary school teachers is to enable the mastery of the French language, which is the key to any further school success or failure and the acquisition of reference points for a lifetime (methods of work, transferable study skills) and civics (*Education civique*) which is '*l'éducation à la morale de la responsabilité*', to be found at all levels and which relates to all aspects of social and personal life: environment, health and justice. The *Contrat pour l'école* also introduces a compulsory daily initiation of 15 minutes per day to a foreign language, in the last two years of all primary schools, using video tapes prepared for schools and audio-visual methods. In every school where it is possible to do so, and at the request of pupils or parents, the teaching of regional languages is 'a desirable objective offering a form of cultural and linguistic enrichment'.

Following five years at primary school, children spend four more years of compulsory schooling at a *collège* to which entry is automatic for pupils whose primary school report states that they have acquired the necessary basic skills. There is no entrance examination or selection on the basis of the school report. In 1959, secondary schooling in France was reorganized: compulsory schooling was extended to the age of 16, *collèges* were created to cover the four-year first cycle of secondary education, while the *lycées* catered for upper secondary education, or second cycle, which was diversified to incorporate technical and vocational courses in *lycées d'enseignement professionnel* (LEP). The 1975 Education Act reforming secondary education marked the abolition of the system whereby pupils were grouped according to ability: the reform led to what is known as the *collège unique* or comprehensive school. The changes imposed on secondary education with the creation of the *collège unique* reflected a determined effort to achieve homogeneity, integration and equal opportunities, but led to some reluctance on the part of both parents and teachers. Education Priority Zones (ZEP or *Zones d'éducation prioritaire*) were also created. The role of the *collège* is to ensure that pupils acquire basic knowledge and to help them make educational choices. The law stipulates that educational decisions are a family responsibility and that parents must be consulted on these choices. With the *Contrat pour l'école*, the *collège* has to fulfil a double objective: ensure some form of success for all and provide solutions for children experiencing difficulties. Repeating a year is now possible only, if necessary, at the end of each *cycle* (Bayrou, 1994). The first two years at a *collège* constitute an 'observation cycle' during which all the pupils follow the same course. However, any pupil experiencing difficulties may in addition receive special help for a total of up to six hours per week, according to need. The next two years constitute the 'preparatory cycle'. In addition to the core subjects, pupils must choose one of the following options: a second modern language other than their own, a classical language, a regional language, or a more intensive course in their first modern language. At this stage, special support arrangements may be made for pupils experiencing temporary difficulties, whereas pupils with more serious learning problems are entitled to receive special tuition on a 'contract' basis. For pupils in the fourth year, it is possible to follow a new 'integration' course (*classe d'insertion*).

In the *collège*, the curriculum is limited to core subjects (French, mathematics, history and geography, modern language, sciences and technology, art, physical education and sports). Throughout the 4 years 4.5 hours per week are devoted to French and 3 hours to the study of a modern foreign language: in the last 2 years of the *collège*, there is an option of 3 hours a week for the study of the regional language.

The *lycée* provides for three more years of post-compulsory schooling, leading to the *Baccalauréat*, which is the entrance examination to university. At this stage, there is no provision for any remedial support.

Teachers are trained at *Instituts Universitaires de Formation des Maîtres* (IUFM) which provide teacher training for both primary and secondary sectors. Currently, there is a core training course common to all trainee teachers, giving them a professional culture regardless of teaching level, specialist field or subject area. The training course lasts two years. In order to teach at primary level, candidates take the CRPE (*Concours de Recrutement des Professeurs des Ecoles*), while the qualification awarded for secondary teaching is the CAPES (*Certificat d'Aptitude au Professorat de l'Enseignement Secondaire*), giving them the title of *professeurs certifiés*. *Collège* or *lycée* teachers are also recruited by competitive examination, the *Agrégation*, from among candidates who hold either a *Maîtrise* (after four years at University) or a CAPES. All qualified teachers are civil servants.

PROBLEMS OF LITERACY

The teaching of reading has been a paramount issue in all policy documents on education for many years, but it became a key issue in François Bayrou's *Contrat pour l'école*. The methods used have not been entirely successful as illiteracy has still not greatly diminished, according to recent studies affecting 20 per cent of the adult population. As opposed to *analphabétisme*, which applies to someone who has never learned to read or write, *illettrisme* applies to someone who has learned to read but who has difficulty in understanding a passage of some 70 words. It is a very serious phenomenon, which becomes particularly noticeable at two levels: when a child enters the *collège* or later on at the time of what used to be a young man's national service, when systematic screening took place for anyone who might have left school without any qualification.

A survey conducted in France by the *Groupe permanent de lutte contre l'illettrisme* for the *Institut National de la Statistique et des Etudes Economiques* (INSEE) in 1990 revealed that one adult out of every four had serious difficulties in coping with reading and writing; 3.3 million were unable to read and understand a simple text in French; while 6 million had difficulties with a written text and were unable to read a label or a newspaper, to fill in a form or to write a cheque. The test used is based on a simple written text of 70 words. The survey further revealed discrepancies between the abilities of men and women, as 60 per cent of those who experienced difficulties were men. More recently, the Ministry of Defence acknowledged that out of 420,000 young men called up for National Service, 1,000 were classed as *analphabètes*, 30,000 as *illettrés*, and 14,000 were considered as non-readers, having forgotten, through lack of practice, any notions of reading and writing which they had acquired during their compulsory schooling.

During 1994, 6,000 young soldiers, according to statistics provided by the Ministry of Defence, were able to take advantage of the 'second chance' offered by the army, using tutors trained through an agreement between the Ministry of Education and the Ministry of Defence's Bureau *d'insertion professionnelle*. What is referred to as the *dispositif carcéral* (the prison system) is another domain where the reasons for illiteracy are analysed and the needs of the prisoners are investigated.

It is clear that a variety of levels of failure in this can be encountered. Yet all research points to the evidence that a child who does not master the spoken form of the language has little chance of entering into the written forms of language and therefore to be successful in school. The Fauroux Commission estimated recently that 15 per cent of pupils are rejected by the school system without the benefit of a 'survival package' indispensable for later life. Of these children experiencing various degrees of difficulty, half came from a working-class background (*paysans ou ouvriers*) and only 5 per cent from the middle class (*cadres*). There is no evidence in this context, however, of any relationship between intelligence and the ability to read: normally it is an issue of motivation, of choice, or of enjoyment. Interestingly enough, such screening does not apply to women, but research suggests that the problem is less serious for girls.

The crucial question is why so many children slip through the net and leave school unable to read. Lack of motivation is an obvious key factor, but also important is the lack of understanding of the many mental operations which need to be coordinated in order to master reading. Ninety per cent of children learn quickly and are able to read within a year, but, for the others, illiteracy is the supreme form of *exclusion*.

The inability to read is a grave social problem, a factor of *exclusion*, eventually leading to marginalization, for someone who is unable to read is unable to communicate, to get about, to go shopping, to write a cheque, or to vote as a citizen. Even with the advent of information technology, our world is still dominated by the written word.

France's struggle against illiteracy is perhaps at the most advanced stage of any European country. The French *Mouvement de lutte contre l'illettrisme* is a powerful lobby which has recently produced a report stressing the impact of illiteracy on exclusion and offering a number of suggestions for its prevention. These include the proposal for a *Carnet culturel* (cultural record), similar to the *Livret de santé* (health record) which is already created for each child at birth, to be given to the child's parents at birth in order to sensitize them to the educational issue as well. Another proposal is the daily hour of reading to be made compulsory in the primary school and beyond, with older pupils acting as tutors for younger ones.

The percentage of the population who are unable to master reading does not show any discrepancy, as one might have expected, between the *Français de souche* and the *Français issus de l'immigration*, that is, children born of French parents and those of immigrant parents. It is worth signalling the existence within the French education system of a significant number of *collèges et lycées à sections bilingues* and of *lycées internationaux*, where certain core subjects, like mathematics, history and geography, are taught in a modern foreign language other than French and where the pupils prepare for the French *Baccalauréat* as well as foreign examinations, like the International Baccalaureate, the English General Certificate of Secondary Education, or certificates in the Teaching of English as a Foreign Language. These *sections bilingues* are a significant departure in the French education system (Vigouroux-Frey and Convey, 1994).

TEACHING THE MOTHER TONGUE TO CHILDREN OF IMMIGRANT PARENTS

The teaching of French

French policy concerning immigrants has always been one of integration. It is essential, however, to differentiate between the recently arrived (who are very much fewer than they once were) and the children *'issus de l'immigration'*, that is the second, third or subsequent generations (often referred to as *'les Beurs'*, in French slang) . The latter are French citizens, having being born on French soil, and they are mostly referred to as *'la jeunesse arabe ou maghrébine née en France'*. The march of *les Beurs* through Paris for equality and against racism in 1983 was also the start of awareness of the problem by *maghrébin* youth, born in France of immigrant parents. As one of them said: 'Culturally, I am French, born in France, I went to school in France, I am an Arab born in France.' They stride two cultures – as does someone from another area of France (a provincial) who has come to Paris – and they are really fully accepted and integrated. But others, who refuse integration, refer to themselves as *'Musulmans franco-maghrébins'*. A survey conducted by the SOFRES with the weekly magazine *Le Nouvel Observateur* and *La Marche du Siècle* (a French television weekly documentary programme), asked *les jeunes Beurs* which were the best areas for integration and the answers were as follows:

- at school   70%
- at work   54%
- in sports   35%
- in associations   15%
- in the street   11%

Most of these young people speak French as their first language if not their mother tongue. A large number of them also speak, understand or 'get by' in Arabic. They will often explain that they have understood Arabic since an early age and many will have been pushed, when visiting their families in Algeria or Morocco for holidays or weddings, to start learning Arabic systematically in order to be able to communicate with the family over there. In addition, they will often speak another language in the slang of *Verlan* or *le Boucher*. But all of them state that in cases of trouble or difficulty they turn to their culture of origin, which is French.

What is the attitude of these groups towards the French language? They are aware that any real improvement in their status cannot take place outside education and that any opportunity for progress is through education, particularly through success at university. Asked about their motivation for success in their schooling, the answer is inevitably: *'Je voulais m'en sortir'* (I wanted to get out of it all): school and university represent contact with the outside world, the way out of the ghetto of the suburbs. In this respect, girls are more combative than boys, reacting against the rigid constraints of the family unit: for them school is a means of acquiring a social status. School represents freedom and social promotion and this promotion comes inevitably through a mastery of the French language. *'Sans diplômes, on n'est rien'* (Without qualifications, one gets nowhere). The *maghrébin* community in France now wishes to *'banaliser'* the educational success of its youngsters, that is, to make it commonplace and ordinary. Born and educated in France, these youngsters are integrated *de facto*: integration takes place through the mediation of women, of mothers and daughters. For them in particular, success at school means independence, freedom, emancipation from the family and religious constraints. This is the well-known principle of the pro-active minorities and this explains why the teaching of Arabic mother tongue and culture does not especially attract them; and when it does, its source is mostly from the religious community and the integrationist elements within Islam.

Until the 1981 Education Law, integration meant assimilation and consequently the disappearance of the previous identity, culture and traditions, through the abandonment of the language which is their vehicle. Today, integration has evolved and its meaning has changed: young people *'issus de l'immigration'* want what the French call colloquially *'le beurre et l'argent du beurre'*; they want integration, but they also want the right to be different: these values are, however, incompatible and ambiguous.

This is very different from the situation which pertained to the waves of immigrants from Russia or Poland or even those from Italy at the beginning of the century. As a rule, it takes two generations to reach a state of integration, but, in France, integration of recent immigrants has been extremely rapid. The statistics provided by the *Institut National d'Etudes Démographiques* (INED) indicate that one French person out of every four has foreign grandparents. Confusion has been created over the past 25 years by describing the children of immigrants as being somewhat exterior to the realities of the French school.

In order to clarify the debate, it is important at this point to define the French notion of what is meant by a 'foreigner'. According to the *Haut Conseil à l'Intégration*, an *'étranger'* (foreigner) is an entirely legal notion: 'Any person who does not have French nationality is a foreigner'. A very simple definition indeed, but it does not take into account the complexities of the French *Code de la Nationalité*. A second notion is that of *'immigré'*: *'Est immigrée la personne née à l'étranger, entrée en France et qui y vit en général définitivement'*. According to this definition, an *'immigré'* can be either French or foreign. However, children of *immigrés*, immigrants or migrants, are mostly excluded from these definitions. Three-quarters of them have been born in France and have not inherited an expatriate or migrant culture. They are culturally French before becoming so legally, for most of them at the age of 18, if they are not already French at birth (Schnapper, 1991). This, of course, explains the difficulty which the French school system has in rethinking and redefining its relationship with this new public and in defining clear and precise objectives for their specific needs. The first minister for education to take this issue into account was Jean-Pierre Chevènement, who at a press conference on 19 December 1985, when presenting the Berque Report which he had commissioned, *L'immigration à l'école de la République* (Berque, 1985), stated without any ambiguity that the school had a mission to integrate the children born of immigration. In 1989, for the first time, legislation took into account in school programmes the diversity and richness of the cultures present in France. Too often, nowadays, difficult situations in school are blamed on ethnic differences, while the real problems, particularly in deprived areas of the '*banlieues*', are of a social order. The only meaningful indicator is, in effect, '*la maîtrise de la langue française*'. In principle, since 1970, the school system has established that the main difference between francophones and non-francophones lies in the area of the acquisition of language, as a non-mother tongue, which in schools is the vehicle for all aspects of learning and all subjects in the curriculum. At the same time, however, there is no existing methodology or tools appropriate to the dispensing of efficient teaching methods to allow for more rapid integration into a normal school curriculum. There are, therefore, three different indicators to account for the '*hétérogénéité*' (mixed ability) of the school population: nationality, the notion of migrant/immigrant/*immigré*, and command of the language.

Almost 90 per cent of the children of parents of foreign nationality are now born in France. Any non-francophone child arriving in France between the ages of 7 and 11 is catered for in a '*classe d'initiation*' (CLIN), and after the age of 11 in a '*classe d'accueil*' (CLAD) (*Cahiers Pédagogiques*, 1991). The rule is the *insertion* of the child at the earliest possible time into a system which is already poorly adapted to those French young people who are socially and culturally deprived. *Circulaire* 86–119 (13/3/1986), which set up these classes, states that the objective is total integration of the non-francophone children as soon as possible.

There is no specific pedagogy in place for children of migrants, but rather a differentiated pedagogy and various forms of support. There are modules of *Français langue étrangère* (FLE: French as a foreign language), available in the *collège*, according to age and level, for non-francophone adolescents who first arrived in France between the ages of 3 and 6. In the second year of the *collège*, stress is put on perfecting the written language. The *Inspection académique* allows 12 part-time hours specifically for FLE in the *collèges*, provided a *collège* puts forward a project of FLE for its own pupils. Some *collèges* contribute a further six hours of their own allowance of part-time hours. The *Circulaire* dealing with these '*structures d'accueil*' recommends the use of methods which have been developed for teaching French as a foreign language. These methods are, however, totally unadapted to the teaching of French in a francophone framework. There also appears to be no special place in the training of future teachers in the IUFMs for these specialized situations which are becoming more and more widespread. *Circulaire* 86–119 deals with the teaching of French to foreign pupils who have recently arrived in France and at the same time draws attention to the case of children born in France, or who arrived in France at a very young age, and who have encountered difficulties because of their insufficient knowledge and handling of the French language. This second category of children is very much more numerous than the first. INSEE (1993) gives an annual intake of 41,000 pupils born abroad in the 1970–74 period, which corresponded to the period of the climax of family immigration, as against 18,286 in 1989, with a continued decline since. The *Circulaire* advises that children in these categories who experience difficulties should be taught in the same way as French children who are faced with difficulties or have special needs in periods of support study. The system set up by the *Circulaire* also provided the *Centres de formation et d'information pour la scolarisation des enfants migrants* (CEFISEM), but so far such centres are not integrated in any way into the normal school structures, though the aim is quite clearly to make it possible for these pupils to be so integrated as soon as possible. At present, the maximum time allowed in the *Classes d'initiation* or the *Classes d'accueil* is not more than two years.

The Berque Report expresses strong criticism of these special classes, as they concentrate on children in a situation of failure or on those who have fallen behind, even though their problems do not necessarily relate to language difficulties. Such classes may well become ghettos or sets from which it is practically impossible for pupils to rejoin the normal school structures, and which may, therefore, lead to further forms of marginalization. The *Bulletin Officiel*, No. 43 (30/11/1989), published a document from Lionel Jospin on immigration, in which he observed that the major problem is not that of non-French-speaking pupils, but that of pupils experiencing difficulties (Jospin, 1989b). The article points to a confusion between the linguistic and the social aspects of the problem and to the inadequacy of marginal structures such as the CEFISEM, which can only worsen the issue of marginality and marginalization. The existence of local associations, run by groups of people themselves from immigrant backgrounds, such as the *Service social d'aide aux émigrants* (SSAE), or the *Centres d'information et d'orientation* (CIO), which are attached to the social services of the *Inspection académique*, is worth emphasizing.

It is also important to keep in mind that most of these pupils with difficulties are to be found in the *Zones d'education prioritaires* (ZEP), created in 1981 in an attempt to fight against school failure and social inequalities in school (Bourgarel *et al.*, 1991). By 1989, there were some 300 city ZEPs, which usually corresponded to areas and districts reputedly '*difficiles ou défavorisés*'. The criteria used for setting up these zones have been threefold: a high rate of education failure; socio-economic difficulties in the population, and the presence of a high number of pupils of foreign origin. Areas that come to mind, perhaps because of their high profile in the media, are les Bosquets, Montfermeil and les Minguettes. In these areas, one is far from the 80 per cent of a *classe d'âge* (age cohort) reaching the *Baccalauréat*, which was set as a target by the *Loi d'Orientation* of Lionel Jospin, and one wonders whether the real role of the ZEP is not to manage the 20 per cent of pupils left by the wayside (*Actes du Colloque: Petite enfance*, 1993). There exist discrepancies between the discourse and the reality, with the *traitement social de l'échec scolaire* (a two-speed school system). Unless, as François Bayrou would like to see, the ZEPs become *des Zones d'excellence pédagogique!* This could perhaps become a reality if a greater number of teachers themselves were '*issus de l'immigration*'.

Arabic as a second language

The estimated overall number of foreigners living in France is about four million. About three million are *maghrébins* and Muslims. Of these, French citizens of *maghrébin* descent number about two and a half million: their families come from one of the three Maghreb countries in North Africa (Algeria, Tunisia and Morocco). There are also half a million Harkis, Muslim French citizens from Algeria, who fought on the French side during the Algerian war of independence and so had no choice but to come to France in 1962 after the war (Ammar, 1988).

The question of teaching these pupils their mother tongue has to be seen in a context where the supreme aim of the French education system is one of integration. The teaching of '*Langues et cultures d'origine*' (ELCO) in the primary school to pupils of Algerian, Moroccan, Tunisian, Italian, Spanish, Portuguese, Turkish or Yugoslav origin, has to take place within a school timetable which provides for a maximum duration of three hours per week, and which is entirely optional. The teachers concerned are often recruited in their country of origin and remunerated by their own governments. With very rare exceptions, the methodology and practices used are those of the country of origin and they are not integrated with the pedagogy normally used in the class the children attend. In other words, there are no formal links or concerted action between the teachers of the two languages. Not infrequently, these classes are viewed as serious disruptions to the smooth functioning of normal lessons. It is estimated that the total number of pupils studying Arabic under the ELCO scheme in 1990–91 was only 40,000. No proper evaluation has been conducted of such teaching. Criticism of ELCO is not lacking: the inter-ministerial committee dealing with integration issued a statement on 31 January 1990 claiming that teaching of ELCO was even detrimental to the pupils concerned. The Hannoun Report (1987) is equally critical. It is also easy for persons so inclined to predict that, being taught by personnel paid by a foreign government, these classes can become instruments of propaganda, religious intolerance and other excesses. There is no proper approach to bilingualism and to the teaching of authentic biculturality.

Whereas the teaching of Arabic in the primary school tends to be poor due to inadequate working conditions imposed on ill-prepared teachers, in the *collège* and the *lycée*, Arabic is one of the 11 languages that can be taken as a subject in the *Baccalauréat* and it is taught by qualified teachers who have one of the two teaching qualifications: the CAPES (created for Arabic in 1976) or the prestigious *Agrégation*, which already existed. Over the past 20 years the teaching of Arabic in France has greatly increased, as a result of immigration, the oil crisis and the need for France to increase her foreign trade and exchange with the Arab world. These developments have resulted in the need to diversify the foreign languages taught at secondary level. Though the number of pupils choosing Arabic is on the increase (356 pupils in 1969–70 to 7,924 in 1981–82 and 11,000 in 1990–91), it is still low compared with the overall percentage of pupils learning other foreign languages, with a striking discrepancy between the numbers of pupils of *maghrébin* origin and of those who have chosen to study Arabic as a foreign language at school (less than 10 per cent of the *maghrébin* population of secondary school age). At this level, obviously, Arabic is no longer considered as ELCO but as a foreign language, and little is done to take into account that the majority of pupils are second-generation immigrants: in fact, any previous knowledge of the language is often discounted. In terms of language needs, the learning of Arabic was formerly viewed as a step towards a possible return to the country of origin, but this is rarely the case now. French citizens of *maghrébin* descent have become a European minority, although this is not currently recognized.

Over the years, France has become a melting pot which has absorbed a large diversity of cultures, from various African countries, South-East Asia or from other European countries, including Turkey. Yet the issue of immigration in France is dominated by the Maghreb and integration paradigm: any talk of immigration immediately brings to mind immigration from the Maghreb countries and the underlying implication is the equation: immigrant = Arab = *maghrébin*. Now, the country is dealing with second- or third-generation 'immigrants' and it is worth remembering that the young *Beurs* in the *banlieues* have never been immigrants. A large proportion of the French population has not yet become aware that this immigrant population is a permanent stable population, which comes from countries that have acquired their independence after fighting French colonialism, and who have no desire to return to the country of origin of their family, particularly if such a country is going through a period of political or religious instability. The passing of time makes it less and less possible for each succeeding generation to return to their 'home' country.

The Portuguese community in France

This is particularly true of some of the other foreign communities which exist in France and do not wish to be treated in the same way as the *maghrébin* immigrants. One such community, which has a very specific place in the context of immigration in France, is the Portuguese one. It is characterized by its autonomy, its ethnic homogeneity and its internal need for socialization. It saw its greatest growth during the 1960s, particularly in the south-west of France and the Aquitaine area. Unlike the *maghrébin* immigration, the Portuguese have relied heavily on an associative community movement, whose activities ranged from the reception of the new migrants (accommodation, employment, paperwork) and all aspects of the socializing process, which revolves mainly around the celebration of traditional feast days. The Portuguese immigrants who arrived in France as adults have maintained strong links with their home environment, in many cases buying houses in Portugal for their retirement. They have always been keen to transmit to their children some elements of their national identity and particularly their language. At the same time, in areas of strong Portuguese immigration, parents have objected to classes made up essentially of children from a Portuguese background which some schools found a convenient way of organizing the timetable. What they want for their children is their total integration with French children in the same classes at school. The young people of Portuguese descent, born and educated in France, who do not have the same experience as their parents of belonging to two different communities, see the issue of school success or failure as a key challenge in the process of integration and social promotion. For the parents' generation the teaching of the mother tongue is perceived as a way of consolidating one's family roots.

They also view the whole process in the light of a likely return, eventually, to the home country. This perhaps is the main difference between the *maghrébin* situation and that of other migrant groups. There is evidence of the existence of bilingualism in Portuguese families in France, with Portuguese being more commonly spoken between parents and children, but French between siblings or with other youngsters from the same background, showing the influence of the school within the family. For some, this may be in response to adults who do not speak French very well. In other cases, the need to speak Portuguese becomes important at holiday time when the family goes back home (72 per cent of Portuguese migrants go back to Portugal at least once a year for holidays), as young people are ashamed to speak Portuguese badly in front of their grandparents. In the relationship between parents and children, Portuguese is often genuinely the mother tongue, that is, the language spoken with the mother until the child goes to the playgroup or the nursery school. This is where the learning of French comes into play, both for the child and sometimes the mother, in the case of primo-migrants, because the mother often learns French from her children. When it comes to the next generation, the majority want their children to be able to speak Portuguese, as the relationship with grandparents and the participation in festivities are essential factors. Portuguese then ceases to be a minority language and regains its function of socialization and the dynamics born from these situations of forced bilingualism ('*bilinguisme obligé*'). The role of radio and television has been a tremendous bonus in this respect. The next stage of *valorisation* of the mother tongue is when it is chosen as a second foreign language in the *lycée* or as a subject of study at university. In more recent years, degrees in Portuguese language and culture have been developed in some universities, which have attracted mainly those born of Portuguese parents. European Union policy on minorities has been another strong factor (CNDP, 1989, 1994).

As is the practice for teachers of other mother tongues, Portuguese teachers are recruited by the Portuguese government and their methods tend to be mainly communicative, because the main objective is to be able to communicate with members of the extended family. It is noticeable that parents prefer that Portuguese lessons should take place in contexts such as a Portuguese school organized and managed by parents, in parallel with, rather than integrated within, the French school. Portuguese is mostly taught outside school hours, but when it is taught on school premises (in primary school mainly rather than the *collège*), the teaching amounts to two to four hours per week. In Marmande (Lot-et-Garonne), for instance, the teaching of Portuguese takes place on school premises on Wednesday afternoons, which is the pupils' free day. The free day had originally been created to allow parents to have their children instructed in the religious faith of their choice, the French schools being '*laïque*' (secular) and so included no teaching of religion. It is ironic that this free time should now be used for teaching a mother tongue.

At first this approach to the teaching of Portuguese as a mother tongue was not well received by the authorities, in the name of the principle of integration. Nowadays things are different and the teaching of mother tongue is viewed in the light of improved integration and is encouraged by the '*contrats de ville*', as part of global projects on '*la ville et les banlieues*'. There are a number of initiatives being taken at local level, usually co-ordinated by the *Inspecteur d'Académie* (regional schools inspector), such as the practice of building bridges ('*passerelles*') between playgroups and nursery schools ('*garderie*' and '*maternelle*'), which starts at the age of two, and in which mothers take part in order to be better equipped to deal with the separation later on between mother and child. Another area of links is through the centres for protection of mothers and children. However, the priority remains first and foremost the linguistic and cultural integration through the learning of the language of the host country. The learning of the home language is increasingly being encouraged, even when this is two generations removed, and this is no doubt in response to European proposals for action in the field of regional or minority languages and cultures, which the French government has not endorsed. When it comes to secondary school and the learning of foreign languages, of the 80,000 pupils of Portuguese origin, only 15,000 chose to study Portuguese as a foreign language in 1989, of whom 3,000 were of French parents. This is a very different situation from that of Spanish: the Spanish immigrant population is a third of the Portuguese one in numbers and nearly one million pupils study Spanish at French secondary level. Whether this situation is going to change with the compulsory introduction of a foreign language at primary school level remains to be seen.

THE TEACHING OF THE MOTHER TONGUE IN A REGIONAL CONTEXT: THE CASE FOR CORSICAN

'*La nationalité qu'on porte sur son passeport n'est pas une donnée linguistique*' (One's passport states one's nationality, it does not carry any linguistic information) – Escarpit, 1979. One may well have two or even three 'mother tongues', but one's acquisition of fluency in one of them will be determined by its status in school and society, particularly if it has a written form as opposed to being a language that is only spoken and understood. Unless a language is taught at school, and therefore allows the pupils to develop all the basic skills of listening, speaking, reading and writing, it will remain a purely oral medium, as stated in the *Arrêté ministériel* of April 1985.

Robert Escarpit, former professor of communications and media at the University of Bordeaux and a fluent speaker of what he called 'three mother tongues' is particularly well qualified to express his views since his personal experience of mother tongue and language learning consisted of three different elements:

- a language, French, acquired through imprintation from early childhood, then systematized by the school system that provided the written status for it;

- a language, 'Gascon', also acquired through imprintation from early childhood, ignored and censured by both school and society and left in its oral state, only spoken by his grandmother in her native Béarn and totally forbidden at home by his father, a primary school teacher brought up in the Republican tradition;

- a third language, English, also learnt through early experience, because his mother used it with him, and later on it was systematized by his school and university education.

At a time when the French language is striving to retain its international status, including fighting the invasion of foreign idioms, the *Comité français du Bureau européen des langues moins répandues* issued a publication entitled '*Quelle(s) langue(s) pour nos enfants*', written in nine different regional languages as well as in French, which underlined the several roles fulfilled by regional languages. These roles include retaining the roots of the community, and form the basis for the identity of the groups which use it (CFBELMR, 1993).

In January 1951, the Deixonne law made it possible, although it is only an option, for certain regional (or 'minority') languages to be studied in French schools at all levels: these were Basque, Breton, Catalan and Occitan. At that time, the Corsican dialect was in a situation of non-being ('*une situation de non-être*', as Monsieur Pascal Marchetti, professor at the University of Paris-III describes it). Probably because of the disturbances on the island, Corsican (like Flemish and Alsatian) was not considered as a foreign or a regional language, instead the pejorative term of '*patois*' or dialect, was used. Corsican was only added to the original list in 1973.

The text of the Deixonne Law is enlightening in its aims: to encourage the study of local languages and dialects in those regions where they are in use and to authorize teachers to use local idioms in nursery and primary schools whenever they could be of value in their teaching, particularly of the French language. Teachers who apply are allowed to spend one hour a week on activities designed to give their pupils some elementary notions of reading and writing in the local dialect ('*le parler local*'), and to study selected pages from its literature, as well as the folklore and popular arts of the region. There is an optional examination in these local languages in the *Baccalauréat*.

As far as Corsican is concerned, the 'influence zone of the Corsican language' is officially recognized by the *Décret Fontanet* of 16 January 1974, and Corsican is taught today from nursery school to university. Of the schools where Corsican is taught, 93.6 per cent are in the maintained sector, only 6.3 per cent are private schools. It is taught at degree level at the University of Corte and the first CAPES examination, giving qualified teacher status to teachers of Corsican, took place in the summer of 1991. But a decree of 30 July 1982, confirmed by that of 22 July 1983, relating to the cultural identity of Corsica, specifies that the activities relating to the teaching of the Corsican language and culture are optional and may not be substituted for any other aspect of the official curriculum.

Since the 1983 law on decentralization, the responsibility for the teaching of Corsican has been shared between the Ministry of Education and the local authorities. This is referred to as '*les compétences partagées*'. Until recently, teachers who volunteered to teach regional languages were paid for these activities by the local authorities. Further legislation, dated 15 April 1988, describes objectives and contents, singling out the acquisition of language skills, the study of texts and, in Article 3, mentions language awareness:

'*L'enseignement des langues régionales s'attachera donc à respecter les grandes orientations suivantes:*

1. Acquisition ou approfondissement des connaissances en vue du développement progressif de la compétence et de l'autonomie d'expression personnelle en langue régionale, orale et écrite.

2. Etude de textes et documents divers (écrits, sonores, visuels, graphiques, etc.) facteur d'un enrichissement culturel structuré.

3. Réflexion progressivement affinée sur le fonctionnement de la langue et sur le langage.'

(Arrêté du 15 avril 1988)

The 1992 Council of Europe European Charter on minority or regional languages was perceived in France as the first international legal document guaranteeing for those countries who signed it protection for regional languages and for their use as a basic human right.

In 1993, for the first time in the history of the French Republic, a minister for education, François Bayrou, has dared to approve openly of minority languages: 'It is high time to work together and preserve the treasures of our common inheritance ('*patrimoine*'), to go out and speak in Basque, in Breton, Occitan or Alsatian.' Bayrou is himself a Béarnais and an Occitan speaker. However, when meeting representatives of the Corsican, Basque and Breton primary schools, he made it plain that the centralized French system would never allow schools where all subjects were taught in a minority language, although this is a reality in bilingual or international *collèges* or *lycées*, where most lessons are taught in English or German. This was in response to the Breton movement which in 1977 had founded some private nursery and primary schools, known as '*Diwan*' schools, financed by families and public subscription. There is no chance at present that these schools could ever become fully integrated in the French educational system, while retaining their linguistic independence.

The campaign for the revival of regional languages in France has been linked with the ecological movement, the anti-nuclear front, independence and autonomy movements, all looked upon as the same fight. The seven ethnic groups that make up the movement are very different, but they all are part of France, and they have formed an association for the '*Défense et promotion des langues de France*'. Each one is a special case, but none more so than Corsican, because of its insularity and the microcosmic approach it allows. The tradition in Corsican schools was that the first child who spoke Corsican in class was given a coin, which was passed on in turn to any other children who did not speak French in the course of the day: the last child to be in possession of the coin took it home and was punished. For the families, school was the only means of getting out of poverty, of perhaps becoming a civil servant, of having security of employment, of going off to the 'continent': Corsican was the language of '*la misère*', it was the synonym of poverty and lack of education.

In Corsica, quite predictably, the fight for the Corsican language has been linked to the nationalist movement and has therefore not been taken as seriously as it should have been by the French authorities. Indeed, if one wants to save Corsica and its language, the priorities ought to be the fight against unemployment on the island particularly for the young. It involves the relaunch of the economy, the defence of the natural geographical environment and the promotion of Corsican cultural identity, which means, first and foremost, the Corsican language. But above all it is essential to put an end to the destructions and the murders perpetrated by the various branches of the *Front de Libération nationale corse* (FLNC), and to re-establish on the island the rule of law. The fight to reintroduce the Corsican language in the school curriculum has been pursued with passion by its pioneers, who saw it as a '*Santa cruciata per a salvezza di la lingua materna*'. It is seen as the only way of protecting, restoring and saving the national and cultural heritage of the island.

Scola Corsa is the association which regroups all the local Corsican language associations (Cervoni, 1990). It was founded in 1970 in Corte and its objective is a common action to promote the Corsican language and culture. Even *Scola Corsa* recognizes that, although Corsican is both spoken and written, bilingualism does not exist in Corsica: they prefer to talk of diglossia, of two languages existing on the same geographical territory, but with very different status. French is the 'dominant' language, imposed by school, army and religion: all the official texts and documents are expressed in French. Corsican is the 'dominated' language, only in use orally and in the family context. Today, there are still many people who speak Corsican as a mother, or rather grandmother, tongue, particularly in the rural parts of the island. It is often the older generation which keeps the flame going, the younger generations tending to understand and read Corsican rather than actually speak it. Although no official study has been conducted, it is accepted that between 10 per cent and 15 per cent of youngsters are more or less active Corsican speakers; they are aware of the existence on the island of a language that is spoken comparatively widely by adults to which they have no access. This may account for the apparent willingness among pupils to learn Corsican.

It is worth noting that originally Corsican was a spoken language with no distinctive written tradition, due to its close connections with Tuscany. The campaign of *francisation* took place in Corsica when Italian was replaced by French as the official language. The lack of a written tradition has made it a priority to publish books in Corsican. *Scola Corsa* has been publishing four or five books a year over recent years and, more recently, it has organized a day to promote Corsican publications (*Foire au Livre*). It is now actively involved in offering a Minitel service and producing an interactive dictionary on CD-ROM. There are also a number of regular twice-daily programmes on local radio and the FR3 regional television network.

However, to be successful, it is crucial that the mother should speak Corsican within the family, that it should be a true 'mother' tongue. Nowadays, parents do not seem to have the same time to talk with their children, even in Corsica where the rhythm of life is more relaxed than in some other parts of the country. In the nursery and primary schools, the teaching of Corsican is carried out by Corsican speakers (genuine *corsophones*) – however, statistics suggest that only 5 per cent of primary trained teachers are corsophones.

Some very exciting experiments have taken place recently. The autumn of 1994 saw the introduction of initiation to the Corsican language for nursery school children in two *écoles maternelles*, in Ghisonaccia and Fiumorbu, so that children may use both the French and Corsican languages at school, and also the creation of the '*Classes Méd*' (*Collège de Finusello*). The '*Classes Méditerranées*' correspond to the specific application to Corsica of the 'European classes' created in 1992 elsewhere in France. This is effectively a new section in the first year of the *collège*, with a small pupil intake and an adapted timetable, to allow the study of three Romance languages; French plus either Italian or Spanish and three hours weekly of Corsican, as well as an initiation to Latin. The aim is to create a new form of humanism with a threefold objective: to enable the pupils to move from one linguistic system to another; to place the Corsican language within its original Tuscan area, and to renew the common links with '*latinité*'. Within the four years of the first cycle of secondary schooling, the pupils should be able to cope with a genuine trilingualism, since other subjects (particularly history and geography) are to be taught in those languages, as Ghjuvan-Maria Arrighi, the Regional Pedagogical Inspector for Corsican, puts it: 'to move from teaching languages to teaching in those languages – and more specifically Corsican.'

Since the autumn of 1994, three hours a week of Corsican are offered in all the *collèges* on the island. These are optional for the pupils and all parents have been informed by a personal letter from the *Recteur d'Académie*. Of all first-year pupils, 60 per cent have opted for Corsican. The main concern is for quality and professionalism. Teachers will say that it is essential for the teacher to be '*passionné et militant culturel*'; they have a message to get over: 'Corsican is our ancestral language, our mother tongue'. But there are as yet no official programmes or curriculum and the paper for the *Baccalauréat* consists of a commentary on a text, where candidates have to write on points of grammar, as well as to analyse the literary value of the passage. At first, teachers of Corsican were part-time and paid for by the local authorities. Now, since the creation of a CAPES in Corsican, some 15 specialist posts have been created and the quality of teaching has improved, although there are very few hours specifically devoted to the teaching of Corsican at the IUFM. With no specialist tutor for Corsican, teachers have to rely on in-service courses once they have qualified. Because there are so few of them, they meet regularly and on a voluntary basis, within the teaching day, working as a team with the regional advisors. At first it was mainly a question of producing a '*référentiel*', a reference document listing communication competencies and linguistic objectives, on the model of FLE. At present teachers spend time enthusiastically preparing teaching tools for tomorrow.

As in the teaching of any modern foreign language, the first rule is to conduct the class in the target language. Communicative methods are widely used, as well as music (based on the tradition of the Corsican *polyphonies*), drama techniques and role play. Lessons usually start with pictures, slides and videos for the first five minutes. The teaching is based on civilization and culture, with stress on the geography of Corsica in *seconde*, Corsican history in *première* and literary texts in the *terminale* class of the *lycée*. Cartoons and '*bandes dessinées*' are used: a history of Corsica has been published on the model of Astérix and, according to several teachers, pupils love the history and geography because they can retrace their roots. The objective is the passage from competency to performance and the emphasis is on the oral performance. Corsican is a difficult language to speak, it is relatively easy to write and the passage from the oral to the written form is quite rapid. Language laboratories and Information Technology are used as they become more widely available.

However, one has to guard against any optimism for the future: at the present time, the Corsican situation has to be assessed in terms of violence and murders, of economic crisis and *illettrisme*, and against the risk of the French government pulling out of Corsica and giving it its autonomy which would spell disaster for the island.

CONCLUSION

We have come a long way from Jules Ferry's *Lettre aux Instituteurs* and the forbidding of the use of regional dialects and *patois* within the school. In France, perhaps more so than in other countries, the question of languages is largely political. The regional communities which have become 'minorities' through the process of national unification are finding their place in the national context: the attitudes linked to the nationalism of the past still exist, but cultural and linguistic specificities, linked to economic and social inequalities, have become a political issue. France has become a composite society, not only because there are French nationals and foreigners, national and regional cultures, but because many belong to several cultures, have dual nationality, even plurinationality, and because many families form a patchwork of nationalities and languages within themselves. ELCO itself is based on two contradictory principles: equality of opportunities and respect for differences. Is it possible in France to place on the same level French, *maghrébin* and Corsican children? One wonders, though, whether we are talking of a true multicultural policy or some symbolic gesture in response to the mood of the day, in an attempt to satisfy cultural or political aspirations and to conform to the principle that schooling in one's mother tongue is part of one's human rights (OECD, *L'Ecole et les cultures*). The danger is that children may become hostages to a culture because of their ethnic origin. Key figures in the Breton movement predict that by the year 2020 there will be no Breton speakers left, unless a strong political will plays a role for a revival of regional languages. The irony is that, nowadays, children have got to go to school to learn their ancestral language, which has ceased to be their 'mother tongue'.

Chapter 10

Teaching the Mother Tongue in Spain

Antonia Ruíz Esturla

HISTORICAL INTRODUCTION

The Spanish Constitution of 1978 finally established the right to autonomy of the regions and nationalities which form the Spanish State. The 17 Autonomous Communities (ACs) which comprise the state were constituted between 1979 and 1983, and each passed its own statute of autonomy, the basic institutional legislation which regulates the organizational aspects of the community and its authority. Not all ACs have the same degree of self-government nor the same authority. Only seven (Andalusia, the Basque Country, the Canary Islands, Catalonia, Galicia, Navarre and Valencia) have full authority over educational matters. In the remaining 10, the administration and regulation remains in the hands of the central government and education is administered by the *Ministerio de Educación y Ciencia* (MEC) in Madrid, although steps are being taken to grant it to the ACs in the future.

Article 3 of the Constitution determined Castilian as the official language of the State and also that 'all Spaniards should know it and have the right to use it'. It also granted regional languages official status and stated that 'this language diversity should enjoy special respect and protection by institutions and citizens alike'. The Balearic Islands, the Basque Country, Catalonia, Galicia, the Valencian Community and some areas in Navarre are the communities in which a regional language is also spoken.

Since the early 1980s the different parliaments passed their own laws of *Normalización lingüística* to ensure that all citizens living in the community would be able to acquire the skills to communicate in both the official language of the state and that of their respective community. This has not been an easy process, especially if it is remembered that in pre-democratic Spain there was not only political but linguistic centralism. Castilian was the only language used in the government, in the press and broadcasting, in the classroom and in public generally, with very few exceptions.

The arrival of the Bourbon dynasty at the beginning of the eighteenth century brought with them their ideas of uniformity and centralization in the administration of the state and reinforced the status of Castilian as the official language of the monarchy. The remainder of the languages, Basque, Catalan and Galician, were increasingly consigned to a marginal situation as local languages without relevance in teaching, culture and the administration. The use of the

Figure 5: The regional languages of Spain

The Graphics Unit, School of Geography, University of Leeds

regional languages by sectors of the population with greater influence on the social development of the region was a key factor in determining the different status of these languages within the regions of the country.

In Catalonia people in power continued to promote Catalan and this contributed greatly to its status. This was supported by an existing strong literary tradition. In Galicia, where the population, predominantly rural, did not perceive Galician as a language of culture, this was not the case. It was only in the nineteenth century that the Romantic movement brought a different perspective and regional languages, such as Galician, improved in status.

The lack of a literary tradition, together with the political and social environment, also did not help the development of the Basque language. The changes brought about by the industrial revolution, with the immigration of people from other regions of Spain who did not speak Basque, held back its development in urban areas in the nineteenth and the first two thirds of the twentieth century.

The arrival of the Republic in 1931 meant a change of scenario. The Constitution declared Castilian as the official language of the whole Republic and recognized in law the languages of the provinces and regions of the country. This gave rise to the different statutes of autonomy for the Basque Country, Catalonia and Galicia, which granted the vernacular languages of these regions equal status with Castilian. The outbreak of the Civil War, however, prevented the Statute of Galicia coming into effect and the statutes referring to the Basque Country and Catalonia were abrogated.

The Public Instruction Act of 1945 established 'the Spanish language as the fundamental means of communication of the Spanish community'. For three decades, 1939–69, there had been no official acceptance of the regional languages until the General Education Act of 1970 recognized their study, where appropriate, as part of the school curriculum. What the law did not do was to make provision for their introduction into the school timetable nor for the training of staff charged with teaching them. The Decree of 31 October 1975 eventually stated that all regional languages were to be considered as official languages in their regions and consequently they could be used by the media (Diez *et al.*, 1980).

THE PLACE OF LANGUAGE IN THE OFFICIAL CURRICULUM

Castilian

The study of Castilian has been implemented in the curriculum throughout Spain with restrictions where the regional languages are official. In 1990 the *Ley de Ordenación General del Sistema Educativo* (LOGSE) was passed. It affected the whole structure and organization of the various educational levels: infant, primary and secondary. Education is compulsory from 6 to 16 years of age, however, 90 per cent of 4-year-olds and 100 per cent of 5-year-olds enjoyed full-time schooling in the academic year 1987–88 (Centro de investigación, 1991). In the same year 50 per cent of 16- to 18-year-olds also attended full-time school. Although the LOGSE established Castilian, alongside the other regional languages in their autonomous communities, as compulsory throughout schooling (6–18 years of age), in this section reference will be made only to mother-tongue teaching until the leaving age of 16 and the Official Curriculum published by the Ministerio de Educación y Ciencia. This is because the different departments of education of the Autonomous Communities have approved a global treatment concerning the issue of language teaching, including official and foreign languages alike, in agreement with the MEC. This makes the study of one foreign language compulsory from the ages of 8 to 18 years.

The Official Curriculum is laid down by the MEC in terms of 'General Aims', 'Contents' and 'Assessment Criteria'. These are statutory and were specified in agreement between the central government and the departments of education of the ACs with full authority over educational matters, by committees of experts and practising teachers on secondment, who were in charge of drawing up the different programmes. This ensures that all the programmes in Spain, regardless of the language medium, are similar.

The Official Curriculum applies to private and maintained sectors alike. The Programmes of Study for the five different stages (6–8, 8–10, 10–12, 12–14 and 14–16 years of age) are left to the ACs to stipulate. Schools are responsible for implementing them through the school curriculum and the different subject departments' schemes of work that must be handed in at the beginning of each school year. These should address, among others, aspects related to contents, didactic strategies and assessment. Non-statutory methodological guidelines and assessment criteria are also included.

In the late 1980s the MEC and the seven ACs with full educational autonomy set up committees to discuss and agree upon the General Educational Aims for compulsory education (6–16 years of age) and the different attainment targets of the various key stages. Attainment targets were laid down in terms of procedures, strategies and values. Once agreement was reached, both the MEC and the different ACs published, through Royal Decrees, their own curricula which, in the case of the ACs, did not have to be submitted to the MEC for approval.

At the beginning of each academic year, teachers agree upon their *Proyecto curricular de centro* (School Curricular Project), which includes among other matters the different programmes of study. This project is submitted to the *Consejo Escolar* (School Governing Body) for approval, where there is a representation of the teaching staff, parents, pupils and non-teaching staff of the school. Once this project has passed the Consejo Escolar it is submitted to the local authority, where it is then examined by inspectors.

In its introduction, the Official Curriculum stresses the fact that language serves a double function, that of communication and that of representation, through which individuals regulate their own conduct and that of others. Language provides the main instrument of learning and of acquisition of skills. In accordance with its stress on a functional concept of language, teaching moves away from the previous normative approach. The general aims of the Official Curriculum stipulate that language should be taught at discourse level, which implies helping learners to adapt their discourse to the situation and to produce coherent and cohesive texts. The ultimate aim of education in language is to help learners develop their personal command of the four skills: listening, speaking, reading and writing, with special emphasis being placed on writing skills and reflection upon language at secondary level. Children should be encouraged to develop an awareness of how they and others use language. Since learners are active agents in the process of communication, the classroom and the school environment should provide opportunities for the active use of language.

It is acknowledged in the curriculum that children already come to school with language experience. Therefore, work in the language classroom should arise from the children's real use of language. Their language environment together with cultural and socio-economic factors determine that use and bring about important dialectal, lexicographic and phonological differences in their language competence. Teachers should use this experience as a starting point and from there promote language patterns that enlarge the children's opportunities of communication and social mobility. Pupils are encouraged to appreciate language varieties, not only among different languages but also within the same language as spoken by different users, and to respect those varieties that may be felt to be socially devalued but serve the legitimate functions of communication and representation in a given social milieu. Pupils must also respect the other languages spoken in Spain that co-exist officially with Castilian. In this sense, education must cherish the knowledge and positive appreciation of the multicultural and multilingual reality of the Spanish State and, from there, that of the world as a whole. It is everybody's concern in Spain that young people should be educated in democratic values and, consequently, come to acknowledge and respect this reality. This concern may be taken to refer to the citizens of all 17 ACs that comprise the state as well as the immigrant population of the late 1980s and 1990s.

The emphasis in primary education is on developing literacy skills within a framework of construction of meaning. At the end of the primary phase of education, the children should quickly associate graphic representations and corresponding phonemes. The command of both written and oral codes and the assimilation of language conventions, as regards use and usage, must give way to fluent communication between transmitter and receiver. The reading of printed texts is encouraged both for recreation and inquiry.

The contents laid down by the MEC are grouped into five targets, four in the case of primary education:

- Uses and forms of oral communication.
- Uses and forms of written communication.
- Language awareness and knowledge about language.
- Systems of verbal and non-verbal communication.
- Literature, which is not a separate target in the curriculum for primary education.

Each target is then expressed in terms of concepts, skills and attitudes. The responsibility for the details of the programmes of study is that of the autonomous governments. The competences expected from pupils at the end of compulsory schooling are:

1. To understand the main idea and purpose of a variety of oral texts of different degrees of formality, and reproduce their content in writing.
2. To summarize in writing an oral exposition or debate on a familiar topic, showing the main lines of argument and point of view of the participants.
3. To speak about the overall meaning of written texts of different degrees of formality, identify purpose, main and secondary ideas, recognize possible ambiguities in their content and give personal opinions.
4. To incorporate personal viewpoints on a given topic to those found in other texts so as to elaborate a synthesis on the topic.
5. To speak about a given topic following an outline, adapting language to the content and situation so as to gain the attention of the listener.
6. To make use of organizational skills to produce different types of texts: narrative, descriptive, expositive and argumentative, adapting them to the situation.
7. To make use of reference skills to plan and carry out different tasks, individually or in groups.
8. To classify literary texts according to genre, identify the elements and types of rhetorical procedures used, as well as express personal opinions.
9. To make use of personal ideas and experience to produce literary texts, consciously

employing structures of genre and rhetorical procedures as well as turning to traditional literary models.

10. To establish relations between those works, authors and literary movements that constitute key elements in the history of literature and the cultural, social and historical context in which they appear.

11. To reflect upon the elements and mechanisms of language so as to broaden comprehension of texts and linguistic versatility.

12. To identify, locate and describe points in common between the different languages and main dialectal varieties of Spain.

13. To identify some linguistic features characteristic of different social uses of language through direct observation and comparison of different types of speech.

14. To identify various images and expressions in oral and written texts which denote some kind of social, racial, or sexual discrimination and explore alternatives to avoid them, making use of those alternatives in writing and speech.

15. To produce messages in which verbal and non-verbal language is incorporated.

(Secretaría de Estado de Educacíon, 1992)

The Official Curriculum also includes some non-statutory methodological guidelines for the teaching of language and literature. The methodology favoured in the language classroom is one which ultimately aims to develop learner autonomy and to enable pupils to control and evaluate their learning processes. Pupils are no longer expected to learn grammar rules but to have a knowledge of language functions which allows them to communicate effectively, both orally and in writing, in a variety of contexts. Teachers are expected to adapt the curriculum to the pupils' general cognitive competence, pay attention to their interests, needs and abilities, and acknowledge their progress by inviting their participation in classroom activities so as to enhance their motivation. This attention to diversity should be reflected in the teachers' ways of delivering the curriculum, in their classroom organization and in the skills used to diversify work according to pupils' abilities, within the general framework of aims and contents expressed in the Official Curriculum.

Education authorities at central and autonomous levels were faced with the challenge of providing teachers with specific training to meet the teaching skills necessary to deliver the new Official Curriculum.

Education of teachers

Teachers are required to hold a diploma (after a three year university course) or a degree (after a five year course) to teach in primary and secondary schools respectively. In the first case teaching practice is incorporated in the programme of study. In the latter, university institutes of education are in charge of initial teacher training, including both the theoretical and practical elements. This can be combined with the last year of study at university or after graduation. To qualify for a permanent position in the public sector teachers must pass a competitive examination set annually for the different subjects by the MEC and the departments of education of the ACs. Since 1993 Spanish nationality has no longer been a prerequisite for people who wish to sit the competitive examination.

In-service training (INSET) for language teachers has to be examined in the context of continuing teacher training as a whole.

In Spain, INSET is mainly provided by a network of Teacher and Resources Centres with a body of advisory teachers responsible for each subject area, the new technologies and cross-curricular subjects. University departments or institutes of education may also be asked to provide INSET. In the past few years, the MEC and the ACs have concluded agreements with the universities in their regions, so that these provide professional training for both primary and secondary teachers. The results seem to be encouraging. This is part of a much wider framework of collaboration between these institutions by means of which, for example, a small number of secondary school teachers are offered secondment at a university department. After a two- or a three-year period they return to school or, after successfully passing the required public examination, they become full-time university lecturers.

The MEC and the ACs have laid down the priority areas for in-service training within the statutory guidelines of the LOGSE. One of these is the supply of training courses and activities directly linked to the implementation of the new school curricula, with special emphasis being placed on methodology and criteria for assessment and evaluation. The Teacher and Resources Centres concentrate their staff and resources in fostering school-based INSET, which starts with the analysis of the school needs and continues with the planning, development and evaluation of the teaching processes.

Priority areas in language education

The implementation of the LOGSE requires a very wide range of teacher-development activities in order to equip the teaching staff and the governing body of schools with the necessary skills which will enable them to face and deal with all the demands that will be placed upon them. There are some courses that are being offered throughout the country which are specifically related to language teaching, for example:

Modern foreign languages courses for non-specialists

Since the introduction of a compulsory foreign language at the age of eight – previously it was eleven – this course has become an area of particular attention. Courses, both in Spain and abroad, are directed at improving the teachers' own linguistic competence as well as their methodological skills.

Cross-curricular courses

Cross-curricular courses on topics such as co-education, media studies, information technology as well as certain multi-cultural issues fall within the scope of language teaching. The co-education programmes have been planned in conjunction with the Women's Institute of the Ministry of Social Affairs. One of its main aims is to raise awareness among teachers of sexism in language.

Published educational materials are being analysed and some will be reprinted to avoid such occurrences. Equally, in the academic year 1985–86, an agreement was signed with the Association of Newspaper Editors. This has contributed enormously to the introduction and development of discussion of the press in the classroom.

Multicultural issues

Teachers working in a multicultural environment have been offered training facilities in areas such as initiation into Spanish as Second Language, and cultural and social integration in the school environment and the community in general. This has not been a problem in the Spanish education system, except perhaps for children from the Romany community in certain areas. However, as more immigrants arrive in Spain, especially from North and West Africa, for example, Senegal, this is one of the issues being addressed.

The issue of inter-culturalism is dealt with in the Official Curriculum under the so called *temas transversales* (which include co-education, sexism, equal opportunities and health education). The idea is that these issues should be incorporated in every school subject. It is then up to the different schools, in their curriculum projects, to establish their priorities according to their particular needs and contexts.

As this is a new phenomenon, there is no national or regional framework that provides a general setting for all the initiatives being undertaken by different institutions. Both the MEC and the ACs have published Decrees to address intercultural and multicultural issues. In some cases Education Authorities have signed agreements with the Department of Social Affairs, the Local Authorities or Trade Unions. Teachers' centres are offering in-service training to help teachers address these matters in the classroom. Adult Education is also offering courses in Spanish Language and Culture for immigrants and specific materials are being published.

As for the Romany population, there has been recognition of their cultural features, but not 'positive integration'. Measures have been taken (using social workers) to respond to specific problems, such as low school attendance and 'abandonment', that is, early withdrawal from school. Areas with a strong Romany population are designated as educational priority action zones, with reduced teacher–pupil ratios and the appointment of support teachers.

The MEC has a central office for Special Education and Attention to Diversity, responsible for setting up programmes to cover the areas mentioned. There are two units of inter-cultural education in the office, one in charge of organization, management and evaluation; the other in charge of materials design, methodological innovation and teacher development. There exists at present one mother-tongue programme of Portuguese language and culture, which reaches 63 primary schools and more than 3,000 pupils. It is completely integrated into the school curriculum and can assume one of two formats: either, both teachers, Spanish and Portuguese, work alongside each other in the same classroom or, they each work separately, though delivering the same area of the curriculum in their respective languages. This project involves the teaching and learning of language, humanities, natural sciences and arts. Because of timetable constraints, secondary school pupils attend Portuguese classes outside school hours. In 1994 an agreement was concluded with Morocco to integrate Moroccan teachers into Spanish schools. Apart from the programmes just mentioned, local councils and regional governments set up their own schemes to deal with cultural diversity specific to their area.

THE REGIONAL MOTHER TONGUES

Basque

Basque, *Euskera*, is spoken in the three provinces that constitute the Autonomous Community of the Basque Country in the North of Spain, where it is the official language, alongside

Castilian. It is also spoken in Navarre and in the French Basque Country. Due to the topography of the region up to seven distinct varieties can be distinguished; the two main ones are *guipuzcuano* and *vizcaíno*. In all these provinces the use of Basque is not evenly spread. It is widely spoken in Guipúzcoa (43.76 per cent), not so much in Vizcaya (17.54 per cent), where it is mainly found in rural areas, and its use is very limited in Álava (6.71 per cent). (Information according to the Secretaría General del Gobierno Vasco, 1991). It is difficult to establish the exact number of Basque speakers. Some quote a figure of up to 500,000–600,000 speakers in Spain and approximately 70,000–80,000 in France. It is widely agreed that for almost one in four inhabitants, Basque is their first language.

In 1983 a Bilingualism Decree was passed by the Basque Parliament that established a bilingual education system based on the criterion that both Basque and Castilian are compulsory subjects in infant, primary and secondary education. The use of the two official languages at these educational levels is structured around three models of bilingual teaching, A, B and D. A further model, teaching exclusively in Castilian, is now practically phased out.

- **Model A**
  Castilian is the language of instruction while Basque is taught as a subject.

- **Model B**
  Both languages are used as languages of instruction, with more emphasis being placed on Basque in the first years to counterbalance the knowledge of Castilian and familiarity with its culture, especially among children from a non-Basque speaking background.

- **Model D**
  Basque is the language of instruction and Castilian is studied as a subject. This is essentially the reverse of Model A.

This spread of models is intended to promote the specific culture of the Basque people and to favour the maintenance and recovery of the Basque language. The teaching of children under Model D will no doubt reinforce the position of Basque speakers, compensating for the constraints of the Castilian-speaking environment. Apart from these models of education, *ikastolas*, schools teaching solely in Basque, have existed in the Basque Country for the greater part of this century and flourished particularly in the 1960s and 1970s (Tarrow, 1985).

According to the *Secretaría General de Política Lingüística* of the Basque Government, in the academic year 1982–83 models B and D accounted for barely 21 per cent of the total number of pupils in infant, primary and secondary education. Yet, in the academic year 1990–91, these models represented 38 per cent of the total. In the case of infant and primary education alone the total reached 50 per cent, which would seem to indicate that in the next few years the overall figure will increase further, including also the secondary level.

The main problems faced when introducing Basque as the language of instruction were the shortage of staff able to deliver any teaching in Basque and the lack of suitable teaching materials. For example, in the academic year 1976–77, only 4.6 per cent of the teaching workforce of state nursery, infant and primary schools were Basque-literate.

In 1983 the Education Department of the Basque Government launched the IRALE programme (*Programa de alfabetización y euskaldunización del profesorado*) which was directed at teachers of all educational levels. Each year 700 teachers were seconded from classroom teaching for a maximum of two years to pursue language courses which were designed especially to help them acquire enough Basque, or the literacy skills necessary to teach in Basque. This programme is now about to include a period of teaching practice for these teachers to smooth the transition from Castilian to Basque as language of instruction.

These models of bilingual education have been criticized in some sectors for not being generous enough in favouring bilingual education. However, according to the education authorities, they correspond to the socio-linguistic configuration of the Basque Country and no radical changes are expected to take place in the short term, though it is accepted that by the end of compulsory secondary education, the knowledge of Basque reached by 16-year-olds is limited. They can get by in a Basque-speaking context but they are far from being bilingual.

The 1991 census showed that the Basque-speaking population had increased by 200,000, despite a fall in the population as a whole. Nevertheless, and although it is used in the government, education and the media, this has not produced a mirror effect in society in general. Basque is learnt but it is not used as much as it could be, having to compete with Castilian-speaking settlers from other parts of Spain (Intxausti, 1995).

Catalan

Of the more than 10 million people in the Balearic Islands, Catalonia and Valencia communities, Catalan is understood by a large majority (88.5 per cent) and is spoken by nearly 60 per cent. The ability to read and write it is much lower (Departament de Cultura, 1992).

In 1983 the *Llei de Normalització Lingüística* was unanimously approved by the Catalan Parliament. Its purpose was to protect and encourage the use of Catalan in Catalonia, to guarantee its status as an official language in the public service and in education and to secure for it a stronger position in the media. As a result of these measures as well as initiatives by private individuals and organizations, the use of Catalan has been restored and expanded in many fields. Parliamentary sessions are conducted in Catalan and it is also widely used in the public services. At the University of Barcelona, in 1985–86, between 25 per cent and 87 per cent of lectures, seminars and classes (depending on the faculty) were conducted in Catalan and 31 per cent of the theses and dissertations presented in universities in Catalonia were in Catalan (Hall, 1990). The development of radio broadcasting and, especially, television in Catalan has been remarkable. In 1983 the Catalan Government set up its own station, TV3, broadcasting entirely in Catalan. In 1988 a new channel, Canal 33, was introduced. All this has caused an enormous impact on the knowledge of Catalan by residents of all ages and social and cultural backgrounds.

It should be added that Catalan in Catalonia, unlike in Valencia, even at a time when it did not have official status, had always been widely used in private circles regardless of class. Furthermore, it enjoyed prestige as the language of the middle and upper-middle classes with above-average educational standards, as opposed to Castilian, the language of large numbers of immigrants from other regions in Spain that settled in Catalonia in the 1960s in search of a better standard of living.

The following can be considered the general principles that underlie the language policy for education in Catalonia:

- Catalan, as the mother tongue of the majority in Catalonia, is also the language at all educational levels.

- It will be taught progressively to all levels, grades and courses of non-university education.

- All children regardless of their language when starting compulsory education shall be able to use Catalan correctly and appropriately by the end of their studies.

In 1992, the education department of the autonomous government, *Departament de Cultura Generalitat de Catalunya*, published a report which stated that for the academic year 1989–90, 56 per cent of primary school pupils had Catalan as the language of instruction against 10 per cent that had Castilian. The remaining 34 per cent enjoyed bilingual education (Departament de Cultura, 1992). All pupils had Castilian and Catalan as compulsory subjects with similar timetable allocations per week. These figures are very different at secondary level. According to the same source, though all schools offered Catalan as a subject, only 40 per cent were offering it as the medium of instruction for the minimum of the two areas of study in Catalan as stipulated by law. Private schools might not even reach that percentage.

To extend the use of Catalan to all levels of compulsory education, especially in the industrial towns surrounding Barcelona to where most of the immigration had gravitated, programmes of 'immersion' were introduced in the early 1980s. Schools could take part in them if approved by the school council, which apart from representatives of parents, teachers, pupils and non-teaching staff includes a member of the local government. However, for the academic year 1993–94, the *Generalitat* extended 'immersion' to all children of up to seven years of age, regardless of their cultural or language background, with recommendations to schools to make provisions for those families whose native language is Castilian and who wish their children to be taught in that language. The methods currently employed to that effect are that either the child is taken out of class to have individual or small group tuition in Castilian for a fixed number of periods a week, or a support teacher works alongside the form teacher helping the Castilian-speaking children by addressing them in their own mother tongue and generally ensuring that they follow the classroom activities. These measures have encountered considerable opposition in some sectors of the Castilian-speaking community in Catalonia, who claim their constitutional right to be taught in Castilian as the medium of instruction is being violated.

The guidelines sent to schools from the Catalan Education Department at the beginning of the academic year 1993–94 stated very clearly that it was the responsibility of the school to help pupils acquire and develop their features of national identity through the use of Catalan for all purposes within the school, and for all communications between school and the outside world. Headteachers must ensure that all staff meetings and school council meetings are conducted entirely in Catalan. The individual school curriculum must also include details of its language teaching and learning policy. Schools still using Castilian as the language of instruction must offer, apart from Catalan as a separate subject, one or two areas of study, Sciences, or Humanities, or both, in Catalan.

Similar language policies have been adopted in the other Catalan-speaking communities of Spain. In 1986 the *Llei de Normalització Lingüística* in the Balearic Islands established the official status of Catalan at all levels in the islands. Three types of schools emerged from the enactment of the law:

- Schools using only Catalan as language of instruction.
- Schools offering one or two subjects per year in Catalan.
- Schools offering pupils a choice of instruction in Catalan, in Castilian or both.

At present one can safely say that the majority of secondary schools are delivering the whole, or at least part, of the curriculum in Catalan, and it also seems that most pupils will choose the Catalan or the mixed option of instruction in preference to the one entirely in Castilian. However, the percentages for the use of Catalan in the private sector are considerably lower than for those of the maintained sector.

In the Community of Valencia the situation is somewhat different. The territorial duality of the region with a Catalan coastal strip and an Aragonese area further inland, together with a tendency in the past to regard Castilian as the language of prestige and a symbol of social promotion, as well as the Castilianization of cities like Valencia and Alicante with the arrival of Castilian-speaking immigrants, have given rise to two completely different views on the language issue. One view supports the linguistic substitution of Castilian for Catalan; the other endorses attempts at recovery and linguistic and cultural *normalització* in favour of Catalan.

The Statute of Autonomy declared *Valencià* (Valencian) as co-official with Castilian. There has been a long controversy as to what the language spoken in this region should be called. It is generally agreed that *Valencià* is a variety of Catalan which presents some differences in pronunciation and vocabulary. Despite this, different regional governments have put strong emphasis on the term *Valencià* as a way of marking the specificity of the language spoken in the region. In November 1983 the *Llei d'Ús i Ensenyament del Valencià* (LUEV) established *Valencià* as a compulsory subject at all non-university levels of education, though in the Castilian-speaking territories its introduction would be gradual, ensuring that all pupils received instruction in their first language. However, the ultimate goal was that all children should be able to communicate orally and in writing in both languages. Parents in Castilian-speaking areas could obtain exemption from *Valencià* for their children.

The law also decreed that teachers should know the two official languages, Castilian and Valencian. Those who did not have the skills were expected to acquire them through a policy of voluntary and gradual professional development. In the province of Castellón 80 per cent of primary school teachers could speak both languages with about 64 per cent in Valencia.

The use of *Valencià* in compulsory education falls under one of two categories: a percentage of the intake has either Castilian or *Valencià* as the language of instruction, or some of the subjects in the school curriculum are delivered in *Valencià*. In either case the study of the other language as a separate subject is compulsory.

The sound economic position of Catalonia, coupled with the widespread knowledge of Catalan, has favoured the vigorous language policy of the autonomous government and helped the production of teaching materials.

Galician

Galician and Portuguese constitute a subgroup within the Iberoromance languages. There are approximately 2.5 million people who understand Galician with just over 2 million who are active speakers (Green, 1994). The language is spoken in Galicia and also in parts of neighbouring Asturias and Castile-León, and also by large communities abroad, in particular in Latin America and elsewhere; in the United Kingdom alone, for instance, there are more than 25,000 Galicians.

In 1983 the law of *Normalización* was passed by the Galician Parliament, with the aim of introducing Galician in all sectors of society, school, public administration and the media. The aim was to combine individual language rights with the abolition of the existing inequality of the two official languages of the Galician Community. In the same year Galician became a compulsory school subject, with the same time-allocation as Castilian, though pupils from other ACs or abroad could be exempted. Nevertheless, this proved insufficient if children were to acquire full proficiency in the language at the end of their schooling. Consequently, in 1988 Galician was decreed the official language of educational administration and also the language of instruction for at least part of the curriculum. All school councils are responsible for ensuring that there is a balance between Castilian and Galician as languages of instruction in Galicia.

Infant education was to be delivered in the children's first language, Castilian or Galician as the case might be. From 8 to 14 years of age, apart from Galician as a subject in its own right, one area of studies, Humanities, was to be delivered in Galician. From 14 to 18 years of age, two subjects of the curriculum, apart from Galician, were to be taught in that language, to be chosen from a range including Sciences, Humanities, Technology and Philosophy. In response to the demand of the Galician-speaking families settled in the United Kingdom, Galician is one of the options offered by the Spanish Ministry of Education (MEC) at its school in London.

The growing demand for lessons in Galician made it necessary to make provision for courses specially designed to improve teachers' competence in the language. These courses were structured at three levels: initial, improvement and specialization in language and literature. Similar courses had been taking place since 1971 run by university language centres and other educational establishments. These courses are promoted by the education authorities both because they represent a way of introducing Galician in the classroom and because they lend an element of prestige. For infant and primary school teachers there are specialization courses of 280 hours, containing elements of literature, history, geography and teaching methods. This is a way to supplement the limited offer of Galician in teacher-training colleges. In 1992, 72 introductory and 99 advanced language courses were offered, as opposed to 42 and 49 respectively in 1990. The number of teachers attending them increased by 55 per cent (Comisión Coordinadora, 1993). These courses are available to all teachers, inspectors, non-teaching staff and parents' associations.

According to the same source, 95 per cent of infant and primary school teachers know the language at threshold level, 80 per cent at an advanced level and 38 per cent have specialized in Galician. In secondary education these percentages are somewhat lower. The figures seem to indicate that, in theory, there are enough teachers to meet the requirements of a minimum of two subjects of the school curriculum to be taught in Galician. Nevertheless, the courses represent only a first step, because teachers require specific training in the language and teaching methods of their speciality in order to encourage them to use Galician as the teaching medium.

Several other measures have been pursued in order to extend the use of Galician in schools. Teachers of different subjects constitute a cross-curricular department in charge of promoting the use of Galician within the school. The school curriculum must include in its language policy the number of subjects to be delivered in Galician and also the kind of extra-curricular activities devised to promote the language. Printed and audio-visual materials have been produced in order to provide support for teachers, including the publication of specific glossaries for the different subjects, especially those related to vocational training. Higher education lacks a common legislation; nevertheless universities have subscribed to agreements with the Department of Education of the autonomous government, the *Xunta*, to enhance the Galician language.

CONCLUSION

The languages discussed show a very different degree of acceptability, which can be ascribed to a clash between the distinctiveness of the medium itself and the degree of its standardization and the personal situation of its speakers.

In all, the study of mother-tongue teaching in Spain provides an important illustration of the difference between rhetoric and reality in terms of liberal governmental policies of a language-diversification scheme on an impressive scale.

Chapter 11

Teaching the Mother Tongue in Germany

Ingelore Oomen-Welke and Guido Schmitt

THE GERMAN LANGUAGE SPEAKING AREA

German, a member of the West-Germanic family of languages, is the mother tongue of about one hundred million people in Germany, Austria, Switzerland, Liechtenstein, Alsace, Southern Tyrol and Luxembourg among others. There have been attempts at standardizing the language since the early Middle Ages and notably since Luther's translation of the Bible. Even so, the existence of a multiplicity of sovereign German states within the various political union groupings until 1918, and of several independent German-speaking states today, has worked to preserve a number of distinct regional dialects despite frequent internal migrations, especially during the last hundred years or so. In the eighteenth century the German standard language, *Hochdeutsch*, gained recognition through the fact that a vibrant national literature written in it had developed, and that it had become the only language of compulsory school-ing. Later, *Hochdeutsch* also came to be considered to represent and be an integral part of German political unity. Formally, the German Empire did not come into existence until after the Franco-Prussian War in 1871, under the leadership of Bismarck's Prussia but excluding the Austrian Empire.

Immigrants

Until World War One the largest group of immigrants from outside Germany consisted of Polish and Italian workers seeking employment in the German Empire. They were only able to preserve their own languages at home and in private cultural societies and religious practices since German was the only language of instruction in public education, a policy which remained much the same right up to the 1950s, when the second strong wave of immigration from the Mediterranean countries began. Recent research (Auernheimer, 1990; Bade, 1992) has shown that the cultural and religious ties and mutual ethnic social support played a signifi-cant role in keeping the immigrants' identities alive.

Since the mid-1950s three different policies towards newcomers arriving in Germany that affect their right to and the provision of mother-tongue education can be distinguished.

Figure 6: The regional languages of Germany

The Graphics Unit, School of Geography, University of Leeds

Workers from the Mediterranean countries

Since 1955, about five million workers (including their families) have come to the Federal Republic of Germany from Italy, the former Yugoslavia, Greece, Spain, Portugal, Turkey and also Tunisia and Morocco as a result of bilateral labour recruitment agreements. From the end of the 1960s onwards their almost one million children had to be recognized as a group of pupils with special educational needs in the then West German school system. Priority was given to measures aimed at integrating them into German schools and society at large. Even so, quite often migrant workers' children born in the host country did not learn German, their second language, because of inadequate everyday social and linguistic contact. Since the 1970s several of the countries of origin have organized, with some financial support from Germany, more formal teaching of the children's mother tongues through their consulates.

Refugees

Following the large movement of refugees from Central Europe at the end of World War Two, Germany, with its liberal immigration laws, became one of the principal destinations of refugees from Africa and Asia as well as from Eastern Europe. This influx has continued, becoming stronger at the end of the 1970s and increasingly so in the 1980s and mid-1990s. Often the refugees applied for and were granted political asylum. Their mother tongues are even more numerous than those of the immigrant workers and only some are taught in any organized way since, under law, school attendance for them is not compulsory. Adults may learn German in privately sponsored courses.

Aussiedler

Since the end of World War Two a third group of immigrants, the *Aussiedler*, has also been identified, whose numbers have grown in the last few years because of the political changes in Eastern Europe. These are families whose German ancestors had emigrated in former centuries to the more easterly parts of the German or Austrian empires or to independent foreign countries even farther away. They now come from Poland, Russia, Hungary, Romania, as well as Kazakhstan and other states within the former Soviet Union. Their total number between 1950 and 1990 was 2.5 million, with half of them arriving since 1980, encouraged by the generous 'homecoming' policies of the Christian Democratic Union government.

According to German nationality laws of descent these people are Germans, even if their home language is no longer German, which is often the case. Extra provision of German language and history lessons for them is in order. Teaching the children their non-German home languages is not usually desired by their parents. All recent immigrants, whatever their origin, can be subsumed in one of the above groups.

THE GERMAN EDUCATION SYSTEM

In the Federal Republic of Germany there is no centrally controlled education system. Every *Land* (state) is independent when it comes to matters of education, with the state governments

(*Landesregierungen*) responsible for the school curriculum and the leaving examinations. Schooling is compulsory for all children and youngsters living legally in Germany aged from 6 to 18 years. A tripartite structure is characteristic for the school system. After four or six years in the *Grundschule* (primary school) pupils go on to secondary education either in a *Hauptschule*, a *Realschule* or a *Gymnasium*, which after nine, ten or thirteen years of schooling respectively prepare them for different careers. The selective *Gymnasium* alone, terminating with the *Abitur*, entitles pupils to study at a university. Some comprehensive schools (*Gesamtschulen*) also exist, particularly in the Länder of Nordrhein-Westfalen and Hessen, which combine all three types of school and usually offer an *Orientierungsstufe* (orientation stage, grades 5 and 6), a programme of teaching which enables pupils to prepare for transfer to a course considered suitable for them. *Förderschulen*, or special schools for physically disabled children or those with learning or behavioural problems, are also the responsibility of each Land. In all these schools teachers are free, with very few restrictions, to choose their own teaching materials. Because of the increasing demand for qualifications, there is a trend towards combining the *Hauptschule* and *Realschule* into a *Sekundarstufe I*, which involves 10 years of schooling. Children of immigrants are integrated into this system; extra teaching and counselling being provided for those who have problems. There are some private schools in Germany, however, in matters of curriculum and leaving examinations they are subject to Land regulations and supervision. They are also in receipt of financial support from the Land.

Vocational training takes place in the so-called 'dual system'. After the end of compulsory schooling at age 15, apart from practical training with a firm, trainees spend one and a half days a week on release at a technical college. Alternatively, this teaching can be concentrated into six-week intensive programmes. Normally training lasts for three and a half years so that everyone completes their secondary education (academic or vocational) at the age of 18 or 19.

Discussions on fundamental matters relating to education in all the Länder of the Federal Republic are held at the Conference of Ministers of Education and Culture (*Kultusminister-konferenz*) at which the ministers of education from each Land are represented. It was in 1964 that reference was first made to the teaching of classes attended by foreign pupils leading to the *Kultusministerkonferenzbeschluß*, which recommended that foreign and German pupils should be treated equally (Mahler, 1974). A practical recommendation became law in 1971. In accordance with European Community guidelines preparation for integration into German classes should be accomplished by means of special German classes or courses for those children who needed them. At the same time discussions were held about the provision of teaching foreign pupils' mother tongues: for example, Spanish, Italian, Modern Greek, Turkish, Portuguese and Serbo-Croat, with only the first two appearing as regular subjects on the school curriculum. Although school attendance is not compulsory for the children of refugees, they are, as a rule, admitted alongside German citizens and immigrants.

PROVISION AND STUDY PROGRAMMES FOR LANGUAGE EDUCATION

German mother tongue

German mother tongue is taught at the *Grundschule* for six 45-minute lessons per week and at the *Sekundarstufe I* for four or five lessons. German is a compulsory subject for all pupils, it is a core subject, as are mathematics and one or two modern foreign languages depending on the type of school. A pass in these subjects is required for transfer to the next grade. Those failing have to repeat the year. Extra lessons are given to weaker pupils.

The school subject 'German' is divided into four working areas or programmes of study: 'Oral communication', 'Written communication', 'Literature and other texts' and 'Reflection about language'.

Oral communication

The main aim of this programme is to improve pupils' competence of oral communication in all respects. From the beginning pupils learn how to communicate adequately and the rules to respect in communication. This involves training in listening to their partners, in narrating, recounting and reporting events and stories. Pupils are taught how to convey information and how to present arguments in discussions as well as giving a lecturette or presentation, the level of which depending on the grade and the type of school.

Pupils are first given the opportunity to observe communicative situations to enable them to understand the different roles of the speaking partners in the process, to play fair when listening and speaking, to make sure their communications reflect their expectations as well as their interests and the topic, and to act appropriately as the situation demands. Increasing their vocabulary, as well as stylistic awareness, is all part of this programme.

Written communication

The main aim of this programme is active and productive participation in a literate society. Reading and writing techniques have to be mastered in the early grades. Pupils learn to write fluently and legibly, ensuring that their handwriting enables them to take notes and to communicate easily in the written medium. They have to learn the standard spelling, which is difficult, takes time and is decisive in cases of selection for the more prestigious, academic secondary schools.

Pupils are taught to express themselves in writing: to narrate, to report, to write letters and to impart information. Much attention is given to the structure of written texts and to stylistics. In the higher grades pupils formulate interpretations, considerations, arguments and prepare lectures and presentations. One important item is to show pupils how to prepare a dossier on a special topic.

Literature and non-literary texts

This area covers the more receptive part of a literate society. Progressing from shorter to longer texts, children learn that reading conveys information and is fun. They can read aloud to others (who listen), read silently (for themselves), or engage in individual or joint reading with peers. Pupils deal with literary texts which can be interpreted in discussion or they can be performed by being turned into a play. Later this study is expected to lead to the reading of complete works of classic and modern literature and drama, the study of the theatre and other media. Suggested lists of works from the older to the newest German national literature are included in the syllabuses for secondary schools.

The term 'other texts' refers to political and pragmatical texts, such as newspapers, instructions for use and descriptions. These are texts with a practical application which are often difficult to understand. This also includes texts that encourage pupils to reflect individually on the implications of a topic as well as texts written by themselves.

Reflection about language

In this programme pupils are introduced to an awareness of language. They are taught grammar rules and trained in linguistic criticism. Language is seen as a product of human activity in society and as an instrument of communication. It can be used for direct and indirect actions and for reflection and thought. Pupils learn the structure of the German language, looking at word categories and the parts of a sentence. At the secondary level they proceed to more complex syntactical structures and study stylistical variety and language change. Subgroup language, dialects and the historical aspects of language change are taught in the higher grades of *Sekundarstufe II*. Until recently non-German languages were used mainly to illustrate structures different from German; meanwhile language diversity in the classroom is being regarded as a topic for study in its own right, leading to intercultural education. Much is left to teachers' discretion which, as shown below, has both advantages and disadvantages.

All German mother tongue syllabuses insist that these four programmes should not be taught in isolation, for instance, reflection about language can start with a literary text discussed as part of a lesson in oral communication or with an essay written on the same topic. In the lower grades, teaching is expected to start with topics dealing with the childrens' immediate surroundings and experiences. In the higher grades, thematic approaches should combine the activities of language study with the training of language skills. Widespread project work clearly reflects joint language activities of all kinds within one context.

Hochdeutsch

In the early grades a regional dialect is accepted, but in the long run pupils are expected to learn Standard German, *Hochdeutsch*. This means that their range of oral communication is not restricted to their region and that they are aware there has to be a common standard language spoken and understood by people throughout Germany, whether coming from the North or South. It is accepted that any participation in public life and democracy requires the use of a standard variety of the official language.

What Standard German is exactly has not been defined other than in terms of an oral code, which is close to written German as far as vocabulary and syntax are concerned, and capable of being widely understood with the potential of being used as a vehicle of communication throughout the country. The acceptance of *Hochdeutsch* in schooling means that regional varieties are excluded though not slight regional accents. In the case of problems it is usual to consult the standard reference book, the *Duden Enzyklopädie,* which has become accepted as a prescriptive authority in the matter of language standards.

Other mother tongues and modern foreign languages

The rights of national minorities to teach their own mother tongues in the state system exist only for the Danes living on the German–Danish border in Jütland. For the 50,000 Sorbs living in the former German Democratic Republic cultural minority and mother tongue teaching rights were guaranteed until 1990 but these are no longer significant in the present-day Länder of Brandenburg and Sachsen. There is no nationwide legal entitlement to non-German mother tongue teaching for the children of immigrant minorities.

Although the home languages of immigrants are not generally accepted as school languages some Länder do make provision for teaching them. Measures to include them are described in a later section. According to the laws of German descent, the *Aussiedler* are Germans even if their family language is no longer German. For their children special language teaching provisions are made which are similar to those for the children of immigrant workers where available. Since teaching in the language of the country from which they have come is often not desired by their parents, the resulting language loss often causes problems for the children's further development (Hoffmann, 1994).

According to the official view the Federal Republic of Germany is still, in spite of the physical fact of immigration, not designated as an immigration country. Therefore there are no special immigration policies in operation and there is no entitlement to tuition in the mother tongue except in some Länder, such as Hessen and Berlin. This particularly affects those home languages which are different from the mother tongues recognized as the official languages in the countries of immigrants' origin. This is so with Kurdish, certain dialects of Arabic, African and Asian languages which have a low status, are not regarded as official languages and consequently are not included in the lists of officially sponsored school languages. The embassies and consulates of the countries of origin responsible for tuition will not organize language courses for people who left the country because they oppose their government; thus the Turkish government does not organize courses in Kurdish. Poor knowledge of these languages is not, however, a bar to educational progress.

The long tradition of teaching the so-called prestigious modern foreign languages in Germany, in former times confined to the *Gymnasium*, has since the 1960s been extended to all school types. Of the languages taught, English is the most popular first foreign language (two languages at least are required in the academic schools) followed by French, Spanish and Russian. Italian as well as Latin are also available, with Latin being the most prestigious. Immigrants' languages, except for Italian and occasionally Modern Greek, are not part of the regular schedules although some Länder, for example, Hessen, provide more opportunity for studying them to examination level. Neighbourhood and exchange programmes exist at primary level in the border areas of Nordrhein-Westfalen and Baden-Württemberg, with the relevant languages being Dutch and French.

The ability to speak a foreign language and bilingualism have a high status in Germany, but this does not apply to the languages spoken by immigrants and refugees, whose own language competence or bilingualism are not held in high esteem. Their so-called 'social bilingualism' is regarded as inferior unlike the 'cultured bilingualism' in those modern foreign languages which are taught in the selective schools. French and English are especially in demand.

TEACHING ARRANGEMENTS FOR MOTHER TONGUE EDUCATION IN SCHOOL

Normal classes in German schools consist of 16 to 32 pupils. Teaching materials are given free or are lent to pupils. The extent of financial provision for them varies from Land to Land and/or according to the school type. Extra lessons to support small groups of weaker pupils are free. There is no difference in treatment between German and non-German pupils in this respect. At the higher secondary level of *Sekundarstufe II* teaching is more often than not akin to lecturing.

After 20 years of educational assimilation the proportion of children from immigrant worker families attending the more academic *Realschulen* and *Gymnasien* is, on the German average, still less than about 10 per cent in any one school year. However, there are considerable variations, for example, in some conurbations in western Germany the number of immigrant children can be about 70 per cent or more. In comparison children of refugees and *Aussiedler* are spread all over the country. This is due to the German policy of dispersal to avoid agglomerations of these families. Even so, every school in the country can be said to be confronted with non-German mother tongues, with bilingualism and the use of German as a foreign language.

Catering for the immigrants

Immersion classes, preparatory classes and support teaching

On reaching the compulsory school age of six all children are usually put straight into the regular beginners' class unless they have been placed in a special pre-school class because they are not ready for schooling or, in the case of children with other mother tongues, because of their inadequate knowledge of German. This special provision usually takes the form of a pre-school or nursery class, depending on age and maturity on admission. Children who have already attended school in their country of origin are placed in a preparatory class. These classes can be linguistically heterogeneous as in Nordrhein-Westfalen, or homogeneous as in Bavaria. The aim is to prepare children to cope with the German language and the course content when they join the regular classes. A preparatory class is set up when there is a sufficient number (between 8 and 12) of immigrant children. The children of the *Aussiedler* are taught in their own preparatory classes called 'support classes' (*Förderklassen*) as far as possible. In Nordrhein-Westfalen it was possible to set up preparatory classes (principally of Turkish children) of short or long duration (up to grade 6) and often taught by Turkish teachers. The long duration classes have since been abolished because of their failure to integrate the pupils, and duration has been reduced to a maximum of two years.

The mixed multinational, multilingual preparatory class is a particular educational problem area. The childrens' second language, German, serves predominantly as the language of communication, which means that competence in the foreign childrens' first mother tongue is neglected or completely ignored. Because of the high multicultural concentration in Germany and the ethnic and cultural diversity of schools (with pupils of different ages frequently spread over several classes because of the need to repeat a grade and pupils' varying school careers) language inadequacy can be widespread. Pupils are likely to suffer a severe language and culture shock as early as the first phase of their settling in. Indeed, after moving to a class which is relevant to their age, most pupils continue to require additional support lessons in German as well as in other school subjects. Recession has led to cuts in these services.

Research has shown that the foreign pupils' overall progress is slower than that of their German counterparts (Chrysakopoulos and Oomen-Welke, 1986; Oomen-Welke, 1985, 1993). Even pupils assessed as 'able' managed to achieve only an average mark of '4' on a scale of '1' (very good) to '6' (poor). The analysis of the amount of subject matter learnt by the pupils in oral and written German showed that they had developed 'normally' in the general areas of, for example, drawing conclusions, structuring their language and acquiring vocabulary. They were shown, however, to be suffering from a 'fossilizing of their language mistakes'. Continuing to repeat their mistakes acted as a barrier to their overall progress. Investigations carried out jointly by the author with Greek and Turkish colleagues led to the assumption that progress in the children's first mother tongue would be similarly affected. For children to develop both bilingually and biculturally methods other than teaching in separate classes would have to be tried, but such classes also have their critics.

Bilingualism trials at Grundschule level. Turkish as first and second foreign language at Sekundarstufe

In the 1980s schools were set up in Krefeld (Nordrhein-Westfalen) which were both bilingual and bicultural: German/Greek, German/Italian and German/Turkish. In the first half of the school year foreign and German children were placed in separate groups to begin with. Parallel lessons in basic literacy were given in both the first and the second languages. Mathematics and German were taught in the mother tongue and to immigrant pupils also in German. Other 'factual' lessons were similarly categorized into first- and second-language classes, being taught to immigrant pupils in their mother tongue and also in German. Teaching foreign pupils through the medium of their mother tongue decreased progressively during the four years of the *Grundschule*. At *Sekundarstufe I* these pupils were able to continue with their non-German mother tongue lessons as a modern foreign language, which was recognized as an examinable school subject. To enable pupils to receive this tuition 'busing' had to be accepted, notwithstanding the possible adverse repercussions on the pupils' social integration in their home areas. The Krefeld model was abandoned in favour of the 'Meeting Languages' concept and the 'Language Awareness' project in Nordrhein-Westfalen (Luchtenberg, 1992, 1995; Pelz, 1989), which enabled the pupils to learn more about language in general and to learn each other's languages in border areas through studying them.

Regular extra classes for the children of immigrant families

In Bavaria and in some schools in Baden-Württemberg linguistically homogeneous regular classes called the 'Open Model' were introduced in the 1970s to cater especially for the children of Turkish and Greek immigrants. Children were taught predominantly through the medium of their mother tongue, receiving about six lessons of German a week only. Ten years later, from the 1980s on, the teaching language had become predominantly German and taking up more than half the timetable, the intention being to accelerate social integration.

At first glance this model seems to meet the needs of everyone involved. It satisfies the foreign parents who do not wish to lose their children to the supposedly too liberal German culture. It protects the children from the pressure to fit in after receiving the shock of having to compete against their German peers. It calms the fears of the German majority that their own children's career prospects are being endangered by their having to study alongside allegedly academically weaker foreigners. The older teachers are happy that they do not have to change their traditional educational practices, while the traditionalist schools themselves, reluctant to introduce the processes of transformation to educate pupils for the 'one world', are relieved of the need to do so. An important consideration is that the teaching can take place in the morning, which is rarely the case with extra lessons in the non-German mother tongues. Co-operation between German and immigrant teachers is made easier because the ethnic teachers are employed by the German school authority and are not required to return to their native countries after the usual spell of between two and five years in Germany. Their own German improves as a result.

Advantages and disadvantages of these teaching arrangements

The reason for making this system permanent was to provide bilingual and bicultural education for the children. The linguistically homogeneous mother tongue classes are intended to qualify them for life in both their countries of origin and in Germany. The advantages are the opportunity to teach reading in two languages and, where there is good co-operation, also mathematics through the medium of two languages. The co-ordinated acquisition of writing and speaking skills intensifies the process of learning to read. By the second half of the first school year all children had already started with some reading. Reading in turn encourages the acquisition of German because the reception channels and learning processes alternate and support one another. Nevertheless, extra teaching and social help are necessary especially for those children, of whom there is a significant number, who are not fluent in German and who take longer to adapt to learning in the school context and to life in the German school, its written culture and the consumer society.

The disadvantages are the separation according to nationality from the German peer group, situations where the children's knowledge of German could be tested, used and become automatic. Lessons intended to be attended together with German pupils in such subjects as sport, music and art are insufficient for striking up lasting pupil contacts. Language mistakes can be reinforced when there is little opportunity to experience authentic German, especially since outside lesson time pupils use their first mother tongue almost exclusively. Although German is the language used when speaking to the teachers, they do, however, sanction the use of the mother tongue on most other occasions in school. The lessons in German tend to be run on the lines of teaching a foreign or second language with little opportunity for spontaneous communication. Too little is done to stimulate the alert and the quick learner.

Additional non-German classes: content, method of organization, degree of commitment

The intention of additional teaching in the pupils' mother tongue is to enable them to increase their competence in their own mother tongue and, with the help of lessons in their country's geography and history, to develop a cultural identity based on their own nationality. Teaching in the mother tongue is also meant to foster links with the society of the host country. The teaching of the Muslim religion to Turkish children can be included under this heading, because schools financed privately by religious groups can provide some communicative tuition in the minority language. They also provide religious education in those religions which are not part of the Christian denominations recognized for state schooling. Increasingly, Muslim teaching is being made available in maintained schools in Hamburg and Nordrhein-Westfalen, although it has been refused in Baden-Württemberg.

Additional lessons in the other mother tongues under the control of consulates are offered almost exclusively to the children of immigrant workers. This teaching can assume various forms and shows varying degrees of commitment. Attendance at lessons, which are usually held on two afternoons a week, is voluntary. In several Länder, where additional mother tongue teaching is carried out under the auspices of the German school authority, it is integrated into the regular timetable and attendance is compulsory. The foreign teachers are then employed and paid by the Land.

As already mentioned, where lessons are organized through the consulates only the official languages recognized by the respective governments are taught. Since teaching usually takes place outside the normal morning school hours, teachers and their pupils are to a large degree isolated from the German school system. This prevents meetings and discussions with regular German teaching staff with the result that the ethnic teachers themselves have one opportunity less to learn German language and culture. Teachers, moreover, are not allocated their own classes and have no say in their composition. This makes long-term lesson planning and grouping of pupils, which could make for more efficient teaching, extremely difficult. Integrating the teaching in the regular timetable of the school could help with such problems.

Education specialists and teacher trainers have been demanding that the teaching of the other mother tongues should be built into the regular school timetable. The simplest way is to put such lessons at either end of the school day. This has in fact been happening in some areas. Indeed, in a number of schools German pupils have actually been attending non-German mother tongue classes alongside their foreign peers. There are good educational reasons for this integrative approach. Acknowledging the existence of the other mother tongue reinforces the foreign children's self-confidence, which in turn improves their general motivation and increases their interest in study, with the newly acquired skills playing an important part in the learning development of all pupils.

Devising and teaching appropriate progression programmes is made that much easier. Our own research (Oomen-Welke, 1990) shows that pupils make significant progress when taught both the German and the non-German mother tongues. The resulting prestige of the immigrants' languages and speakers works for better intercultural peer relations. Recognizing these languages as regular school subjects further encourages contact between teachers of different nationalities who can get together to tackle wider educational problems arising from intercultural teaching.

Despite the positive results, many German teachers tend to advise against additional other mother-tongue courses which they consider an extra workload. The better informed and more committed teachers recommend such classes to all pupils, including the children of refugees, though their languages, unlike those of immigrants, are less widely available. On the other hand, many ethnic pupils prefer to adopt the German language and culture, a stance in which they may have the support of parents (Tulasiewicz, 1994). Pupils may, of course, simply wish to get out of a second school session in the afternoon during a time when their German peers are mostly free. In any case children dislike this dislocation, the extra travel involved and the clash with homework. The teaching methods of the ethnic teachers can often be rather 'conservative', which also puts pupils off attending their lessons.

Attendance at non-German mother tongue classes

When a part of the regular school programme, non-German mother tongue lessons are attended by 90 per cent of the children, making it easier for them to be integrated in all curriculum activities. Attendance drops to less than 30 per cent, although consular statistics, taken at the start of the year, tend to be less than absolutely reliable where the children are taught separately.

Bilingual classes

Traditional bilingual classes and schools which cater for the professional and social advancement of members of one national group by which they are financed, such as the American, Japanese or European schools, and which work on the immersion principle are acceptable to society at large. They provide for the prestigious cultural bilingualism and also prepare the children of professionals working abroad for their return to jobs and study in the home country. As far as this kind of language tuition is concerned society generally closes its mind to the needs of immigrant minorities, with the countries affected providing few secular institutions to meet this demand. Religious instruction is not bilingual. In Germany the Krefeld experiment involving immigrants was short-lived. Nevertheless, there exist a few less well advertised bilingual schools for both territorial and non-territorial minority languages such as Dutch/German, Modern Greek/German. Their main aim is the reciprocity of language learning where members of the majority and minority cultures and languages can be seen coping with the other language and making progress. Despite the suggestions from interested educational staff there have been hardly any serious attempts to set up such schools in the 'ethnic' languages of immigrants.

TOLERANCE OF VARIANTS OF GERMAN MOTHER TONGUE AND MULTILINGUALISM IN SCHOOLS

The average German school class is made up of children from the local German majority who speak either the regional dialect or the standard *Hochdeutsch*, together with children from immigrant families. Depending on their personal histories, pupils and especially many immigrants speak German with varying levels of deviation from the standard, ranging from very close to the standard to barely comprehensible variants. The latter dialects are known as 'immigrant workers' speech' (Linke 1993; Linke and Oomen-Welke, 1995).

Teachers, who in the lower school grades are alone responsible for assessing their pupils, show varying degrees of tolerance towards their language variations. These can be summed up as follows:

- A slight colouring of the language through dialect on the part of German children is accepted, but strong dialect is tolerated only during a child's initial period at school and predominantly only in South Germany. It is acceptable to use local dialect when speaking as long as, in the opinion of the teacher, progress in written work (spelling, essay writing) is not affected. In the written language some lexical elements of dialect are more likely to be tolerated than syntactical features such as the use of different gender, case, conjugation or prepositions. The micro-variety of youth culture is sometimes tolerated in oral communication, but not by all teachers.

- Foreign accents and, to a certain degree, their lexical variants are tolerated; strict attention is paid only to grammatical accuracy. As soon as no accent can be heard, and especially when an immigrant child picks up the regional German accent, teachers tend to ignore the grammatical mistakes in the same way as they do in the case of German children. In a subtle way accent becomes an instrument of selection and works as a filter. When the teachers are not aware of 'oral mistakes' or of the variations which are typical for foreigners, for example in the use of article and case, then strategies for covering up linguistic errors are hardly noticed.

- Not much thought is given to the fact that there are differences between the spoken colloquial language, the logically based language of teaching (the possession of which is called Cognitive Academic Language Proficiency), and the language of science and the professions. These variations are not taken into account when assessing success at school and in training, and are not pointed out to pupils. Pupils have to achieve a stylistic competence by critical reflection on the written language: a difficult task.

- Mistakes in spelling and grammar are not acceptable in written work. Teachers feel obliged to correct such mistakes because of the curriculum requirements and what is seen as the general duty of the school to educate. When correcting mistakes they remind pupils of examination requirements. On the other hand some will insist on keeping to the language of the written word in oral work, where their interference cannot really be justified. Therefore they frequently insist on answers being given in full sentences.

- Children who are speakers of other mother tongues are often forbidden to use their own language in school when communicating on the grounds that in a German school only German is allowed to be spoken. Not all German teachers insist on this, usually it is the same teachers who discourage attendance at non-German mother tongue lessons.

- Female teachers, predominantly in the *Grundschule*, often speak German using an indirect style with softening modal clichés resorting to questions instead of commands or weak responses instead of reprimands. This is a language variety known from research on womens' speech in the USA, Britain and Germany (Linke, 1993; Oomen-Welke, 1993). The friendly tone is well understood by German middle-class pupils, but it is often misunderstood by pupils whose mother tongue is not German. This is so especially if the ethnic pupils have been used to authoritarian methods of education, when their own language experience at home and the use of their mother tongue with teachers of their own nationality has been markedly different from the German school. This can lead to uncertainty in their dealings with the teachers who use an educated middle-class way of speaking.

RECENT INNOVATIONS IN LANGUAGE TEACHING METHODS

In the last 20 years in the Federal Republic of Germany, as in other countries, mother tongue and modern foreign language teaching has changed significantly. The traditional established position of the reader or reading book at the centre of language teaching has come under criticism. New grammatical theories, for example content-orientated grammar according to the Glinz and Erben interpretation (Erben, 1980; Glinz, 1973), found support in sociological, psychoanalytical methods and are based on critical theory. They began to be accepted in some cases. In parallel to the various innovations in modern foreign language teaching generative transformational grammar was more widely adopted. Even in the structural study of political lyricism much socio-political and cultural information about the society dealt with was taught (Hessen: Kultusminister, 1972).

Teaching German mother tongue

As a holistic approach the project method of teaching German was rediscovered more than 20 years ago and this spilled over into the teaching of other subjects (Fritzsche *et al.*, 1992; Geisler *et al.*, 1976; Schuster, 1994). The straitjacket of the 45-minute lesson has, up to now, prevented this method from being properly exploited. Most recently experiments have been undertaken which take the form of active German teaching: pupils no longer have to explain grammatical phenomena and produce text interpretations expressing themselves in words. Increasingly, they can do so using alternative symbolic devices, such as pictures, puppets and other objects, or playlets. This approach appeals particularly to children who are educationally disadvantaged (see Freudenreich and Sperth, 1983).

The child and childhood have been rediscovered as a centre of interest with the autonomous child taking the lead and determining learning processes by organizing activities which are better understood. Teachers have been giving much thought to finding ways to help children growing up in a technical world dominated by the media, by unemployment, by the break up of traditional values and by the challenges of a multicultural society. These are reflected in the working texts used in both mother tongue and modern foreign language teaching.

German teachers differ in the way they teach pupils who are bilingual in German and another language influenced as they are by their own home backgrounds, their own school experiences and their professional training, as well as by their personal educational convictions and political conscience. Many of them have a good analytical understanding of the school subject mother-tongue German. On the other hand, because of lack of proper training, many are unfamiliar with the concept of bilingualism and its relevance (Schmitt, 1992). Teachers inclined towards educational reform try hard to encourage their pupils to be active in lessons, although many do so without a grounding in the neuro-psychological sciences and without a knowledge of the relevant Russian culturo-historical and psychological theories of learning of Galperin, Vygotsky and Leontiev (List, 1981). Language Awareness is now becoming an innovative field of study providing an element of language education in lessons which further the acquisition of communicative skills and tap the language resources provided by the pupils themselves.

The problem-formulating method of Paulo Freire, with its visualizing technique and the link of action–word–understanding of meaning, which he developed when he was teaching literacy to agricultural workers in Brazil, was adapted during he mid-1970s by student groups and has also been used in language teaching with immigrants and their children. Conducting investigations outside the school, composing and exchanging texts, letters being sent to classrooms, printing them with a hand press, individualized language learning using a learning menu with cupboards full of materials and a stimulating learning environment in a studio or workshop with open monitoring of achievement: all these techniques when taken together constitute the independent method. This is further supported by genuine pupil and teacher cooperation in class councils and joint programme planning sessions, providing ample opportunity for language use in the classroom and introducing pupils to communication in real-life situations.

Modern foreign languages and German second language

The above innovations can also be found in modern foreign language teaching (Appeltauer, 1987; Butzkamm, 1993). The co-operative activities are rich in active language use and are meant to facilitate the acquisition of the second language. However, in this respect, there is little evidence that teachers recognize that German as a second language also involves communication for problem solving and inducing social interaction. It is intended as an introduction to the ways of the host country, exposing injustice and aimed at overcoming prejudice and hostility through intercultural education. The average modern foreign language or German as a foreign or second language teacher still believes that learning requires no more than the acquisition of a vocabulary and the rules of morphology and syntax, totally unaware that dialogue as well as culturally defined behaviour in typical situations may encourage social interaction and help solve some of the problems arising.

SCHOOL TEXTBOOKS

As part of this development, a change in schoolbooks has also occurred which now combines the previously discrete working programmes in the form of pupil and teacher tasks, and they are also more attractively produced. In the 1970s and 1980s textbooks were created with the aim of integrating the children of immigrants. Later, in the 1980s and 1990s, books were also developed for the use of *Aussiedler*, some appearing in bilingual versions with the two languages printed on facing pages. For pupils who try not to use their non-German language, they probably provide only a limited opportunity for experiencing Language Awareness.

In Freiburg an educational construction kit, also called the Freiburg Model (Henrici, 1986), was developed by the co-author of this chapter (Schmitt, 1980). The kit starts with an initial non-verbal visual stimulus and develops into a dialogue, providing role play and text-writing opportunities under guidance with all the required linguistic, lexical and grammatical information supplied which can be used in communication for problem solving. For example, for a dialogue 'in the swimming pool' the text is introduced or it is composed together by the user of the kit and the tutor. In the next unit factual issues are inquired into (for example, 'water cleanliness') and dealt with using a similar method. Intercultural remarks and reflections are exchanged, then there is room for further role play, text production, grammatical exercises and application as before. The conclusion takes the form of a review of the entire teaching unit.

The construction kit concept is intended as a guide to productive and creative mother tongue and modern foreign language teaching, providing the necessary grammar, listing mistakes and expected models of teacher performance, and involving pupils in authentic social communicative situations. The general teaching goals can be used by teachers as a framework for practical planning and evaluation of tasks, as well as by pupils at different levels of achievement in determining their own course content according to what they consider useful (Lührs, 1985).

TRAINING OF MOTHER TONGUE TEACHERS

There is a shortage of teachers of German in the regular school system. This is the result of the large number of compulsory German lessons prescribed by the curriculum for the regular classes as well as the amount of teaching required in the *Vorbereitungsklassen*, the *Immersion* and other types of special classes. Depending on the children's age and the school type in which teachers want to teach, their training can be started right after the *Abitur* and can take between three and five years, with an additional period of practical training lasting almost two years. Again, depending on the type of school, two or three school subjects have to be studied together with subject methods and education foundation disciplines. A significantly higher percentage of education and theory study as opposed to subject expertise is prescribed for primary school teachers (about 30 per cent) than for the *Gymnasium* (about 5 per cent).

Teachers of mother tongues other than German have been trained almost exclusively in their countries of origin, being sent to Germany for a limited period of time and often without any knowledge of German, unless at the time of appointment they were employed permanently in Germany. In-service language teaching experience exists in theory. Such practice can be acceptable only if it is education policy to leave the teaching of other mother tongues in the hands of the foreign consulates. Educationally, it makes better sense to train and retrain mother tongue teachers in the country where they will be, or are already, working. A start has been made with such training in Hessen and more recently in Nordrhein-Westfalen.

With regard to the function and acquisition of German as a second language the significance of the second language as a means of socialization and education in the host country must be emphasized, especially under the conditions of a virtually monolingual school system. Within this context the relevance of, and necessity for, fostering the other mother tongues to help children's development with the ability to cope with problems generally, the pressure of the German environment on non-German peoples and the high motivation to learn German as a second language are increasingly important (Gogolin, 1994a, b).

Offers of further training to native-speaking teachers alone or of training together with German teachers have been made by various Land-run teacher-training institutions. The take up has not been enormous, with native teachers preferring to take further education to qualify for a profession in their countries of origin through correspondence courses (in the case of Turks), or to prepare for another occupation in Germany (in the case of Italians). However, a common future in Europe puts an obligation on everyone to understand each other. This means that school systems have to encourage bilingualism and all teachers have to learn more about it so that the multicultural society can become a valued society where all languages enjoy an equally high status.

Chapter 12

Teaching Majority and Minority Mother Tongues in Denmark

J. Normann Jørgensen and Anne Holmen

> The Danish language is the beginning of everything and the end of everything.
> (*Det danske sprog er altings begyndelse og altings slutning*, Education Minister Haarder, 1991, 2)

> He manages so well that one never notices that he is not Danish.
> (*Han klarer sig så godt, at man aldrig tænker på, at han ikke er dansker*, teacher quote, Kristjánsdóttir, 1990, 60)

INTRODUCTION

Compared to a number of European countries, Denmark is often said to be linguistically very homogenous. The overwhelming majority are native speakers of Danish, even when the two outlying parts of the Kingdom, Greenland and the Faroe Islands are included. However, in the Kingdom as a whole there is heterogeneity, with considerable variation within the Danish language itself, which is used as a mother tongue, as a foreign or second language, and in a number of regional varieties as well as minority languages. In Denmark, this heterogeneity is often ignored, probably for ideological reasons, as national identity is often perceived as closely linked with the use of a Standard Danish, spoken by middle- and upper-class Danes. 'Standard Danish' is understood as a variety of the language with no localizable features (Jørgensen and Kristensen, 1995).

The teaching of Danish is considered the core subject in both primary and secondary school education. Majority and minority pupils from all parts of the country are expected to understand, read and write national Standard Danish and to a certain extent also use it when speaking. This chapter looks at the main features of the teaching of Danish and discusses them in a wider perspective through comparison with the teaching of other languages in Denmark, and language policies in the two outlying parts of the Kingdom. We shall start with a short description of the historical evolution of the majority and minority groups on the Danish linguistic scene.

MAJORITY AND MINORITY GROUPS

The Kingdom of Denmark consists of three parts. The earliest part of the Kingdom is the southern part, with the peninsula of Jutland and the surrounding islands. The northern parts

Figure 7: The regional languages of Denmark

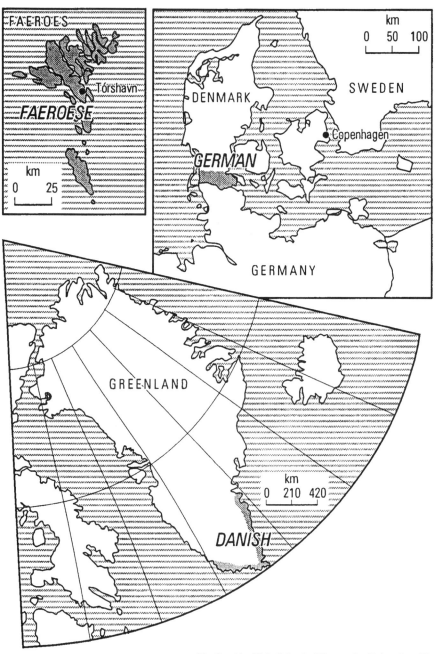

The Graphics Unit, School of Geography, University of Leeds

are Greenland and the Faroe Islands, settled over the centuries. Native speakers of Danish comprise a large majority (more than 90 per cent) of the Kingdom's 5.2 million citizens. In Greenland the majority are speakers of West Greenlandic, an Inuit language, although many are bilingual with Danish. In the Faroe Islands the vast majority is bilingual with Faroese, a Nordic (North Germanic) language as the first language and Danish as the official language. There is also a bilingual German minority in Slesvig.

Until World War Two immigrants were by and large from neighbouring countries, especially Germany and Scandinavia, but since the 1960s immigration has changed, first with the immigration of labour, in particular from the Mediterranean and the Middle East, and later with waves of refugees from a number of politically unstable corners of the world. In 1995 about 200.000 citizens from abroad resided in Denmark, that is around 4 per cent of the population. Apart from those who hold Scandinavian and German passports (Denmark does not accept dual citizenship), the largest groups of foreigners are persons with Turkish passports (including Kurds), Pakistanis, Iranians, followed by immigrants and refugees from the former Yugoslavia, Sri Lankans, Poles and Vietnamese. The labour migrants have mainly settled in and around Copenhagen and the major towns of Denmark, whereas the refugees, as a consequence of a deliberate policy, are dispersed all over the country.

Greenland is now considered a bilingual, monocultural society with West Greenlandic as the official language of the elementary school system and Danish as the language of the administration and of the major part of secondary education. Since home rule in 1979, Greenland has strengthened the West Greenlandic language and judging from observations of the younger generation there are now signals that this effort is succeeding. However, in the process, Greenland has had to realize that gaining ground on a former colonial language is an uphill battle (Møller, 1988), and that one important factor in Greenland's development is the economically and politically powerful Danish-speaking minority.

The Faroe Islands maintain a linguistically purist policy of Faroeizing, which is seen in the new syntactical constructions and vocabulary used instead of Danish (or English) loan words. On the other hand, Faroese society is close to being universally bilingual in Faroese and Danish as a result of the early introduction of Danish in schools, and the pervading Danish cultural influence in The Faroes (Hagström, 1987).

It can be said, therefore, that the Kingdom consists of three widely different linguistic entities: southern Denmark, in which the intellectual élite tacitly maintains that the whole country is monolingual; the Faroes which are genuinely bilingual; and Greenland, with a growing bilingualism as part of a strengthened Greenlandic identity.

EXPLICIT AND IMPLICIT LANGUAGE POLICIES

In 1955 Denmark signed a bilateral agreement with Germany to support the linguistic identity of minority groups on both sides of the border. Apart from this, Denmark has no other overt language teaching policies with regard to Danish abroad and no language academy or similar institution to protect the language in Denmark itself. This may reflect the fact that the Danish language is in a very strong position in Denmark and not threatened by other languages. The Language Commission (*Dansk Sprognævn*), an independent agency supported by the Ministry of Culture, is given the responsibility of registering new developments in the Danish language, publishing a spelling dictionary and giving advice on language matters, but not of acting on its own initiative. If we look at patterns of language use this seems to be the case. All official transactions are carried out in Danish: court rulings, military manoeuvres, trade union negotiations and parliamentary sessions (including contributions by members from Greenland and the Faroe Islands). The same applies to the language used in utilities such as public transportation, the health system and the major part of the mass media. In schools, it is taken for granted that children speak and understand Standard Danish by the compulsory school age of seven, and compensatory measures are taken when this is not the case. These include reception classes in which children from minorities are taught in isolated groups for intensive training in the Danish language at the cost of the rest of the curriculum.

Furthermore, the role played by the standard language carries a heavy ideological weight (Holmen and Jørgensen, 1989). The Romantic idea of one nation, one culture, one language seems to have survived as an important element in the Danish national identity of the 1990s, possibly strengthened through the public debate on the European Union and the Maastricht Treaty (Gregersen, 1994).

Recently, schools – and with them a number of linguists – have been criticized for the naivity of this view. It is claimed that by subscribing to this they inadvertently suppress all varieties of the Danish language other than the national high-status 'Standard' (Kristiansen, 1990). At the same time, Danish educators and scholars have been criticized for being complacent when it comes to the status of Danish *vis-à-vis* the more powerful European languages, especially English (see Jørgensen, 1991).

The privileged role of Standard Danish is taken for granted in school language teaching and is not really an issue of public debate. This is not the case with the teaching of minority languages. They have a limited and unstable status in the educational system and often form the focus of school curriculum discussions. Moreover knowledge of minority languages coupled with inadequate knowledge of Danish is also the concern of those involved in developmental problems of underprivileged urban areas (Jørgensen, 1994).

General educational policy in Denmark is assimilationist, though not overtly so. Government and bureaucratic discourse is careful not to appear racist, none the less there is only minimal support for the maintenance of minority languages, and among Danes awareness of the legitimacy of linguistic minority rights has a very low priority. There is little interest in Danish as a second language.

SCHOOLS IN DENMARK

In Denmark, education – but not schooling – is compulsory for children between the ages of 7 and 16. Parents are free to choose a maintained or a private school for their children, or to provide other kinds of education for them. In practice, 90 per cent of the children attend maintained schools, and almost everybody else a private school.

The maintained school is a 9–10 year comprehensive school. The vast majority of children attend mainstream classes, which are not divided by ability level or otherwise, throughout their schooling. Private schools, which also receive considerable financial support from the Danish state, are usually based on a particular religious, political or educational outlook. They cover a wide range of organizational models, of which the majority are not very different from the maintained schools and are also comprehensive.

Compared to most other school systems the Danish system is very decentralized, every school having its own school board, consisting mainly of elected parent representatives but also including elected teachers and pupils. These boards, however, have little influence on the everyday teaching in the schools, because the choice of methods, teaching materials and topics covered lies with the teacher and, to a lesser extent, also with the pupils. It is a well-established principle in the Danish educational tradition that children must learn to take responsibility for their own learning, and therefore teachers are required to choose themes and activities in close co-operation with their pupils.

The new 1994 Education Act emphasizes that the school should base its work on an individual child's personal background: their language, culture, ambitions and needs. As a consequence the concept of differentiation of teaching has come to the fore. The simultaneous teaching of all pupils in classrooms that can be very mixed with respect to backgrounds and abilities calls for constant adjustment by the teacher to new situations, new motivations and new demands. The materials and themes must appeal to all the children, and the activities must apply to the different learning styles required by pupils within the same classroom.

THE ROLE OF DANISH AS A SCHOOL SUBJECT

The centrally issued set of guidelines for schools suggests a fixed number of weekly lessons of 45 minutes duration of Danish for each school grade. These appear in the table:

Table 12.1 *Weekly number of lessons of Danish in Danish maintained schools*

Grade	1	2	3	4	5	6	7	8	9
No. of lessons	9	8	7	6	6	6	6	6	6

Source: Undervisningsministeriet, 1988

Pupils in the lower grades have more hours of Danish than those in the higher grades because it is accepted that two important developments in the children's education take place in Danish language classes: these are the pupils' acquisition of literacy, and their adjustment to social norms and learning activities in school.

Compared to a number of other countries, formal, systematic literacy instruction in school begins quite late in Denmark. It does not start before the age of 6 or 7. Before that most children attend a non-compulsory year in a 'kindergarten class'. Although this takes place in the school building (and not in a special kindergarten or day-care centre) the activities include play, art, storytelling and excursions with a clear focus on furthering the children's general cognitive and motor development rather than their literacy skills.

Traditionally, the teaching of literacy is based on the alphabetic principle and the phonetic character of Danish spelling. After linking sounds with letters children are often supposed to develop literacy skills through putting letters together to make words and words to make texts. In more recent coursebooks this bottom up approach has been replaced by a more holistic top down approach in which the children are supposed to progress from a pragmatic awareness of the meaning of texts to the semantic meaning of words and finally to a mastery of orthographic principles. For the past 10 years the two approaches have led complementary lives in schools, the choice between them being considered part of the individual teacher's freedom to choose a method. However, results of an international study on reading have led to a vehement discussion about the relative validity of the two methods in school circles and in the country at large. The study (Mejding, 1994) placed Danish grade-3 children very near the bottom in reading skills of a long list of countries. The study also included a comparison between grade-8 pupils, which gave a more encouraging picture of reading skills in Danish schools with the Danish group placed at the top end of the scale.

It is most likely that the difference between the comparative results in the two age groups has to do with the multifunctionality of the teaching of Danish. Literacy acquisition is not considered a subject in its own right, but one of many disciplines forming the subject of Danish mother tongue. In Danish schools there is a tradition of letting the Danish teacher be the 'form teacher', that is it is the teacher who is responsible for the social ethos of the class-room, for the general development of each child, and for co-operation with parents. To secure continuity and development of more stable relations in class the form teacher follows the same class for all nine years of basic schooling In most cases the role of form teacher is given to the teacher of Danish. Consequently, the class will have the same Danish teacher through-out their basic school careers. Besides taking care of the major part of the language curriculum (including literacy) the Danish teacher is responsible for traffic and sex education, and for arranging school trips, theatre performances and the like. All in all the Danish model, as described, emphasizes the role of Danish as the main subject in the school's socializing and culture transmitting function.

THE ROLE OF DANISH AS A TRANSMITTER OF A NATIONAL IDENTITY

To the description of educational aims of the state maintained school, as formulated in the 1994 Education Act, a paragraph was added about all pupils becoming familiar with Danish culture as well as acquainted with other cultures. This paragraph has been the subject of much discussion. Some see in it a necessary return to certain shared cultural values, for example the study of 'good' literature within the school subject of Danish. Others see it as an unnecessary list of priorities ignoring the cultural variety represented in the country as a whole. This dis-cussion confirms the view of the teaching of Danish as at the core of the curriculum, not only in the everyday life of the school, but also in a wider national perspective. Insofar as national identity is ideologically linked up with the idea of one 'National Culture' and one 'National Standard Language', all attempts at introducing multiculturality or multilingualism into the concept of the Danish school are bound to be perceived as threatening by the educational establishment. The only exception is found in the curriculum of a few private schools run by parents which aim at maintaining the minority pupils' languages and cultures without neglect-ing their competence in Danish.

Another example of the general concern appeared in a recent debate about the concept of language awareness, or language consciousness, in teaching Danish. As with respect to the notion of culture there has been a marked tendency among some educationalists to move the school towards more traditional grammar teaching, away from the communicatively oriented teaching of both the Danish language and of other languages. The trigger was a report to the Ministry of Education (Undervisningsministeriet, 1992). The ensuing debate was full of harsh criticism of this report (Risager *et al.*, 1993). The report considers the notion of communi-cative competence as of little use, and the communicative teaching practised in the schools a deficit version of language teaching. The teachers' reaction maintains that there is little evidence in the report of real understanding of the notion and purpose of communicative teaching, and suggests a further development of this line of thinking instead of its abandonment and a return to the narrow, structural and monolingual view of language of 20 or 30 years ago which concentrated on rules and correctness.

NEW GUIDELINES

As a consequence of the debate, the redefined goals and activities of the state-maintained school system expressed in the 1994 Education Act are once again under review. Teaching guidelines are being rewritten all across the curricula. For subject Danish this means that the guidelines will now distinguish between Danish as a subject for all students and Danish as a second language. A further outcome is that the Ministry of Education will issue an entirely new set of guidelines for the teaching of minority languages as mother tongues, that is, languages such as Arabic and Berber for immigrants from Morocco, Croatian for immigrants from Croatia, or Kurdish and Turkish for immigrants from Turkey. The guidelines took effect from the school year 1996–97.

THE TEACHING OF OTHER LANGUAGES AS MOTHER TONGUE

The focus of this chapter has been on the teaching of Danish and minority mother tongues in the Danish schools and did not include the well-established tradition of teaching several modern foreign languages to a fairly high level of competence, as is the case in most other European countries, starting with English as a compulsory subject in grade 4 (age 10), followed by German as an optional language in grade 6 and French from grade 8. French may replace German as the second foreign language chosen. In high schools, starting at the age 16, a number of other languages are available as options in some schools: Italian, Spanish, Russian and, in specific schools, also Turkish, Arabic and Bosnian.

However, the new guidelines for the teaching of minority mother tongues are unlikely to suggest a fixed number of weekly lessons in the minority tongues equal to the number of weekly lessons in Danish. The 1984 guidelines (Undervisningsministeriet, 1984) suggested between three and five mother tongue classes a week. This makes it considerably harder for the minority pupils to become literate in their mother tongues to a degree that can compare with that of the majority. In spite of good intentions in some places, relying on becoming biliterate only through the work of the maintained school is very difficult indeed (Jørgensen and Holmen, 1990).

Some private schools offer instruction, partly or fully, through the medium of languages other than Danish, including French, English, German, Urdu, Arabic, Turkish and others. Only certain specific minorities are entitled to public instruction entirely in a non-Danish language, namely the Germans in the border areas with Germany, and Sign Language users.

Any analysis of the teaching of minority pupils is complicated by the fact that the minorities are very unevenly distributed in the country. Altogether minority children make up approximately 7 per cent of pupils in maintained schools in Denmark. However, the minority children constitute more than half of the student body in some school districts, especially in certain working-class districts in Copenhagen and a few other major towns, while they are totally absent in many other places. The linguistic criteria chosen to register minority pupils may be misleading as only children in 'whose homes languages other than Danish are spoken' are registered as minority pupils, and children who have mastered a comparatively near-native standard of Danish beside their mother tongue are rarely included. The researcher responsible for the field study found that the real number of minority pupils in one typical Copenhagen school was at least 30 per cent higher than the official number given (Lørring, 1988).

The debate about the education of minority children is part of a larger public debate about integration. It is taken for granted by many majority members, including as it seems powerful figures in the main political parties, that immigrants and refugees assimilate to Danish ways, which includes making a language shift as quickly as possible. Having a non-Danish language as one's mother tongue is considered a burden, not only to the individual concerned but also to society, unless this language is an acceptable form of English, German, French, Norwegian, or Swedish. This attitude is shared by a good number of the teachers and administrators in the school system, and it has characterized much of the debate. The result is that it deals with questions like: 'how can we best help the immigrants to learn Danish ways?', rather than questions of mutual adjustment, language maintenance and bilingualism. The Danish debate is probably not any less informed than that which goes on in the rest of Europe but it is not any more enlightened either.

In school circles, however, there has been a continuous, although low-key, discussion about bilingualism, bilingual development, and bilingual and bicultural education. The decentralized organization of schools and teachers' extended freedom of method makes it possible for such a debate to set its mark on individual schools in the country, thereby allowing non-assimilationist approaches to gain ground regardless of the general political discourse.

TEACHER PREPARATION

The lively and openly critical discussion about bilingualism, bilingual development and bicultural education among teachers and others may seem odd in view of the rather rigid language education policy and practice in Denmark. The very recent reforms to introduce changes in the four-year teacher training for teachers of the *folkeskole* pays increased attention to the two specialist subjects teachers are required to teach and the raising of standards. In the circumstances there is rather less opportunity to explain the reasons for language teaching policies and priorities. As it is teachers pick up ideas in the generally liberal climate of discussion and free choice of teaching methods in Denmark. This is reinforced by the influence of untrained and unqualified persons who can be hired to teach, among whom there is an increasing number of foreigners.

SUMMARY

This chapter was headed by two remarks typical of school politicians and teachers, both of them expressing the strong position occupied by the Danish language in the educational system particularly when compared with the large number of minority languages. However, Danish is not only a dominant majority language. It is also a dominant subject in Danish schools as the main transmitter of the national culture as well as the centre of school socialization and parent co-operation. Furthermore, traditional literacy instruction has placed Standard Danish as the only language variety used in schools all over the country. Altogether, the dominance of Standard (and majority) Danish is taken so much for granted that it is rarely an issue in the debate about the development of the Danish state school. When challenged by support of linguistic diversity, both inter- and intralingual, the educational establishment strikes back with monocultural and monolingual arguments based on the ideology of the nation state.

Figure 8: The regional languages of Poland

The Graphics Unit, School of Geography, University of Leeds

Chapter 13

Teaching Mother Tongue Polish

Anna Berlińska

INTRODUCTION

Approximately 38 million Poles in Poland and some 12 million Poles and people of Polish origin living abroad use Polish as their first language. There are large numbers of Polish people residing in the USA – 5.6 million; within the boundaries of the former USSR – 2.5 million; in Germany – 1.5 million; in France – 1 million; in Canada – 400,000; in Brazil – 200,000; in Australia – 150,000; in Great Britain – 140,000; in Argentina – 100,000; and tens of thousands in other countries (estimated numbers culled from *Rocznik Statystyczny*, 1993).

Polish is the official language in the Republic of Poland and the language of instruction in Polish schools, both maintained and private. The latter, reopened in Poland after 1989, are partly subsidized by the government and follow the state curriculum except for minority-interest programmes. Instruction in Polish is also available to pupils in larger Polish centres abroad and is often financed by Polish embassies and consulates.

The ethnic minorities in Poland, listed alphabetically, are: Belorussian, Czech, German, Greek, Jewish, Lithuanian, Macedonian, Romany, Russian, Slovak and Ukrainian. It is difficult to provide the exact numbers of people in minority groups because accurate statistics have not been kept. The estimated figures published officially under Communist rule, before 1989, were apparently understated as 1.5 per cent of the population. On the other hand, the representatives of minorities themselves tend to overstate their numbers and so their data is also questionable. One can assume that ethnic minorities now make up no more than 3 per cent of the population of present-day Poland, compared with the period before World War Two when the figure was as high as 30 per cent.

HISTORY OF THE POLISH LANGUAGE AND EARLY POLISH EDUCATION

The formation of Polish as a national language, emerging from a group of territorial dialects, dates from the turn of the tenth century; with the reigns of Mieszko I and Bolesław Chrobry and the arrival of Christianity, which coincided with the beginning of the Polish state (Klemensiewicz, 1981). The process of the creation of common speech must inevitably have been gradual and long. It is assumed that some inter-dialectal ways of speaking were first developed within the royal court and Church administration. The royal court assembled people from different regions. The Church authorities recommended in the thirteenth century that the most important prayers should be said in Polish because the common people would not understand Latin. However, sermons were occasionally delivered in Polish, or rather in one of the Polish dialects, even earlier. As the court, initially settled for a short time in Gniezno, later moved to Poznań, then to Kraków (the capital of Poland from the eleventh century) and to Warsaw (the capital from 1596), no particular dialect was to play the role of the one, common medium of communication. This has, in fact, gradually evolved largely from the two dialects of Western and Southern Poland (Wielkopolska and Małopolska).

Parochial and convent schools, of which there were very few in the Middle Ages, often with foreign teachers who did not speak Polish, and with Latin as the language of instruction, did not contribute significantly to the process of linguistic unification. The oldest Polish university, founded in Kraków in 1364, though still dominated by the Latin language, exercised in the fifteenth and sixteenth centuries an important influence on the process of refining and unifying the Polish tongue, which was used outside lecture hours and sometimes even in courses – as an auxiliary medium (Taszycki, 1964).

The written form of Polish probably did not emerge until the thirteenth century (Klemensiewicz, 1981). The oldest preserved documents in Polish date from the fourteenth century. Older ones, written in Latin, occasionally contained Polish proper names (in the *Bulla* of Gniezno from 1138 we find about 400 Polish names of people and places). The Bible of Queen Sophia from the middle of the fifteenth century, preserved only in part, is the oldest known translation of the Bible into Polish.

Latin as the language of education, science, religion, and partly of state administration, was used in Poland until the mid-eighteenth century, although it was being progressively replaced by Polish. In the sixteenth century, the Renaissance period in Poland, the literary output in Polish became considerable. The writings of important authors contributed to the great upsurge of Polish, the creation of the literary language of that epoch. Modern Polish spelling also evolved in the course of that century from the policies of the first Polish publishing houses in Kraków. Polish vocabulary was enriched by coining new words from Polish morphemes as well as by borrowings from other languages. Borrowings from Latin, Czech, German, Italian, French, Ukrainian, Belorussian, Russian, Turkish and Hungarian (and more recently from English) can be found in large numbers in the Polish language. The influence of the Belorussian and Ukrainian languages occurred not only in the vocabulary but also the grammatical system of Polish.

The period from the mid-seventeenth to the mid-eighteenth century is generally regarded as the time of the decline of Polish, which had become permeated by many Latin borrowings, especially in its written form. The noblemen most often chose to speak Latin. Among aristocrats and at the royal court it was fashionable to speak French. Polish was treated as a language of the lower classes. People of high culture and education used in their writings a cumbersome and unnecessarily complicated style, ornate and full of obscurities, an 'elegant Latin'. Latin was still the language of instruction in schools. For boys only, these were established and conducted mostly by Jesuits from the end of the sixteenth century till 1773 when the order was disbanded. They either tolerated the mother tongue as an auxiliary medium in the two lower forms and during recreations, or banned it completely. Girls from rich families were educated in schools managed by nuns, where mainly French but also some Polish was taught (Klemensiewicz, 1981). The majority of Poles at that time were illiterate.

The situation changed during the reign of Stanisław August Poniatowski in the latter half of the eighteenth century, when a group of enlightened people set out to make the upper classes of society appreciate their mother tongue. The first periodicals written in Polish began to appear. Under royal auspices the Commission of National Education (*Komisja Edukacji Narodowej*, KEN), regarded as the first ministry of education in Europe, was created in 1773 to prepare and execute an educational reform. The Society for Elementary Handbooks, established in 1775, took care of the preparation of Polish textbooks for teaching reading and writing, grammar, arithmetic, religion, history and other school subjects. Onufry Kopczyński wrote the Grammar for National Schools (*Gramatyka dla szkół narodowych*), published in 1778–83. It was one of the first books of Polish grammar intended not for foreigners learning Polish but for Polish schoolchildren and officially recommended for classroom use.

The Commission of National Education directed that all the teaching in elementary parochial schools was to be conducted through the medium of Polish. Only in secondary schools and in the universities was it recommended to teach some subjects in Latin. The Jagiellonian University in Kraków with its still medieval structure of studies was reformed and modernized. In place of the closed Jesuit schools many progressive schools conducted by the religious order of the Piars were created. Some of the clergy contributed significantly to the reform of culture and education, indeed many KEN members were priests. The reformers of the educational system realized that learning foreign languages (mainly Latin, German and French) was useful, but as one of them, the professor of rhetoric and poetry Filip Golański, insisted that only a thorough knowledge of the rules of language (with its various structures of meaning, ways of speaking and expressing one's thoughts) acquired while learning their Polish mother tongue would enable pupils to learn one or more foreign languages easily and effectively (Klemensiewicz, 1981). Unfortunately, members and supporters of KEN were unable to execute all the reforms they had planned because of the political situation which led to foreign occupation.

At the end of the eighteenth century Poland lost most of her independence in three partitions. The neighbouring states, Russia, Prussia and Austria, which had seized Polish territory, gradually banned the use of Polish as a language of instruction – particularly in Prussia and Russia after the uprisings of 1830, 1831 and 1863–64. It was the most difficult period for Polish when, in the foreign occupiers' administration, judiciary and school system, mainly German or Russian was used. At the end of the nineteenth century in the part of Poland seized by Russia even Polish sermons and prayers in the Roman Catholic Church were banned. Priests who in spite of that ban continued to say them were persecuted. Strict censorship was enforced on everything that was published in Polish. Preserving the Polish language and culture in such conditions – by clandestine private education, church services and reading books published abroad – was seen as one of the most important actions of patriotic Poles. Language became the hallmark of national identity. The writings of the great Polish romantic writers, living and working abroad, first and foremost those of Adam Mickiewicz and Juliusz Słowacki, contributed much to the flourishing of the Polish literary language of this period.

During the enforced instruction in German or Russian in the latter half of the nineteenth century the defenders of Polish tended to be national purists who sought to purge the language of foreign elements, even those well adapted to Polish and which were sometimes necessary. However, this never assumed the same dimensions as, for example, in Czech. Words of Greek and Latin origin present in many European languages were not rejected. Most of the German and Russian borrowings of that period disappeared gradually when Poland regained her independence in 1918. In the interwar period education and instruction in Polish was restored.

CONTEMPORARY POLISH

Modern General (also called Common) Polish (*polszczyzna ogólna*) is characterized by a high degree of homogeneity. In the spoken language one can observe some regional features: Cracovian, Varsovian, Poznanian, Northeastern, but they are generally limited to lexical differences. The local dialects are richly diversified, yet endangered and quickly disappearing varieties of Polish. Only the oldest villagers still speak their dialects, using some borrowings from the general variety as well. The middle-aged and the young living in the country most frequently speak what are called semi-dialects of General Polish, containing a certain element of the dialectal features of the area in question. The language of the first-generation intelligentsia also often contains a dialectal element, a legacy of the dismemberment of the country before 1918, when there was no single administrative authority. The factors facilitating the homogenization of Polish include: the post World War Two migration of people from the east to the west of the country; from villages to towns; general social mobility; the relatively easy access to education under Communism; and the development of the mass media. The role of social and professional idiolects, however, increases as the territorial diversity loses ground.

It is worth mentioning that there is a local movement sustaining the Kashubian tongue in parts of Pomerania. Linguists and non-linguists continue to discuss its status. In Polish linguistic literature concerning the topic there is a general consent that Kashubian is a dialect of Polish (or rather a group of dialects), though undoubtedly it is the most distant from General Polish and from the central dialects also. The representatives of Kashubian society argue that their tongue is a separate language, as do some scholars from abroad who use the term Pomeranian language in Germany. Among Polish linguists Alfred Majewicz (1986, 1989) is of the opinion that Kashubian is a dialect of Polish, while Witold Mańczak (1995) holds the contrary view.

GENERAL POLISH AND ITS ACCEPTANCE AS 'STANDARD'

General Polish, which evolved as the speech of those social classes whose members came from different parts of the vast country (in the seventeenth century the Polish–Lithuanian Commonwealth occupied the largest territory in Europe) and who had reasons to communicate with one another is, though itself a dialect, given out as common and 'correct' Polish, with no obvious dialectal features. The term 'standard' is not used, but 'correct', on the other hand, crops up frequently. Grammars have contributed to its codification, and its use by writers in administration and education have led to its expansion. In the process of constant use General Polish is likely to undergo change which, in turn, will find acceptance in grammars and other works. Hence the generally tolerant attitude towards General Polish which does not stop recent changes from becoming codified and accepted as 'correct'.

As Polish socio-linguists indicate, 'the quantitative integration is accompanied by a certain qualitative disintegration' of the General Polish language (Kurkowska, 1981). A considerable number of users, especially the less well educated, have difficulties with using this variety of language, in observing the rules of 'correctness' in their speech and at the same time making it clear and precise. The phenomenon contributes to a sort of erosion of the earlier rules of 'correctness' which does not necessarily mean 'fixed'. Being possessors of the common language, most users take an active interest in it and disapprove of the persistent neglect of both grammatical and stylistic rules, particularly in public speeches. Offences diminish their respect for the speakers who are guilty of it, and may even make the latter seem ridiculous, disregarding other merits and competences. For example, former President Lech Wałęsa's way of speaking had a negative influence on his public image. Evaluations of the language of the mass media, too, are diverse in Polish society. It seems that for most listeners to radio and viewers of TV broadcasts and readers of newspapers the language of the media is consciously or unconsciously taken as a model to imitate. They consider it superior to their own everyday language. Educated people, on the other hand, often criticize the usage of the media. They find it careless, abounding in errors and obscure passages. It is noteworthy that most criticism is light-hearted and critics see the funny side more often than they point out mistakes. Professional linguists also make many critical remarks about the language of the media, though their opinion about a particular passage is usually more detached compared with that of average users. Against that, some features of the language of the media, such as the frequency of nominal constructions in news bulletins (which makes their style rather heavy), noticed by those linguists who have done research on the subject (Honowska, 1972), are probably seldom noticed by the average newspaper reader. There is a high readership of newspapers and much watching of more serious TV.

There are many Polish linguists in university centres such as Warsaw, Kraków, Poznań and Wrocław who are engaged in research in the field of normative linguistics, which in Poland is more often called 'the culture of language' (*kultura języka*). The latter term is wider than the former, and concerns not only the grammatical and lexical 'correctness' of a spoken or written text but also takes note of its appropriateness to the subject of discourse, the listeners and readers involved, and the aims and the targets of their discourse. It helps authors to make their speech clear, brief, logical, aesthetically pleasing in form and effective. Their discipline, also used in schools, includes both theoretical reflection on the rules of 'correctness' (criteria of normative evaluation of utterances, and concepts of error) and an element of practical linguistic advice. The accepted task of linguists is to observe the modern usage, to compare it to the traditional ways of speaking and writing, to define the evolutionary tendencies of contemporary Polish and to formulate the rules of 'correct' Polish by preparing normative dictionaries, books and periodicals devoted to the problems of 'correctness'.

As in France, there is general support, almost an affection, for the language and its development. This is less concerned with imposing rules than with encouraging 'language culture' in education and literature. Two important organizations, the Association of Language Lovers (*Towarzystwo Miłośników Języka Polskiego*), founded in 1920 in Kraków by Kazimierz Nitsch, and the Society for the Culture of Language (*Towarzystwo Kultury Języka*), formed in 1966 in Warsaw by Witold Doroszewski, work on disseminating the culture of language among speakers of Polish (indeed, similar efforts were also made earlier). These societies are not official state institutions. Their pronouncements on linguistic problems have no legal power. Only universal acceptance by educated people gives their suggestions a sort of validation. The societies publish two periodicals: the bimonthly, *Język Polski* (Polish Language) in Kraków, and the monthly *Poradnik Językowy* (Language Guide) in Warsaw. They popularize 'knowledge about language' by organizing public lectures, making radio and TV broadcasts with the participation of university professors, secondary school teachers and others, and give practical linguistic guidance over the telephone or in newspaper articles. The title of one of Jan Miodek's popular television programmes bore the characteristic title: Fatherland – Polishness (*Ojczyzna – Polszczyzna*). Contrary to the case in France, in Poland there is no official institution authorized by the government to supervise the language and to codify its rules, nor are there laws regulating language politics. However, some well-known professors have been accepted as authorities in matters of a broadly understood 'correctness'. As the authors or editors of popular dictionaries, they have had much influence on modern usage in respect of the 'cultured' dialect and the literary Polish language. Witold Doroszewski's 1982 dictionary is accepted as standard and authorized for use in schools. The role of the schools and Polish language teachers in the popularization of the culture of language must also be taken into account, though obviously not all teachers are judged to be equally competent in the matter of linguistic 'correctness'. Committees of scholars look at spelling reform and grammatical issues and publish recommendations, but these are infrequent; the last spelling reform was in 1935 and there have been only minor adjustments since.

Many Polish linguists approved of Halina Kurkowska's proposal for three different sets of rules: everyday speech, public (official) speech and model speech rules (the last being the most rigorous) to be applied according to different types of language context situations, (Kurkowska, 1977). However, the acceptance of this is rare in practical language advice and even less common in school teaching. Another linguist, Halina Satkiewicz (1990), distinguishes three different attitudes among people interested in language politics and who include not only professional linguists but also teachers, writers, journalists and ordinary people. These are:

- *conservative* – people should observe all the traditional rules. That was generally the attitude taken by older linguists such as Stanisław Szober and Witold Doroszewski, though it does not mean that they never accepted innovations themselves.

- *liberal* (*lenient*) – the functional criterion should be the basis for the evaluation of utterances (a good example of this attitude is Jan Miodek in his advisory activity and theoretical reflections).

- *democratic* (*even nihilistic*) – linguists should not interfere with the autonomous and free development of the language. This view is seldom maintained consistently and it is difficult to quote any names in support.

The first and the third of these attitudes are nowadays rather rare.

There is now no unquestionable linguistic élite which can be set up as a model to be imitated by the rest of society. As has been shown, maintenance of a 'correct' standard is not imposed from above but depends on the acceptance of the authority of educational linguists and the creative users of the language. Ordinary people can follow the usage of members of the intelligentsia, particularly those working in the humanities, though their language is not beyond reproach either. They are criticized for using too many borrowings from foreign languages, which makes their speech, and especially their writings, less intelligible to the ordinary users. That the usage of the linguists themselves should become the model for students, teachers and all who care about the 'correctness' of speech seems just as problematic, a rather inconvenient and abnormal situation likely to lead to subjectivism as far as their advice is concerned. To avoid this users need another point of reference. In the nineteenth century this was the language of literature, the language of such writers as Henryk Sienkiewicz, Bolesław Prus, Eliza Orzeszkowa and others. Contemporary writers reserve for themselves the right to use the language more freely, in their own individual ways, according to the artistic patterns they pursue in their writings. Linguistic experiments, often present in literary texts, reduce the possibility of treating the language of literature as a model usage for other purposes.

Apparently most linguists now approve of linguistic liberalism and accept all those innovative ways of speaking (propagated mainly by the mass media) which seem useful in improving communication and are widespread, and which are supplanting the traditional ones found in everyday speech. Language politics, or 'language pedagogy' as Zenon Klemensiewicz (1947) preferred to call it, is now understood by professional linguists as the popularization of good usage, of knowledge about language and of attention to beautiful style rather than the spending of time in fighting against errors. This last aspect dominated the normative activity of linguists towards the end of the nineteenth century and in the interwar period. However, in present-day Poland no state institution is responsible for pronouncing on any linguistic rules or trying to influence the shape of General Polish.

Most linguistic experts are of the opinion that thorough research into the system of the language, the history of linguistic phenomena and the dynamics of contemporary language should precede the giving of any professional linguistic advice. Such linguists must also have in mind the social functions of the language, which are accepted as being required in different varieties and styles of speech. That requires suggestions as to what is 'appropriate' in a particular context of communication rather than what is 'correct' in the language (Bugajski, 1993).

Examples of some language 'alternatives'

According to the opinion of Stanisław Urbańczyk (1977), the *usus modernus excultus approbatus et promulgatus* becomes the standard of General Polish. The use here by the author of 'prescriptive Latin' is interesting since professional linguists are usually tolerant of regional elements in texts: that is, the words, inflexional forms or syntactic structures of a limited territorial extent used by educated people living in a particular region of the country. However, such tolerance is extended only to the spoken language. In written General Polish 'correct' structures are preferred. As to extensive borrowings from dialects, they are admitted neither in spoken nor written General Polish. Nor are they welcome in schools. Teachers try to eradicate them and make pupils use General Polish. The exceptions are the names of some specific country specialisms, products and events, for example, *oscypek*, 'a kind of cheese' or *baca*, 'a senior shepherd of sheep', which are borrowings from the dialect of Podhale used in General Polish. It is in fact difficult to draw a strict distinction between regional and dialectal elements when proceeding to evaluate speech.

As far as stylistic variants are concerned, it is hard to pronounce on the choice between them in a particular context using the simple categories of correct or incorrect. In oral communication the freedom of choice of linguistic elements is greater than in a written text, depending on the situation and the listener, and is regulated by somewhat vague rules of linguistic pragmatics, a kind of linguistic etiquette. Some variants have presentational value, to a careful listener they can tell something about the social or psychological characteristic of the speaker. A regional or dialect word or structure chosen from a territorial, or especially from a social dialect, can provide that information: *Ja dla niego powiedział* (I told him) instead of the general *Ja mu powiedziałem* characterizes the speaker as an uneducated man (the verb has a masculine form) from the north-eastern region of Poland. There exist some kinds of pronunciation which mark out the speaker as 'nervous' or 'childish' or 'pretentious': the latter of these is signalled by the exaggerated pronunciation of the nasal vowels especially at the end of a word.

The surplus of accepted equivalents may lessen the communicative effectiveness of language and require speakers to remember too many alternative words and grammatical forms. It is significant that students and adult users who ask teachers or linguists questions concerning the problem of 'correctness' usually dislike getting such answers as: 'both forms are correct', or 'the first form is more suitable in the context but the second will do also'. They would prefer to hear: 'the first form is good and the second is bad' because it is easier for them to memorize such a piece of information.

In familiar linguistic contacts between friends or relations, many occasional, non-standard forms and structures may occur; even dialect or archaic forms may be used on purpose, though the speaker will as a rule avoid them in more official utterances. Therefore, saying *Co słychować* (What's the news?) at the beginning of a conversation rather than the more usual *Co słychać* makes for closer contact and a less stereotypical utterance, on the assumption that the speaker knows which form is the 'correct' one and that his listener also knows this. Using such forms is often an example of playing with language. They are used by speakers who have an acute awareness of language and are able to exploit creatively the possibilities offered by the language system. Poles like playing with their language.

In colloquial speech there is a well-known tendency to use diminutives when this is not at all necessary: *pieniążki* instead of *pieniądze* (money), *ryneczek* instead of *rynek* (market). The phenomenon is widespread but linguists find it undesirable, making speech sound too childish. It seems to be a question of personal preference rather than of correctness.

Considerable harm to the Polish language (especially the type used in public speech) in the postwar period was done by the use of *nowomowa* (newspeak – the notion coined by George Orwell in his novel *Nineteen Eighty-Four*), that is, the use made of language by the official propaganda machine of the Communist rulers (1945–89) in political speeches, newspapers, radio and TV broadcasts. It was also employed in schools, offices and factories with the aim of distorting the information available about events and facts so as to promulgate the official ideology to the citizens and to organize their desired collective responses. A number of books and many papers have been written on the subject which demonstrate how the Polish variety of newspeak was formed and how it worked as an instrument of political manipulation (Głowiński, 1990; Sambor, 1985; Wierzbicki, 1987 and others). Indeed, some of its elements (certain expressions and loaded words) can still be heard in public speeches and in the usage of administration more than eight years after the change of the political system. A language-conscious listener or reader would react only reluctantly to the style of such propaganda. Indeed, it happened that speeches and articles intended to persuade people would occasionally seem absurd and ridiculous when they neglected the common rules of language and good style. Many humorists had a field-day parodying newspeak without being found out.

THE TEACHING OF POLISH IN SCHOOLS

The situation of contemporary Polish discussed above makes the task of the Polish mother tongue teacher rather difficult. There still does not exist an up-to-date, coherent description of the Polish grammatical system and vocabulary which is readily available for school use and would be acceptable to everyone. The approval of normative grammars is after all a subjective matter of choice.

In the eight-form elementary school, Polish is a compulsory subject with six weekly periods in forms I to III (elementary teaching) consisting of combined language (grammar) and literature lessons; in forms IV to VI there is one separate period of spelling, one period of grammar plus four periods of literature; and in forms V to VIII the five weekly periods are made up of one language and four literature periods. In order to move to secondary education (post-15), pupils have to pass an examination in Polish. If they fail the written examination they are given the opportunity to take an oral test. All school programmes are produced by the Ministry of National Education (*Ministerstwo Edukacji Narodowej,* MEN) through joint committees of pedagogues, subject specialists and administrators. The programmes contain detailed syllabuses which the teacher has to teach. There is a compulsory basic list of literature texts plus a longer supplementary list from which the teacher may choose. School inspections are used to check on how far teachers fulfil the programme requirements. This is done by the expedient of comparing entries in the teachers' record books with those of their pupils.

The detailed syllabuses of the subject called Polish Language (*Język polski*) in all Polish schools include teaching about language, as well as literature and cultural achievements. Within the parts concerned with language, the syllabuses are divided into exercises in speaking and writing and (theoretical) knowledge about language, mainly about its grammatical structure and vocabulary. In secondary-school syllabuses this part is enriched by some information concerning the history of the mother tongue, its change, varieties and registers. Teachers are encouraged to link exercises with explanations of the rules of grammar during the lessons as they become necessary. The output of modern linguistics of the last few decades has not until now had much impact on the teaching of what goes by the name of 'knowledge about language'. Mother tongue teaching is strongly rooted in the linguistic concepts formulated by Stanisław Szober before World War Two, continued and developed later by Witold Doroszewski and Zenon Klemensiewicz. The writings of these three linguists constitute the theoretical background used by the authors of basic schoolbooks which deal with language study. The traditional school grammar as taught contains many contradictions and is often incoherent. It has therefore been criticized in some linguistic writings and many improvements have been proposed. Teachers find it difficult to explain to their pupils such items as the category of gender and the inflectional and syntactic features of numerals in Polish.

The elementary school syllabuses (for children aged 7–15) for Polish recommend, above all, the training of pupils' communicative skills. Another important objective 'should be to provide them with some form of (more or less abstract) knowledge about language'. In the first three years Polish Language lessons consist mainly of learning to read and to write and of developing children's ability to express their thoughts in speech. In year four some basic information about sentence structure is acquired in the following forms: knowledge about verbs, their conjugation (which is complex in Polish); syntactic features and their links with other parts of speech which are gradually introduced in the course of teaching. In forms IV, V and VI knowledge about language is presented alongside literary education in the course of the same lesson; in forms VII and VIII some lessons are intended exclusively for education in language.

In secondary schools (ages 15–19, or 15–20), knowledge about language occupies a rather more marginal place. Literary and cultural education dominates most of the time set aside for Polish language lesson. The coursebooks, four volumes of *Język i My* (*Our Language and Us*: I–IV in the secondary schools) edited in 1986–90, were prepared by well-known linguists and methodologists. The books are more up-to-date, compared with those for the elementary schools, in taking account of the achievements of modern functional linguistics, sociolinguistics and lexicology. They contain some information on the history of Polish and its evolution. Nevertheless, some Polish mother-tongue teachers admit that they tend to make little use of the books because, overburdened with literary material, they do not get time during the lesson for 'knowledge about language', which is often considered a less-important component than 'knowledge about literature'. The most common form of practical language education is writing compositions. Many students tend to use a very conventional style (*styl szablonowy*), some of them trying to elaborate a very ornate style which, when awkwardly handled, may turn absurd. This can be observed rather too often in the essays written by candidates for Polish philology studies during their entrance examinations.

After 1989, reading lists for elementary and secondary schools were reviewed, books propagating Communist ideology (kept before on the lists though not seriously studied) were removed and some which had been banned by the censors were reinstated. A thorough reform of all the school syllabuses is now in the course of discussion and preparation. This includes, for example, how language in communicational situations can be shown to pupils in more interesting and instructive ways. For the transitional stage, very brief and concise 'minimal syllabuses' (*Minimum programowe*), which do not entirely abolish but modify the earlier syllabuses, were prepared and announced by the Ministry of Education in 1992 (MEN, 1992). Teachers are encouraged to propose and put into effect their own syllabuses, which have become known as 'author's syllabuses'.

Meanwhile more time has been found for 'knowledge about language', particularly language change. A minimal syllabus of mother-tongue Polish for secondary schools emphasizes the practical skills, precision, logic, force (*ekspresja*) and ease (*swoboda*) required when presenting one's thoughts, editing one's own and other people's texts, an appropriate pronunciation and intonation – in short, summing it up as '*kultura języka*' (MEN, 1992). Secondary school graduates should know the basics of communication, which uses speech, history of Polish, stylistics, phraseology and again 'correctness' and *kultura językowa*, with particular attention to contemporary Polish in its numerous varieties (MEN, 1992).

School teaching methods cannot be said to be exactly 'modern', however, use is made of audio-visual equipment and IT in the general instruction in skills, literature and culture.

TEACHER PREPARATION

Teachers of mother tongue Polish receive their professional education and preparation at university or the higher pedagogical schools (*wyższe szkoły pedagogiczne*), specializing in Polish philology. This includes five years of language and literature studies together with the methodology of teaching mother tongue Polish, ending with a Master's degree. Recently, some private colleges were created to speed up the process of training, requiring three years of study and finishing with a licence. This is only available for existing (non-graduate) teachers on secondment and future elementary school teachers.

Among the subjects taught to Polish philology students are the descriptive grammar of Polish, general linguistics, the diachronic grammar of Polish, history of the Polish language, and also, sometimes, dialectology and lexicology, which are often optional subjects. There is a considerable gap between what the future teachers are taught at the universities as linguistic knowledge and what they are supposed to teach to their school pupils when they start work. It cannot be totally explained by the understandable difference of levels of teaching; it is necessary to take account of the important difference in attitudes. To learn the formal system of Polish grammar is challenging. It demands an understanding of the rules and also a good memory. Spelling is also often regarded as beyond the ability of the average Pole.

As a rule, Polish language specialists are required to teach Polish only; occasionally in small rural schools they may have to teach other subjects. They are accepted for employment after successful completion of study without further tests. However, they have to undergo a long period of probation before their posts are made permanent.

OTHER MOTHER TONGUES AND FOREIGN LANGUAGES

Members of minorities living in Poland are for the most part bilingual. Teaching of their own mother tongue is available where the parents demand it and sign for it. In a few elementary and secondary schools minority languages are the medium of instruction; in rather more they are taught as second languages. Of the modern foreign languages, which are begun in the elementary school, English is the most popular, followed by German and French. Russian has never been popular, although it was a compulsory subject under the Communists. There is a shortage of English teachers.

Polish, when it started being taught in schools in the eighteenth century, was also taught to the other nationalities in the old Commonwealth in the same way as to Poles. The peasantry could receive limited tuition in their own mother tongues. There are not many special arrangements or methods for teaching Polish as a second language. Where it is taught abroad it is taught mainly to ethnic Poles.

Difficulties in the education system have to do mainly with the economic crises of the 1970s and 1980s and the efforts required for completing reforms necessitated by changing ideologies as well as modernization.

Chapter 14

Maintaining the Mother Tongue: The National Identity of the Belorussians in Poland

Elżbieta Czykwin

INTRODUCTION

Belorussians inhabit the river and forest lands of northeastern central Europe. The 10.3 million Belorussians live within the borders of the present-day republic of Belarus, with minorities to be found in the frontier areas of neighbouring countries, especially Russia, Poland, Lithuania, Latvia and the Ukraine. The majority of Belorussians living in the major cities speak Russian as their first language, in the countryside on the other hand most people regard Belorussian, an East-Slavonic language, as their mother tongue. Russian and Polish are widely understood throughout the country.

The Belorussian minority in Poland is an autochthonous community living mainly in the eastern part of the country: south and east of the city of Białystok. The Belorussians reside in larger communities in the rural areas. In some villages and towns they constitute the majority of the population: for example, around the towns of Bielsk Podlaski and Hajnówka.

The population of this community is estimated at 250,000–300,000 people (0.7–0.8 per cent of the total population of Poland), which makes this group the second largest of all minorities: the German being the largest. Unlike the Germans who had immigrated to Poland, Belorussians are a territorial part of what used to be the Polish-Lithuanian Commonwealth, the northeastern areas of which, now the modern republics of Lithuania and Belarus, were inhabited by a Belorussian majority. Generally, most Belorussians, unlike the Poles, are members of the [Greek] Orthodox Church. Because some Ukrainians, Lemks and Poles are also members of the Orthodox Church, the criterion of religion alone is not sufficient to distinguish between them. However, there are not very many Belorussian-speaking Catholics who identify themselves as Belorussians. Some Belorussians have joined the Catholic Church through marrying Poles.

The Belorussians are not always aware of their nationality. For this reason, they behave as a typical borderland community without a specific national consciousness but with a strong feeling of their local identity which is often a deliberate substitute for a declared national identity. Many of these people think of themselves as a 'minority', 'the 'locals' and they call their language 'local', 'ordinary', 'everyday' or just their 'common language', 'the language which is from "here"'.

POLISH POSTWAR POLICY TOWARDS THE BELORUSSIANS

The Orthodox Belorussians under the prevailing influence of the Catholic Poles were exposed to the vagaries of various socio-political and religious movements. Until recently they were often regarded and treated by the authorities as a community less well endowed with a cultural tradition which should be brought up to the level of Polish culture. After World War Two, the Communist government pursued a policy of repression which further limited all distinct Belorussian community and religious activity (Keosten, 1989).

In the 1950s the policy was much liberalized (Tomaszewski, 1991). However, the anti-Jewish demonstrations of March 1968 badly affected government policy towards the minorities. The authorities propagated the slogan: 'Poland – a homogeneous country'. This led to the 1976 resolution of the second plenary session of the Communist Party Central Committee which defined the 'morally political unity' of the Polish nation. It was followed by further discriminatory actions: among others, the Polonization of place names and the names of businesses in the Bieszczady Region of South-Western Poland. As a result, in the 1970s the ethnic minorities became publicly invisible. Their situation 'was similar to the way fishes swim in an aquarium. People shouted, some saw but nobody could hear them.' Although the actual situation of the different minorities varied, this was the position of most groupings (Berdychowska, 1990).

Initially, Belorussians were suspicious of the *Solidarność* (Solidarity) movement at the beginning of the 1980s because it took up mainly Polish national and Catholic values. On the other hand the rise of the movement showed the ethnic groups how to establish their own independent organizations.

After August 1980, the minorities addressed a large number of petitions to the authorities. They demanded, among other things, the award of the status of political representation to their existing social-cultural associations, and the right to be represented in the *Sejm* (the lower house of the Polish Parliament) as well as in local people's councils, municipal parliaments, access to the media, and more subsidies for their publications. At the time the managements of their own societies and organizations were bitterly criticized. In 1981 the authorities defied attempts to legalize Belorussian, Lithuanian and Ukrainian student organizations which were supported by the independent student organization of *Solidarność* and which was operating in the universities at the time.

Later *Solidarność* leaders began to appreciate the importance of the ethnic minority groups for fighting their own cause of political freedom. On 7 October 1981 the First Congress of *Solidarność* in Gdańsk passed its resolution on national minorities' rights. However, this neither appeared strong enough to those communities nor did it much affect their general negative attitude towards the *Solidarność* movement as a whole. The outcome was that the problem of national minorities, tackled in terms of Poland's relations with her neighbour countries, moved into the limelight. The Catholic press and the Catholic political circles, mainly the weeklies *Tygodnik Powszechny*, *Więź* and *Znak*, did much to keep the issue in the foreground (Dawidziuk, 1991). In the middle of the 1980s, the entire *Solidarność* and anti-government opposition became concerned about the problems caused by the split in the opposition and so collaboration was established between minority and opposition leaders.

On 18 December 1988 the National Social Committee was formed as an advisory body to Lech Wałęsa, then chairman of the *Solidarność* trade unions. The Committee appointed the Commission on National Minorities. Towards the end of the 1980s they were rapid and far-reaching changes in the international situation, particularly in what was then the USSR. These developments greatly stimulated the processes of socio-political and economic reforms in Poland.

After the June 1989 parliamentary elections minorities were free for the first time since World War Two to enter the political arena in Poland. Lech Wałęsa's declaration 'To the electorate', a document of great importance, particularly since it was also published in the minority languages, addressed itself to the problems of the religious and national minorities. Włodzimierz Mokry was elected to the *Sejm* as a representative of the Ukrainian minority and of the *Solidarność* movement because many Poles also voted for him. Eugeniusz Czykwin, a Belorussian, supported by the Orthodox Church, was also elected.

On the other hand, the varying amounts of subsidies designated for the Belorussians demonstrate the absence of a stable financial policy towards minority groups. In 1988 the monies amounted to a total of 119 million złotys (equivalent to 11,900 [new] złotys [about £3,500], in 1989 the sums rose to 216,000 in (new) złotys and up again to 1,650,800 złotys in 1990. In the year 1991 they were reduced to 599,500 złotys. The same sum was disbursed in 1992. Berdychowska (1990), quotes the amounts disbursed by the Ministry of Culture and Art for minority cultural activities. Since members of the minority communities live in different provinces, government fiscal policy must be seen as evidence of the strength of support given to particular areas of the country. Clearly, close co-operation between the ethnic groups and the local authorities assumes great importance.

Even so, it must be said that recent government policy has responded to the demands of the situation. An example which illustrates this very well is the attitude of *Solidarność* leaders towards the major petition presented by the communities of the ethnic minorities – to have the law on national minorities passed by the Polish parliament. In 1989 when they first entered the *Sejm*, the Solidarity group had a draft for it. Unfortunately, the government of Tadeusz Mazowiecki failed to put forward the proposal which would grant minority rights in education and local administration before it fell. However, this law is now being implemented in terms of minority schooling and the maintenance of places of worship. Particularly hotly disputed is the right to church property.

TEACHING BELORUSSIAN

Maintaining the mother tongue undoubtedly is the key element for the Belorussians trying to safeguard and nurture their own distinctive culture and tradition. Sustaining their religion is also as equally important. The law which legalizes the teaching of ethnic languages in Poland is the regulation of 24 March 1993 of the Minister of National Education (MEN), which enables the preservation of pupils' and students' national, ethnic and linguistic identities (*Dziennik Ustaw*, 1993). This law stipulates that the minority language can be taught if the parents file a petition within the time required for curriculum preparation for the new school year. The application once agreed will remain valid until the child completes elementary schooling at age 15 or nursery schooling at age 6. The relevant clauses mention the following four models:

Article 4. Other mother tongues will be taught in:

1. nursery schools and schools where the teaching medium is the pupils' mother tongue (other than Polish);

2. nursery schools and schools where the official language (Polish) and the other mother tongue (ethnic language) are both spoken by pupils;

3. schools where the ethnic language is an optional subject;

4. interschool groups teaching ethnic languages.

Under model 1, the Polish language can be taught in nursery schools but only for four hours a week and in groups of 6-year old children also in elementary schools but only in Polish literature and history classes (article 5).

The teaching of languages other than Polish can be made available only if seven pupils of an elementary school or 14 pupils of a secondary school after consulting their parents declare their wish to have such lessons (article 6). The schools for the minorities are financed in accordance with the laws and regulations affecting state schools. According to information given by Piotr Idzikowski, a Provincial School Superintendent, when addressing the Parliamentary Commission on National Minorities on 12 December 1992, the monthly maintenance cost of one minority pupil in an elementary school is 35 złotys (£7) while that of single pupil from a Ukrainian language school is 47 złotys (£10) covering tuition and teaching materials.

Belorussian is taught in 43 elementary schools and two general education secondary schools in Hajnówka and Bielsk Podlaski. The Belorussian classes are conducted as additional lessons for three to four hours a week, that is model 2 above. The total number of pupils who learn the language is 3,651, of whom 3,030 are in the elementary schools and 621 in general education secondary schools, that is schools preparing for universities (Litermus, 1992). Belorussian is taught in no nursery school, neither is there a school where Belorussian is the language of instruction (model 1 above). Unlike children learning other ethnic languages, the number of pupils studying Belorussian is steadily decreasing. Tables 14.1 and 14.2, on page 178, illustrate this trend.

A very limited amount of Belorussian may be taught as part of religious instruction, although this is not official language policy pursued by the Orthodox Church. In fact the language used in such classes is a mixed Polish/Belorussian dialect. Teaching Belorussian in these circumstances is difficult in any case because instruction is mainly oral while religious terms exist in the official language of the Church which is Old Church Slavonic.

It is difficult to explain why the numbers of pupils learning Belorussian is falling in comparison with the trend towards learning mother tongues other than Polish. One of the main reasons is the attractiveness of other languages, not only Polish or English as in the case of the Lithuanian minority, but also of Ukrainian, Russian and indeed Old Church Slavonic, all of which are particularly attractive to Belorussians, according to oral evidence from Belorussian teachers in Bielsk Podlaski and Hajnówka.

The fact that Belorussian is used mainly as a spoken medium further limits its appeal. Particularly unfortunate is the absence of satisfactory cultural contacts with the republic of Belarus, which has its own somewhat ambivalent language priority policies. Belorussians

Table 14.1 Number of schools teaching ethnic languages other than German. Source: Litermus, 1992

Language	School Year					
	1978–79	1988–89	1989–90	1990–91	1991–92	1992–93
Belorussisn	46	59	47	50	48	45
Ukranian	50	47	40	45	45	50
Lithuanian	20	11	12	14	14	13
Slovak	13	23	22	19	19	18
Total	129	140	121	128	126	126

Table 14.2 Number of pupils learning their ethnic language other than German. Source: Litermus, 1992

Language	School Year					
	1978–79	1988–89	1989–90	1990–91	1991–92	1992–93
Belorussisn	4265	4321	3928	3717	3553	3611
Ukranian	440	926	1055	1350	1465	1642
Lithuanian	480	662	670	708	816	716
Slovak	466	549	465	461	471	529
Total	5651	6458	6118	6236	6305	6498

living in Poland think of themselves as loyal Polish citizens. This lack of a positive Belorussian identification gives rise to the schizophrenic situation in which, on the one hand, the Belorussians feel obliged to be trustworthy Polish nationals, while, on the other hand, they feel a cultural affinity not so much with Belarus itself but with the Eastern Slavs in general and most of all with the Orthodox Church.

As far as relations with Poles are concerned it seems that the most important obstacle to being fully accepted in the Polish community is the Belorussians' less than fluent knowledge of Polish. The educational reasons why the teaching of Belorussian is not as effective as that of the other minority languages are the low standard of teaching methods, out-of-date and hastily prepared coursebooks and poorly qualified teachers. Interestingly, Belorussian teachers on the whole are less well qualified than their German or Ukrainian colleagues, with fewer specialists and university graduates.

All language coursebooks for the minorities used to be subsidized by the government and distributed free of charge. This policy has been modified. Due to high publishing costs they will now be sold at prices equal to those of other school books .Their poor quality is not simply the result of poor printing standards. What is more important is that the methodology used is far behind the present demands and expectations of modern foreign and second language teaching methods. In addition their content still reflects the period under the Soviet Union when Belarus was not independent. Therefore, there are no comments in them on current developments in Belarus and their impact on readers. Although published in Poland, their contents and layout are determined by experts from Belarus. The literary Belorussian used is difficult for speakers of the dialect spoken in Poland which consists of many additional Ukrainian, Russian, Polish and Lithuanian elements. Teachers do not pay sufficient attention to this problem, despite the fact that this is the language spoken in class. Since the teachers themselves come from the community in which the dialect with its different elements is spoken, and because they speak fluent Polish and Russian, it is perhaps not so surprising that they are tolerant of those pupils who use the same idiom and make the same 'mistakes'.

Even so, some form of Belorussian is basically known and understood by most of the local minority and extra-curricular approaches to language tuition are popular with learners. Papers such as the weekly *Niwa* with a run of more than 2,000 copies, *Czasopis* (3,000 copies) and the religious monthly, *Przegląd Prawosławny* (6,000 copies) cater for these interests. The local Białystok radio station broadcasts a 15-minute Belorussian programme, *Pod znakiem Pogoni*, on weekday mornings repeated in the afternoons. The other 15-minute afternoon programme *Sobotnia* presents more in the way of cultural and literary issues. The 30-minute Sunday programme has two parts: one is devoted to the Orthodox Church and its rituals, the other deals with local cultural developments. TV programmes are irregular, with Belorussian issues often discussed in Polish. It is possible to see Minsk TV programmes, although reception is badly affected by the long distance. Since October 1956 the Belorussian Social and Cultural Society has functioned in Białystok. The Belorussian Students' Association (BAS), the Białowieża Association of Belorussian Writers, Belorussian Youth Union and the political party, Belorussian Democratic Union, are all active.

LANGUAGE CONTACTS

Belorussian and Polish

Even someone with only an elementary knowledge of both languages will be struck by their similarity which goes back to their proto-Slavonic origin. The Krewa treaty between the Kingdom of Poland and the Grand Duchy of Lithuania of 1385 and particularly the treaty of Union (*Unia Lubelska*, 1569) brought the two languages (Belorussian rather than Lithuanian and Polish) in close contact, with Polish exerting an influence on the development of Belorussian (Smułkowa, 1988). Belorussian borrowings from Polish reflected the emergence of the new socio-political, cultural and religious reality of the eastern part of the Commonwealth in which Poland was the dominant partner. The Polonization of Belorussian and Lithuanian nobles was a swift process, which also affected their speech. By the end of the seventeenth century the language whose standardized literary form had served as an official language and had been used in various religious and secular writings had suffered a decline.

From the second half of the sixteenth century (especially in the mainly Lithuanian-speaking part of the Grand Duchy of Lithuania) Latin, a language widely used in Poland, was felt to be linguistically closer to Lithuanian and further reduced the use of Belorussian (Żurauski, 1967). These developments intensified the process of Polonization. Official approval of the existing state of affairs came with the 1569 resolution of the Warsaw General Conference which provided that official documents should be written in Polish, not in Belorussian (Żurauski, 1967). Orthodox Church practice of writing religious texts in Old Church Slavonic and the use of Russian in sermons were further setbacks for Belorussian. From the second half of the seventeenth century printing houses which used to publish in Belorussian began to print in Old Church Slavonic only. Folk or dialect Belorussian withstood the compelling force of Polonization and survived the collapse of literature by writing in an enriched dialect. This became the source of the rebirth of the modern Belorussian literary language in the nineteenth century. Another blend with Lithuanian was the base for the so-called 'borderland Polish' tongue.

Ironically, it was the Catholic Church that played a key role in the process of the national resurgence of the Belorussians in the nineteenth century. From there came the most active representatives of revival inspired by the *Nasza Niwa* movement with Bronisław Taraszkiewicz. However, Orthodox Church believers soon became the majority of those writing Belorussian literature (Żurauski and Kramko, 1973). The two cultures marked their separateness by using their own alphabets: Latin and modern Cyrillic. In 1859 tsarist censorship banned the publication of Mickiewicz's epic poem *Pan Tadeusz* because it was printed in the Latin script.

As a minority language Belorussian suffers from social as well as linguistic prejudices. The linguist, Ewa Smułkowa, rightly holds to the view that the opinions of many leading linguistic researchers about the 'structural weakness' of Belorussian are wrong. The weakness of the language does not lie in its structure but in the social-political and cultural life of the nation which uses it (Smułkowa, 1988).

Socially, the prestige of Belorussian and Polish is unequal. People have a 'much higher opinion' of Polish. Apart from the legacy of history the reason for this is that Belorussian is used mostly orally and those who speak it cannot refer to written standards. The use of the Cyrillic alphabet is a barrier to those using the Latin alphabet. Those who regularly use spoken Belorussian prefer to read, not to mention write, in Polish. For the present generation of Belorussians living in towns and villages where they are a large or the dominant group, Belorussian is just as much their language as Polish. The generation which was brought up before TV was introduced considered Belorussian to be their first language and their mother tongue. However, the new generation learning Belorussian and Polish regard Belorussian as their second ethnic language.

Belorussian brings back memories of home, farmstead occupations and the local community. It is the language of privacy as opposed to Polish, which is synonymous with the big world: media, politics and career. The distinction between Polish and Belorussian can be perfectly described in this saying: 'The Lord created the village and man created the city'. Belorussian is associated with the authentic realm of nature, worshipping and farming, in contrast to the artificial, anonymous and official world of seductive illusions. Belorussians migrating to the urban areas in large number do this because of the shortage of jobs, and good post-elementary schools as well as poor living standards in the countryside, in areas which are called 'The Eastern Wall'. Such a move is seen as a social rise. Though exposed to Polish, the first generation of migrants does not lose contact with the language of their parents. They often go to see their families in the country and support each other. City-dwellers find it easier to use Belorussian in such situations as counting, reprimanding children, discussing technical details or building operations, telling jokes and singing.

The Achilles heel of the Belorussian tongue as compared to Polish can be identified in terms of the greater attractiveness of Poland. Though the same dialect is spoken on both sides of the border, the long-standing separation and the different economic and political living conditions in Poland and the former Soviet Belorussia favour Poland as the chosen homeland.

The second generation of migrants do not regularly use their grandparents' language. In their case it is the Orthodox Church that prevents assimilation. However, the autocephalous Orthodox Church in Poland stands for the idea of superiority of faith over national issues. It does not support any particular ethnic group of believers. Archbishop Bazyli, the Metropolitan of the Orthodox Church in Poland, said in 1991 that there were at least 60,000 native Poles and Germans in Poland who were Orthodox. Therefore, the Belorussian language is not singled out and favoured by the Church while Old Church Slavonic remains the language of the liturgy and clergymen preach in Russian.

Why not preach in the language of the worshippers? The answer to this straightforward question is not easy. Russian is understood as much as Polish. Like Polish it has great appeal because it used to be the language of authority, an official language. In contrast to Polish, however, which actually belongs to the group of West-Slavonic languages, Russian, as is also the case with Belorussian and Ukrainian, belongs to the East-Slavonic group of languages. Preachers have always used Russian in what was known as the Russian Orthodox Church in contradistinction to the remainder of the [Greek] Orthodox tradition outside Russia. There is no theological literature in Belorussian. The most important bias in favour of Russian is that it is not the language of Catholicism, which before World War Two attempted to convert Orthodox believers and to introduce the use of Polish into Orthodox churches. Russian also 'covers better than Polish' the differences that exist between the dialects spoken in neighbouring villages.

Belorussian and Ukrainian

The convergence of Belorussian and Ukrainian dialects in the area is another example of the lack of a firm, established demarcation for Belorussian. The plurality of languages spoken in the present-day province of Białystok is a living, vital mixture which is a result of settlers who came into the area from three different directions: the West (Polish, Catholic); the South-East (newcomers from Wołyń and Polesie – Ukrainians); and the North (immigrants from Belorussia and Lithuania).

The rural population that makes up the Belorussian minority is well aware of the language plurality. They, however, do not divide the territory into Belorussian and Ukrainian language areas, but according to features of the dialects spoken. For example, neighbouring village residents can call each other *dziekałanie* [*dzia:k*] or *dekałanie* [*da:k*], depending on their using a palatalized or dispalatalized pronunciation of [*d*]. Even the different articulation of the pronoun 'what' (equals *shto* or *shcho*) leads to the split between the *shtokman* and the *shchokman*. The inhabitants of the small towns of Narewka and Lewkowo are known for their pronunciation of [a] [a:ket] for [o] [o:ket] (termed *akanie*)and they call the neighbouring villages round Hajnówka and Bielsk Podlaski *Podliesanie*, those close to the Poles. What distinguishes here is the more Polish pronunciation of [okaæ] and [dekaæ]. Those who reside around Bielsk Podlaski, Orła and Dubicze Cerkiewne call themselves *Korolowcy* (*korol* means 'Polish king'), while the residents of the land which once belonged to Lithuania are called *Litwini* (Lithuanians), though this group meanwhile uses dialects. This shows the coincidence of political sovereignty and dialect. Certainly the Belorussian, Ukrainian, Polish and Lithuanian languages have all mingled together, thus presenting a phenomenon of great interest to linguists and sociologists which is not straightforward to classify either in terms of speech or origin, but which is a fact of everyday life for the inhabitants' ethnic identity. However, Belorussian has wider currency as a language, while Ukrainian is referred to as a Ukrainian-like dialect.

Language is clearly one criterion of national identity but, in these circumstances, not the main one. Religion too must be seen as helping to identify a nationality, distinguishing Orthodox believers from the Polish Catholic majority. Religion is seen as a 'better bargain' than the possession of an 'inferior' language.

CONCLUSIONS

The results of research into the stereotypes of the Belorussian and the Pole show contrasting opinions presented by different generations and the characteristic barriers which make it difficult to shake off an individual or a group identity. The assimilation of the Belorussians continues, leaving behind three distinguishing elements of their identity:

1. Land, seen as a life in communion with nature. Migration is the cause of loss of land as a factor.

2. Language, as an element of individual and group consciousness, which is exposed to the same danger. The second and the third generations of the migrants are certain to forget their parents' tongue.

3. Religion, which is the strongest and most resistant factor, is probably the best evidence of identity.

The example of the Belorussians is a good example of the relative redundancy of language, which is after all only an instrument of communication which can be changed, while religion helps to maintain the self. Orthodox churches in Białystok are full of worshippers on Sundays and religious holidays, although Belorussian is hardly used in public in Białystok city and is not taught institutionally.

Even so, many believe that the language must be preserved to help maintain the national and religious identities of the Belorussians, and they like to quote the example of the revival of Basque after it was introduced as the language of the nursery schools. For this to happen in Poland new language teaching methods are vital. It is necessary to teach it as a second mother tongue along with Polish, not as a foreign language. This approach would make learning Belorussian not an end in itself but a means of achieving self-knowledge. Recent methodologies ignored the fact that for the majority of learners Belorussian is a language which they use daily. This would make it easier for Belorussians to develop a modern culture while not jettisoning their past. A good coursebook would provide new opportunities and challenge the local communities. Erik Erikson's concept of the psycho-sociological stages of identity development (Erikson, 1963) seems to be a proper reference point. Tuition should not be restricted to the structure of language, which has been the case so far, but to the 'nuclear problem' which is characteristic for the developing stage and organization of human activity.

Teaching Belorussian should begin in nursery schools because at that stage of development a child begins to distinguish his or her ego from others. This can be illustrated in these words: 'I was with my grandma', not 'Mary was with her grandma'. Teaching can be improved by developing extra-curricular activities, publications, societies, theatres, music and dancing groups, radio and TV broadcasting which support Belorussian culture and traditions. It is necessary for the government to pursue a stable policy which sees the Belorussians as a minority of citizens with equal rights. Polish-Belorussian relations cannot be traded as 'diplomatic arguments', a *quid pro quo* for the facilities, often inferior, extended to the Polish minorities in the republics of the Commonwealth of Independent States.

The delayed reform of local self-government in Poland, which would provide the regional authority with larger powers and the means to enforce them, should change the position of the Belorussian territorial regions. This would make it possible to oblige teachers, physicians and other professions to learn the local language during their period of employment as part of their contracts. The realization of an intercultural education programme would be very significant for the Belorussian minority's survival. A programme addressed to nursery school and primary school children would make it possible to eliminate prejudice early on and to teach positive attitudes towards 'aliens'. The Catholic majority of the country, which numbers a tiny minority among the minorities in this part of Poland and which was forcibly closed up under the Communist rule, needs to open itself to the others. The significance of this is valid not only for the minorities in north-eastern Europe but for the whole of a united Europe.

Chapter 15

Russian and Other Mother Tongues in the Schools of the Russian Federation and the Former Soviet Union

James Muckle

INTRODUCTION

The upheaval which Soviet society underwent in 1991 ended in the demise of the Union itself. Historians will doubtless argue for decades about the extent to which education contributed both to the grip which Marxism-Leninism maintained on the country for so long and to the speed of its overthrow. The question concerns us only peripherally in this chapter, though political matters do have a bearing on the place of the Russian language in Russian and former Soviet society, and on its teaching.

The basis on which education is now carried out has changed radically. That the Communists are no longer in control is less important than the fact that Communism is totally discredited. New values are sought. Many reject the past utterly and will not accept that any good was done in the Soviet schools. Nevertheless, Soviet science, technology and scholarship in the humanities were widely respected throughout the world, despite the need to discount ideological distortions. We have, therefore, a paradox: a discredited society with an apparently discredited education system nevertheless managed to educate schoolchildren and students to a level which enabled them to compete intellectually, if not economically, with the rest of the world. Universal compulsory education to a very creditable standard was provided free of charge. If there is now dissatisfaction, we should remember it is not only in the former Soviet Union that people have misgivings about the quality of education.

Education in the new Russia is being shaped on a basis of certain reform movements which began a decade or so before the USSR collapsed. The year 1984 brought a much trumpeted but abortive attempt at reform in schooling (Eklof, 1993; Muckle, 1990; USSR, 1984). This was later criticized for conservatism; its limited scope was attributed to the fact that it was instituted before the era of *perestroika* and *glasnost'*, which began in 1985. However, certain outstanding innovative teachers were either already at work or were poised for action. For example, a book by the Georgian psychologist, Shalva Amonashvili, *Zdravstvuyte, deti!*, sold 300,000 copies after its publication as early as 1983, indicating that parents of primary age children were becoming highly sceptical of the education their children were receiving. (Suddaby, 1985, 1988; Sutherland, 1989). The demands that have been heard ever more stridently since that time were for 'humanization', 'democratization', the 'pedagogy of co-operation' and for making children the 'subject' rather than the 'object' of the 'educational process'. It must surely be clear from the words themselves what their import is. The development of individuals was to be the new watchword. We shall see later how much or how little effect this has had on native language teaching today.

MOTHER TONGUES IN RUSSIA

It is not always fully realized that the former Soviet Union was an immensely multi-cultural and multi-lingual state. Only 52.4 per cent of the population in the 1979 census were ethnic Russians, but another 6 per cent claimed Russian as their first mother tongue. (In the Russian Republic, now the Russian Federation, 82.6 per cent were Russians.) The rest of the population spoke any one of about 129 other languages: the exact figure depends on how a language is defined. These other languages are not dialects of Russian. Only two of them, Belorussian and Ukrainian, are at all closely related to Russian; the rest belong to five diverse language groups. There is controversy as to which group some of the more recondite and little studied tongues belong. Some are spoken by a few dozen people, some by millions (Comrie,1981).

The legal and constitutional situation with regard to languages in the Soviet Union was enormously complicated and is very difficult to summarize. There existed no definition of the 'status, functions and sphere of use of either the national languages or Russian'.(Aslan and Fuller, 1989). Even where a national language had some official status, as in Azerbaijan, business of all sorts had been carried on in Russian for decades. To take another example, the Belorussians feared that their language was nearly dead, even though a very high percentage of the population claimed it as their mother tongue; many in fact communicated in a weird mixture of Belorussian and Russian known as *trasnyak* (Mihalisko, 1989). Before the collapse of the Soviet Union a new and quite 'liberal' USSR law on languages was passed (*Current Digest of the Soviet Press*, 42 (22).

Every Union Republic, however, had a tongue regarded as the national language of the dominant ethnic group in that republic, whatever its actual constitutional or practical position; 16 autonomous republics, 5 autonomous regions and 10 national areas in the Russian Republic were created usually for an ethnic group after which they were named. These territories still, of course, exist in the new situation. The growing independence of the former Soviet republics and similar yearnings in the national areas has almost everywhere meant increased enthusiasm for the upgrading, revival or rescue at least of major languages, with all the political, and educational consequences which that entails (Grant, 1989).

Another interesting, extremely complex and politically fraught question, which can only briefly be touched upon here, is the place of the Russian language in multi-ethnic Russia. Policy in the last years of the Russian Empire was to discourage the speaking of other languages in order to deter separatist activity. Ukrainian was banned from 1876 to 1905: a blatant sign of weakness. Soviet language policy varied markedly from one period to another. In the early years of Soviet Russia equality was preached, and indeed much progress was made, especially in the provision of literacy in languages which had never been written down. In the

1930s some of these languages ceased again to be written, and Russian was fostered as a language of intra-Soviet communication: it was, for example, always the language of the army. In the later Brezhnev era, some unsubtle efforts were made to Russify further, and strong reactions were provoked. This happened in Georgia, for example, where it had seemed that Georgian might lose its prestige in the Republic (and as a language in which doctoral theses in Georgian universities could be presented). The theory had been that Russian should be the cement binding together the Union; instead, some foreign observers felt it might become 'the acid that will dissolve the ties' between the nationalities. (Bilinsky, 1981). Kreindler (1982), with 10 other contributors devoted an entire issue of the *International Journal of the Sociology of Language* to this principle.

Dissolved it was, and strong reaction to the dominance of Russia and of the Russian language, too, there has certainly been. Yet Soviet educational policy was not totally unenlightened in this respect. Any educational administrator will sympathize with the difficulties of providing education in 129 languages. It just cannot be done: teachers, materials and quite simply opportunities for former pupils after school cannot be found. Nevertheless, education in all the main republican languages was offered throughout the period of compulsory schooling, and one or more years of instruction provided in many of the less widely spoken tongues. In the 1970s and 1980s between 45 and 57 languages of instruction were recorded in Soviet schools at some level – but not through the entire system – at different times. The dominant position of Russian is illustrated by the fact that it was always available as a medium of instruction in schools throughout the Soviet Union. It was in many, but not all, republics often chosen by non-Russian parents for their children, for obvious reasons of career advancement. It should be remembered that for these pupils, Russian, though taught as a mother tongue, is in fact a foreign language of which they are attempting to seek a very high degree of mastery.

THE LANGUAGE SITUATION TODAY

Education will have to wait at least for partial resolution of these problems, which are in many ways political as well as linguistic. Latvia may be taken as an example. A Latvian Communist Party paper from 1987 had expressed concern that the Latvian and Russian-speaking populations were not in concord; while advocating more stress on the teaching and learning of the Latvian language, it regretted the growing 'one-or-the-other' attitude and the anonymous letters betraying linguistic egocentricity and chauvinism which had been received by those preparing the paper (Commission on Nationality, 1989). The concern was well justified, as in November 1993 the Latvian parliament was considering five new draft citizenship laws, the most draconian of which would bar all ethnic Russians (nearly 50 per cent of the population and many of them Latvian citizens) in perpetuity from Latvian citizenship (*Independent*, 27 November, 1993). Latvia, and also Estonia, were persuaded by diplomatic pressure from the Council of Europe to compromise (see the *Current Digest of the Post-Soviet Press*, vols 46 and 47). Educators will need to consider their response carefully if a situation resulting in inter-community tension is to be avoided. However, and in other places, there is some evidence, beneath the jingoistic distortion, of the enlightened belief among those who form educational policy today that people of all ethnic groups need to identify with their own cultural and intellectual traditions. Important as such issues are, few would deny that there is also a need to recognize the importance of concept formation in the first mother tongue for a child's development, which is discussed by Vygotsky (1986) and colleagues (see Valsiner, 1988).

It is necessary to be cautious in accepting figures for the number of languages used as the medium of instruction in Russian schools: many languages are used for a year or two only with the youngest children, a few for the whole of compulsory education. The World Bank reports that in 1992 Russian citizens could be educated throughout compulsory schooling in Russian, Georgian, Bashkir, Armenian, Tatar, Buryat, Urdmurt, Chuvash and Yakut, while in 1987 only the first five of these had been available. Another source, the Director of the Academy of Pedagogical Sciences of the USSR Institute of National Problems of Education stated that, whereas only 18 languages were used for instruction in Russia in the mid-1980s, between 1990 and 1991 the number increased to 66 (Kuzmin, 1992). The Russian Minister of Education, on the other hand, reported in 1994: 'Within the past five years the number of languages . . . of instruction in elementary school has reached 25' (Tkachenko, 1994).

It is possible to summarize the position as follows. Speakers of the major languages in former Soviet republics can be educated through the medium of that language throughout secondary and in many cases higher education. It seems likely that in many areas there will be increased choice of the language of instruction. Practical constraints will ensure that pupils speaking less widely spoken languages move on to instruction in Russian or another major language within a few years of starting school. Something of the way this works is reported by Canadian visitors to north-west Siberia (Bartels, D. and A., 1989). A well-known Leningrad establishment, the Herzen Institute, was training teachers, native speakers, in 18 of the Siberian languages, which are spoken by between 96 and 24,000 people. Textbooks were compiled and tried out in the classroom. The aboriginal language was taught alongside Russian but used more intensively at first; one was found to help the other. Instruction in the Siberian language continued for up to four years of primary education, during which time Russian was phased in. There is some evidence in the source quoted that this initiative in native-language education came from Siberian educators who saw that the native languages would disappear if Russian exclusively was used as a *lingua franca* in kindergartens and primary schools for children from different language groups.

THE TEACHING OF RUSSIAN AS A MOTHER TONGUE

The nature of the Russian language

We turn now to the principal case study for this chapter: the teaching of the Russian language as a mother tongue (Muckle, 1988). Modern Russian did not really settle down and achieve a stable literary form until the early nineteenth century, after which Russian poets and prose writers began to create what has become a major world literature. Russian writers have asserted the claims of the language to respect in ringing terms: Mikhail Lomonosov (1711–65) wrote that it possessed 'the splendour of Spanish, the vivacity of French, the strength of German, the tenderness of Italian, and the richness, brevity and vivid imagery of Greek and Latin'. Ivan Turgenev (1818–83), in a poem in prose entitled, 'The Russian Language', wrote: 'in days of wearisome meditation on the fate of my native land – you alone are my support and stay, O great, powerful, true and free Russian language!' These statements are very familiar to Russian children through their Russian lessons.

Russians value the spoken form of their language highly. Recitals and radio programmes of poetry are popular, and 'expressive reading' is stressed as a classroom activity. A wide range of literature, prose and verse is available as recordings, many of which are intended specifically for children. Moreover, school examinations in Russia have always been very largely oral. The Russian child who cannot speak up for himself or herself in class and examination room will not succeed in the system.

Russian is the most widely spoken language of the Slavonic group within the Indo-European family of languages. It has a very large vocabulary and is highly inflected, having three genders (which give very young Russian children a great deal of difficulty), six cases of nouns, pronouns and adjectives, but only three verbal tenses. There are many irregularities and anomalies in the endings of nouns and verbs. Words are longer than in English, but the same meaning is conveyed in fewer words. This is because there are no articles, no present tense of the verb 'to be' and because of a strong tendency to abbreviate utterances and to take as understood items which would be expressed in other languages. For example, one Russian story-writer wittily reduced all his plots to two basic rhyming stereotypes: '*Vlyubilsya – zhenilsya*; *vlyubilsya – zastrelilsya*': four words in Russian, but the neatest translation into English runs to 14: 'He fell in love and got married; he fell in love and shot himself.' (Literally the Russian means: 'fell in love – got married; fell in love – shot self'; no pronoun is necessary because all the verbs are masculine singular; prefixes enrich the meaning of the verbs 'love' and 'shoot'; suffixes indicate the reflexive; words for 'and' and 'or' are typically omitted in such aphoristic utterances.) Pronunciation presents some problems even for Russian children: for example, the distinction between 'hard' and 'soft' consonants and the highly mobile word stress. The language is written in the Cyrillic alphabet of 32 letters. Spelling is reasonably logical, but is far from phonetic. Difficulties here include the spelling of unstressed vowels and final unvoiced consonants: a Russian child who had not been taught would not know, working from sound alone, whether to spell the last syllable of the word for 'town', *górod*, *-od*, *-ad*, *-ot*, or *-at*.

Russian dialects do not differ greatly or create serious problems of comprehension, surprising though this may be in a language which is spoken over such a wide area. Spelling was a political issue in the nineteenth and twentieth centuries, and it is interesting that one of the first acts of the revolutionary government was to abolish certain archaic and superfluous letters of the alphabet; street demonstrators saw them as symbols of reactionary élitist attitudes.

In the Russian classroom, standard language is required from children, and emphasis is placed on correct pronunciation and clarity of diction. Clear and literate communication is the priority: the notion that to correct non-standard usage is in some way to infringe a child's 'culture' would be regarded in Russia as the height of lunacy. The language is seen as a priceless cultural possession, which is to be valued, conserved and spoken properly.

It is not clear exactly to what extent Russian teachers think children need help in mastering aspects of the language they would learn anyway, other than pronunciation, that is. Case endings and verb conjugations are learned 'naturally', but the way these are represented in written form presents difficulties. Mother tongue teaching in Russian schools therefore consists of a great deal of analytical study of 'traditional' grammar, morphology, graphics and orthography. Some will therefore consider it dry and perhaps pedantic.

AIMS OF MOTHER TONGUE TEACHING

The principal aim in the 1980s was to give children 'a profound knowledge of the language': consciousness of it as 'an historically developed social phenomenon', feeling for its beauty and the desire to strive for mastery of its richness. Other aims were to give pupils the ability to express thoughts clearly and to instil literate habits in writing the language down. A conscious awareness should be aroused of the use of words and a sensitive attitude to them should be fostered. The purposes of Russian teaching, therefore, are to impart practical skills and a scholarly attitude, to develop powers of thinking and to arouse aesthetic awareness of the beauty of the language. Traditionally in Russian schools language and literature teaching were separated; in very recent years the feeling has been expressed that they should be brought closer together.

The teaching of reading in the earliest stages

The whole word 'look and say' method had adherents in the Soviet Union, and now that experimental non-state schools are permitted again, it is not impossible that exponents of methods other than that described here will be practising them. Literacy is, largely speaking, taught by the 'sound analytic-synthetic method' (*zvukovoy analitiko-sinteticheskiy metod*), (Downing, 1984; Elkonin, 1973) which represents a development of work done by Konstantin Ushinsky (1824–71). In its modern manifestation there is a 'pre-alphabetical period' of a few days or weeks in which children engage in conversation, story-telling and recitation with the teacher. Their vocabulary is enlarged, attention is directed to the structure of simple sentences, words and syllables, and, most importantly, they are taught to recognize the phonemes from which words are made up, and the order in which they come in a given word: *d, o, m, dom,* (house). This naturally leads to the building up of words from cards with one letter on each. At the same time, great importance is attached to the recognition and reading of syllables, since it is argued that children who read letter by letter miss out non-final vowels when they come to write. The correct pronunciation of Russian consonants depends on the nature of the vowel which follows them. By December in their first year pupils were expected according to the 1980 syllabus to know the alphabet and by the end of that year they should be able to read aloud at a rate of 30 to 40 words a minute.

The syllabus

Compulsory education in Russia now lasts for 11 years from age 6 to 17. The first four years are considered 'primary', though most schools are all-through and are referred to as *srednie shkoly*. This is usually translated as 'secondary schools', though the word means 'middle'. It is much more likely now than previously that primary Russian classes will be differentiated into groups on a basis of attainment, but teaching methods in most of them will doubtless continue to represent the full-class 'frontal' tradition of the Soviet school. Before literacy is achieved, pupils are taught to recite poetry 'expressively and using correct intonation', to recount an experience to the whole class, to re-tell a story which they have been told or answer questions on its content. In the teaching of writing, emphasis is placed on the correct handling and care of paper and implements, on posture and calligraphy.

Since 1991 schools have been much freer than ever before in the realization of the curriculum. In the 1980s, 27 per cent of curriculum time, calculated across a child's whole school life, went on first language and literature, and it must be assumed that this proportion will probably not change much for the moment. The following paragraphs summarize the syllabuses which were introduced in the 1980s, and this will be succeeded by some discussion of changes since then. Fuller details of the 1980s syllabuses are given by Muckle (1988). They fall into two broad sections: technical information about grammar, word-formation, punctuation, lexis and the like on the one hand and 'development of continuous language' on the other. There is a very great deal of analytical study of parts of speech, morphology, syntax and sentence structure. A particular preoccupation of Russian educators is with punctuation, which is less a matter of style in Russian and more of knowing the rules: when university entrants do *not* know the rules, it is considered scandalous – and, we are told, they frequently do not. The failure of the education system to teach them these rules has not, on the whole, led to calls for a new methodology or an easing-off on the analytical approach, but to appeals for greater efforts and more effective teaching in the traditional style.

Lessons based on this material can be tedious in the extreme, and frequently are. They may often be counter-productive, in that the pupils may appear to know less about the language they have spoken since infancy than in fact they do. How did anyone learn to speak Russian at all before all this theoretical guidance was given in schools, one wonders? Though good teachers liven up the guidance with songs, action games and quiz-type activities, and dilute it with more interesting matters, the solid core of technical information remains indigestible. Children may need drilling in the spelling and literate production of their own language, but to spend 45 minutes on dry technicalities with 35 or 40 children, sometimes without humour or variety, is far from ideal.

A minor, but rather interesting, part of the 1980s syllabus concerns the efforts to convey a feeling of patriotic pride through lessons on such topics as 'The Russian language: one of the world's developed languages', 'The international significance of Russian' and, in the old days, 'Russian as the language voluntarily adopted by the Soviet people as the language of communication between the nationalities'. A recent article recognizes the changed status of Russian even in the Russian Federation itself. At the same time there is talk of the 'formation of the linguistic personality of the pupil', which develops both the ability to communicate and a feeling for the culture which the language encapsulates (Bystrova, 1994).

A second major part of the Russian syllabus is known as 'development of continuous language'. It is carried on in conjunction with all parts of the syllabus, often allowing the technical material to be lightened somewhat. Its purposes are to teach the 'literary linguistic norm' (whether in its artistic, scientific or colloquial register) and distinguish it from dialect, slang and 'uneducated talk' (*prostorechie*), to teach the difference between written and spoken language and to achieve for every pupil a minimum 'culture of language'. This phrase implies the ability to use language sensitively, persuasively and even artistically. The range of concepts possessed by children is extended by teachers as their vocabulary is systematically enlarged; work is done on (often metaphorical) turns of phrase and proverbs. Attention is paid to the logical organization of thought in children's analysis of texts they have studied and their answers to questions. Phrases and sentence structure are studied. Work on 'continuous language', oral and written, consists of answers to questions, single sentences about pictures, dividing a text into sections and providing a title, short summaries, accounts of the children's games, hobbies and school work. In secondary education, development of language includes studying the concept of a text and its organization and style, the planning of essays, summary and précis, narrative, descriptive and later publicistic writing. 'Home reading' tasks are set from the early stages. In fact, this has a prominent place in foreign language teaching too.

The type of continuous language required from pupils falls into two types: *izlozhenie* and *sochinenie*. Both can be written or oral. The first word means 'analysis' and includes the re-telling of a text, summary, extracting one argument or aspect from a complex text or rewriting a text in a different way, such as telling a story from the point of view of another character than the original narrator. *Sochinenie*, literally 'composition', is more free and is likely to require some imagination or independence. Pupils are trained in narrative, descriptive, reflective and publicistic styles and are expected to use them appropriately.

What British teachers would consider 'creative', personal or imaginative writing obviously comes under this second heading, but it is somewhat less commonly encountered in Russian classes. The writing of poetry, for example, tends to be seen more as an activity for out-of-school activities than the classroom, though I have heard teachers set creative writing for homework.

Assessment

A Russian examination is traditionally of a specific type. As mentioned earlier, the standard examination is oral in all subjects, except that there are written tests in mathematics and the mother tongue. Pupils therefore find it necessary to speak; this is how they are tested throughout their education. Secondly, the questions are known in advance. The official school-leaving examination papers (*bilety*, 'tickets') are sold at newspaper kiosks well in advance; teachers use them for revision and answers are rehearsed.

The examinations in Russian, therefore, consist of an oral examination and written tests. For the oral, about 30 'tickets' each bearing two questions are published. The candidate selects a ticket from a number placed face downwards on a table and has a few minutes to prepare answers to the two questions. The first of these will be about morphology, phonetics or orthography: 'Speak about vowels and their correct spelling in the root of a word . . .', 'Speak about the way common nouns decline and about the spelling of the sounds -*o* and -*e* in the singular . . . Find some indeclinable nouns . . . Insert missing letters in certain words and explain their correct spelling', 'Define a numeral . . ., speak about the declension of numerals . . . explain their correct spelling.' The second question will relate more to syntax: 'Extract from a sentence indicated by the teacher some word combinations (phrases) and analyse them . . . Compose some phrases using "thanks to" or "contrary to" . . .', 'Speak about direct speech and the punctuation signs used in sentences including speech. Insert and explain punctuation into a sentence indicated by the examiner'. Written *izlozhenie* and *sochinenie* are set. Two hundred titles for free composition for the latter are published along with all the other examination questions. Ten of these, which were set recently perhaps give the flavour of the selection: 'Why I love the region where I live', 'My favourite literary character', 'Heroes are born in labour', 'My favourite writer, composer, painter or architect', 'They fought for the fatherland', 'An interesting excursion', 'A good name depends on good deeds', 'The person most dear to me', 'An unforgettable meeting' and 'Reading is the best education'.

CHANGE IN MOTHER TONGUE SYLLABUSES

The syllabus described above dates back to 1984. It differed in certain respects from the earlier prescriptions, but anyone reading the two together might be forgiven for not noticing the difference. Many Russian teachers failed to spot the changes and were duly castigated in official reports (*Russkiy yazyk*, 1985). They had not, according to the complaints, used visual aids, they were not teaching the children to use dictionaries and other reference materials, they had omitted the introductory lessons on the Russian language and its role in the world which had a moral purpose, they were still teaching parts of the old syllabus which were no longer required. This bleating from official sources does little more than indicate that teachers scarcely notice minor tinkering with syllabuses, and that if real change is necessary more radical approaches should be applied.

The real problem is the failure of the theorists of mother tongue education to produce principles on which effective teaching methods can be based. It is frankly admitted that a sizeable gap exists between the presentation to children of facts about language structure, orthography and so on and the same children's ability to apply the knowledge in their writing (Belen'kiy and Snezhnevskaya, 1985). Teachers are teaching and children learning by rote. The authorities assert that rote learning is 'not required', yet it is clear that many of the examination questions encourage cramming. How difficult it is to teach participles, adverbs and particles in class 7! How disgraceful it is that syntax is so little understood! How ignorant university entrants are of correct punctuation! At this stage in Soviet education (1985) the gnashing of teeth was reaching a climax, but it was never questioned that technical information about grammar should have a direct effect on pupils' free writing. It was not considered that a change in emphasis might bring about the improvement so earnestly sought.

What of the present? Perhaps the most straightforward way to estimate the likelihood of change is through a reading of *Russkiy yazyk v shkole*, the professional journal for teachers of Russian language in schools. In it appear articles by practising teachers (of the 'how I do it' variety), by psychologists and methodologists, administrators and researchers. While remembering that such articles will tend by definition to be from the leaders of the profession, a survey of them may help us see the direction which reform is taking.

There is an increasing tendency in the journal to look at the task of learning the mother tongue from the child's point of view. Post-Soviet educators admit that the Soviet system from about 1930 to the late 1980s paid little attention to a child's age or stage of learning, so this is already a step forward. The intensely teacher-dominated classroom, it is said, should give way, and monologue be replaced by dialogue (Bystrova, 1992).

The articles contain a great deal about making the syllabus more palatable to children, about introducing humour (almost taboo in the view of many Soviet teachers). There is a new understanding that school exercises must have a real-life context; thus texts for analysis need to be interesting and relevant; an intelligent reading of literary extracts can raise children's sensitivity to the power of language and possibilities for its use (Pakhnova, 1993). One author from a new humanistic grammar school in Moscow follows a number of others in stressing that it is vital to improve understanding in pupils as opposed to getting them through the examinations by rote learning; she goes on to argue for the teaching of rhetoric in schools (Ivanova, 1992). Computers are meanwhile suggested for routine learning tasks, such as practice in punctuation (Pakhnova, 1993).

There is some evidence of a more radical approach to the psychology of learning. An article on 'The teaching of reading' (V'yushkova, 1993) shows evidence of having gone back to the 1920s, the golden age of Soviet pedagogy when there were progressive schools which have been described as 'democratic', 'child-centred' and even 'romantic', and of an approach to the subject which is close to that common in Britain since the Schools Council Project, *Reading for Learning in the Secondary School*, of 1979–82 (Lunzer and Gardner, 1982). By reason of its happy combination of theory and practice, its intelligent style and realistic awareness of the tasks readers have to perform in the classroom and in real life, it makes refreshing reading. Yet at the same time many articles appearing in 1994–95 show a strong concentration on the minutiae of spelling, punctuation, parts of speech and word-building. Nevertheless, the journal, *Russkiy yazyk v shkole* (see issue no.5, *Russkiy yazyk,* 1994), includes an entertaining list of quiz questions for use in a schoolchildren's *olimpiada*, or extra-curricular competition, in which the stress is on motivating children to look at language and how it is used – and particularly misused. If, at first glance, there appears to be too much about the nuts and bolts of language, there is also a feeling that linguistic humour, expressiveness and communicative power depend on accurate and knowledgeable understanding of Russian (Klyueva and Chupasheva, 1994).

Even though there is some evidence that teachers realize that the present examinations have a 'backwash effect' which militates against change in the desired direction, it must be said that the majority of correspondents in this professional journal do not seriously question the assumptions of the existing curriculum. There is plenty about how to learn the old stuff in new and jolly ways, as in Latin textbooks published in Britain 35 years ago, in which the paradigm of *mensa* was preceded by two paragraphs of information on daily life in Herculaneum before the earthquake. There is little for the average or below-average child, who scarcely needs all the technical information about a language he speaks well enough. And it is the higher education entrants who seem to be failing to convince the examiners that they have learned enough from the course as it stands. Those in Britain who imagine that poor standards of proficiency in the mother tongue are due to a lack of old-fashioned grammar should be warned.

RECRUITMENT AND TRAINING OF TEACHERS

Like everything else in post-Soviet education, teacher training is undergoing extensive reorganization (Bolotov, 1991; Webber and Webber, 1994). The system as it existed at the end of the Soviet era, and largely still exists, makes the following provisions. Potential kindergarten staff and primary teachers leave school at 15 to train for three or four years, or at 17 to take a two- or three-year course, in both cases in a college of education which counts as a 'secondary specialist educational establishment'. In other words, it does not give 'higher education' (what British educators would consider to be graduate status), but a vocational qualification of somewhat lower prestige. Ninety per cent of secondary teachers trained or train in a pedagogical institute, some of which have now been upgraded to the status of 'pedagogical university', for five (or in the recent past possibly four) years. This course gives them a graduate diploma. The remaining 10 per cent are university graduates: all university courses include some perfunctory information on teaching methodology. All professional people in the Soviet Union underwent in-service training compulsorily every five years: structures for professional renewal were therefore well established.

The real problem was the nature of the training offered in these various establishments and the status of staff and institution. College students were much more likely than institute students to be taught by former practising teachers. Institutes gave a great deal of specialist subject training, physical culture and ideological indoctrination (history of Marxism-Leninism and the Communist Party), but relatively little pedagogy or teaching practice (14 weeks in five years only). Half the students had no interest in entering teaching, but were in the institute to work for the diploma purely as a general qualification to enable them to seek graduate employment outside of education. For those keen to go into schools 36 hours per week of face-to-face teaching in the institutes is scarcely the way to train young people to use participatory methods when they start teaching themselves. It also leaves the staff little or no time for research into basic classroom practice; many of the staff lack school experience anyway, and may have little understanding of what goes on in classrooms. Teacher dissatisfaction with in-service training reached over 90 per cent in many cases – it was 83 per cent for initial training courses (Bolotov, 1991). The status and salaries of the teaching profession are lower than any other of what would in the West be considered as 'professions'.

It will be clear from all this that there are deficiencies in Russian teacher training and supply which go far beyond the folklore criticisms that teachers in Western societies sometimes make of the training they received. The official responsible for reforming the system in the new Russia writes (Bolotov, 1991) of two types of reform: the 'common sense' way of improving matters without changing basic assumptions and a more radical 'attempt to create fundamentally new content and techniques of teacher training'. The existence of the teacher-innovators referred to earlier and the enthusiasm their methods have aroused may motivate teachers and trainers both to research and reform in the field of methods. The main problem is that of changing attitudes. The success or failure of teacher-training reforms will depend on whether a majority of the people concerned, not only their leaders, can break away from mindless teacher-dominated lecturing and help young students to see that their task is to develop inquiring minds and critical attitudes in their pupils. Despite the rejection of the education of the past by many post-Soviet educators, it is not hard to find as many good teachers in Russian schools as would be seen in those in other Western countries.

In an effort to improve standards of teaching a process of 'attestation' (advanced certification) has been introduced for teachers seeking promotion. This is voluntary, it aims to assist self-improvement, and it attempts to 'raise qualifications' – that is, in Russian terms, it is an instrument of in-service training. In order to achieve *attestatsiya* a teacher of Russian has to demonstrate extended knowledge of linguistics, pedagogy, psychology and methodology, and must submit to assessment of his or her lessons (*Russkiy yazyk*, 1994).

CONCLUSION

On the face of it, the picture of post-Soviet education in the mother tongue given here may appear to be one of gloom. Political acrimony, linguistic strife, low levels of funding, crisis over the values of education and of its organization. What can the future hold?

Maybe it is too easy to criticize the stress in Russian mother tongue teaching on orthographical and grammatical rules. After all, Russian educators want their pupils to write their native language correctly and literately. They have not yet discovered how to teach them to do it. The rather pedantic approach is the only one that many of them know. At least many are at present trying to brighten up this pedantry and teach pupils in a more lively manner. The Russian teaching profession has always been extremely conservative, and any change will come slowly. Radically innovative teaching may produce an alternative methodology, and the innovators are attracting great interest at present. Some teachers, as we have seen, would harness the undoubted enthusiasm many pupils feel for Russian literature and use it to promote grasp of language, though the traditional separation of language and literature perhaps militates against this. Innovators have in any case yet to show evidence of marked success for any new methods they may advocate.

The linking of language, ethnicity and education could be an immense force for good or evil. If educators allow mother tongue learning to become confused with what Mitter called 'chauvinistic perversions' (1992), the Russian Federation and indeed the whole of the former

Soviet Union will be torn with strife worse than it is already. If, however, the study of native languages is carried on in a liberal and enlightened spirit, it should enhance the morale of language and ethnic groups large and small, and it is not impossible that it might induce respect for other groups and languages. There is a task here for multicultural as well as multi-lingual education.

Part III

Language Awareness in Mother Tongue Teaching

Chapter 16

The Importance of Language Awareness

PREAMBLE

The twofold objective of this book has been to explore the concept of mother tongue, locating it within the context of the variety of other languages most language users experience at first hand, whether as their first, second or foreign language or, indeed, dialect, and the problems which arise from attempts to teach it. The current interest in reforming the teaching of the mother tongues, illustrated in Britain particularly by the Kingman (1988) and Cox (1989) Reports, has led to a re-examination of the phenomena of language acquisition and language learning, setting them against a number of different mother tongue teaching approaches. This has involved revisiting the topics of language and identity and the role of the standard language in the process. In the multilingual continent of Europe, of which the European Union forms but a part, the ability to communicate with fellow Europeans using different languages is especially important, as is the use of a *lingua franca*.

The choking link between language and identity, responsible for separating users of the different mother tongues found in Europe all going their own way, will not be loosened until the desire of many, and the urgent need of all, language users to communicate with each other is taken into account in devising suitable approaches to language education. The task to achieve communication within diversity has to acknowledge the complex nature of all languages but especially those functioning as world languages. As *mother tongues* they are ranged along the many other mother tongues in their respective regional corners but as *linguae francae* they make a substantial contribution to resolving the multilingual and multicultural diversity of the world. The question to ask is: if diversity is a desirable good, can this contribution be made without its permanent destruction? This concern can be met by enabling mother tongue users to perfect their competence and performance of their own language while at the same time helping them to find ways of achieving communication within another.

The twin tasks lie well within the desired objectives of a European dimension in education, that of enabling Europeans to get along with one another. The European dimension in European education is essentially a language education but it cannot be intended exclusively as a training of language skills – clearly there is a limit to the number of languages of which it is possible to achieve command – but rather as encouraging a language predisposition which enables a start to be made with meaningful communication among users of different mother tongues by re-directing some of their existing linguistic resources (Adams and Tulasiewicz, 1995a). If we stress the word 'start' then this is to recognize the difficulties this entails. Even assuming that one mother tongue, as *lingua franca*, can be used for this purpose there will be an unfair variety in the levels of proficiency between those using it as their first, their second, or, indeed, as their foreign language. A link between mother tongue and foreign language teaching, an insight into the other mother tongues as it were, might help resolve some of the difficulties. The Kingman Report (1988) suggested that all language teachers in training might profit from studying an element of language together, comparing languages they are familiar with and so improve their command and teaching skills of their mother tongue and to alert them to the problems facing learners of modern foreign languages. The need to accept a 'whole language' model in education rather than language as 'subject English' was advocated by contributors to *Kingman and the Linguists* (1989) and *Responding to Kingman* (1988).

A relatively novel and controversial component of teaching a language syllabus is variously referred to as Knowledge about Language (KAL) or Language Awareness (LA). In Britain it has been identified with the widely publicized concerns with 'falling standards' in English and the 'slow progress made' with learning modern foreign languages. This approach empha-sizes the cognitive as well as attitudinal dimensions of any learning by linking the simul-taneous processes of language acquisition (L1) with L2 acquisition and learning for which there is considerable support from research findings (Flynn and O'Neill, 1988). This has also found response in modern foreign language teaching. A start, albeit a slow one, has been made with its introduction in the school curriculum of a number of countries where it has been presented as an alternative to the teaching of grammar. Language Awareness can thus be seen as a distinctive approach to teaching the mother tongue, as well as second and foreign languages as part of a comprehensive language education that uncovers elements which the diverse mother tongues have in common.

Harnessing the potential of the mother tongue as an agent for an improved education in language, for an awareness of its role for the individual user and groups of users, a linguistic sensitivity closely linked with the possession of language skills, can make an important con-tribution to overcoming the barriers of multiculturalism and multilingualism in Europe.

THE LANGUAGE AWARENESS APPROACH

The German term *Sprachbewußtsein* appears in 1849 in the report of a philological confer-ence quoted in the *Deutsches Wörterbuch*, the dictionary begun by the Grimm brothers. The interest in the nature of language among German philosophers and the ease with which German can form word compounds are partly responsible for the appearance in German of the term which translates exactly as 'language consciousness' or 'awareness' some hundred years before it is recorded in English. To be sure Language Awareness has not yet gained entry to the *Shorter Oxford Dictionary of English*. Like many such terms it has a number of mean-ings, even its application as an element of the language teaching syllabus has been interpret-ed in a number of different ways.

All language users are aware of their language when they correct themselves or speak more loudly so as to make their point. However, it is necessary to distinguish between a more spon-taneous, intuitive language awareness which is a part of the process of language acquisition (for example in the natural *use* of a particular metaphor) and the directed (taught) awareness, which is a deliberate, albeit temporary, distancing from the language in use, as far, of course, as these two phenomena can be kept separate. Playing with language by both children and adults, for example when *selecting* a metaphor is one feature of such activity. It is the directed Language Awareness or Knowledge about Language which has been linked with the shift in mother tongue education away from literature towards the teaching of language. In his textbook on second and modern foreign language teaching, Hawkins (1984) referred to the Language Acquisition Support System (LASS), a concept aired by Bruner in an Oxford lecture in 1981, which reinforces the previously identified Chomskian Language Acquisition Device (LAD) and which helps the language development process on its way. The difference between its role in the mother tongue and a second or modern foreign language is that when learning the 'rules' of language the use of LASS is more 'visible' in the latter.

Linguistic or metalinguistic awareness, the latter being the 'distancing' stance of the former, is the process of a conscious awareness of one's use of the mother tongue as that language develops. Language education can help learners to organize their language, the process being one of learning rather than an imitation of models (Cazden, 1976), with the learner, unaided, becoming 'aware of language rules which he will eventually use' or arriving at this development helped by sensitive teaching. A combination of the two is a likely procedure with language tuition made available to children very early in life. The process thus proceeds through a progression of awareness of word structure in one's mother tongue, with pupils confronted by the feature (Halliday, 1967; Mackay and Thompson, 1968) when introduced in learning to read and especially so in learning to write, to an ever better understanding of word and sentence formation. The realization that 'come' + 'ing' becomes 'com(e)ing' with a disappearing 'e', and the understanding of the function of '-ing' as a particle acquired in the same process is one of the examples quoted. This ability 'advances' to become a study of awareness of language as such with pupils actually spending classroom time reflecting on what they have been doing when using their language and why. This procedure may also be used in the learning of second and foreign languages. Metalinguistic understanding is 'almost surely acquired later than the corresponding "primary" skills' (Carroll, 1986) because it tells the user that 'he knows that he knows'. Indeed, in some circumstances a learner's language awareness may outstrip his language ability, the possession of skills *per se*. It develops alongside more elementary ways of playing with language (Cazden, 1976), for example in interpreting paradoxical sentences such as 'I went to the pictures tomorrow'. Bruner (1983) remarks that: 'There is no better play material in the world than words' while Cazden (1972) insists that it is important that children monitor their own language behaviour by making their own language games. Language Awareness takes account of the elements which make up language, including spotting the differences between users' own languages and dialects and those of other people. This can be developed further to create language tolerance, a linguistic sensitivity of other languages and their users. The increasing acknowledgement of the multilingual composition of the world's classrooms is not unconnected with the arrival of Language Awareness.

Writing, reading, speaking and listening skills require learners' awareness of the sign and the sound symbols of the language and their functions. The better these skills are developed the more easily do learners understand what is being said to them and the better qualified they are to handle both their reading and writing assignments. One product of this is the recognition that languages which are not phonologically written may create difficulties for learners which are less likely to occur in the case of phonetically written ones, a fact which determines the selection of different methods of teaching reading: whole word, syllable or letter, or a combination of all three. It was in the context of writing down names that Vygotsky became involved in what can now be described as language awareness: 'Literacy depends on, and in turn contributes to, making previously non-conscious or tacit knowledge more conscious' (Vygotsky, 1962). Bilingualism may help to hasten the process of awareness in recognizing, for example, 'the arbitrariness of names' (see Leopold, 1971). Appeal to the cognitive faculty helps to activate users' innate, emotional and attitudinal, faculties in the process of their language development.

The above gives an idea of the complexity of Language Awareness, which like other concepts can be used to emphasize several priorities. The main emphasis in this chapter has been on the 'easily accessible linguistics applied in a language learning and language teaching context' (Tulasiewicz and Zajda, 1996) which does not stress it as the object of an academic study but acknowledges the presence and need of a 'literacy of awareness' (Tulasiewicz, 1997) besides the acquisition of oracy and the other traditional literacies associated especially with mother tongue teaching (Wilkinson *et al.*, 1980).

Language Awareness can be defined (in Tulasiewicz, 1997) as the study of language based on the latest linguistic and pedagogic principles underlying mother tongue and modern foreign language teaching. It is not a purely academic study of language but uses the cultural, social, as well as linguistic aspects of language and combines them with the traditional devices of mother tongue and modern foreign language teaching into an educational concern for learners. This exploits linguistics for its potential as part of a school-based language education in which the pupils are actively performing language skills and games. It envisages the use of language across three dimensions of human development: instrumental, affective and emancipatory. Together they cover the needs of a mother tongue language education which is to empower the pupil (emancipatory outcome), to encourage national and international communication (instrumental aim) and to release the creative (affective) language dimension. While not actually concerned with explicitly teaching the skills of another language, Language Awareness sensitizes pupils to diverse elements of language, structure or intonation patterns for example, which can help to improve their acquisition of language proficiency and increase their language repertoire, enabling them to use their existing knowledge and skills to acquire new ones in wider language contexts. The involvement of emotional intelligence (Goleman, 1996) in this process has been argued by Kron (1998, in preparation) and others. An important further definition sees the language education process as users' ability to apply their language experience for a critical analysis of society (Stubbs, 1990) achieved through an understanding of their own use of language and that of others. This covers the area of critical language awareness (Fairclough, 1990), the ability to discover the manipulative use of language for obtaining advantages.

The two terms, Language Awareness and Knowledge about Language, although similar in their current usage, have rather different philosophies underlying them. Language Awareness (LA) was originally used in the context of the teaching of modern foreign and second languages, including English as a Foreign Language, to promote the teaching of language as both a system and a social and cultural phenomenon. As already mentioned Hawkins (1984, 1992) was among the first to see its potential in the classroom and to develop its comparative linguistic structures side. Knowledge about Language (KAL), by contrast, is a term more frequently used in England in the context of mother tongue teaching following the reports of the Kingman and Cox committees. It may be taken to refer not so much to the comparison of structures, most of them known by school pupils, but to the explicit teaching of how language works as a human artefact, the social and cultural meanings that underlie various aspects of its use, and, recently and increasingly, the relationships that exist between dialect and language. Outside the United Kingdom users of the term 'Language Awareness' (*Sprachbewußtsein*, *réflexion sur la langue, kultura języka*) employ it in the above senses but add an emphasis on greater social awareness as part of their programme of intercultural education and linguistic sensitivity. In both cases the multilingual classroom becomes a living laboratory for understanding the various languages and cultures which comprise it. Multicultural Europe provides an opportunity, and indeed necessity, for the development of programmes of study in both Language Awareness and Knowledge about Language through which pupils can come to an understanding of each other's languages and cultures and learn to communicate and work together in a multilingual and multicultural world. It is important that linguistic sensitivity, taught alongside lessons dealing with the material facts of language change, should encourage tolerance and respect for other languages and cultures and foster the motivation, often absent among pupils, to learn or improve their language to communicate with their peers in and out of their countries (Tulasiewicz, 1989). In the increasingly more multilingual classrooms of today's schools one pupil's mother tongue turns out to be another's foreign language, (Tulasiewicz and Tournier, 1995).

Prescribed official or agreed school curricula differ in allocating the place accorded to teaching what we have called 'language education' and languages other than the national (mother tongue) language in language teaching periods set aside for this purpose. Current experience in the Canadian province of Alberta is the theme of an article by Bilash and Tulasiewicz (1995). Oomen-Welke (1994) has been using the German syllabus in the state of Baden Württemberg to teach what may be described as Language Awareness with a strong cultural component, with reference to, and inquiries about, the societal background of the languages encountered and their users, their difference from German and their perceptions of each other (see also Kodron and Oomen-Welke, 1995).

Reference to the previous language experience of children coming to school, as seen in language arts syllabuses such as those prescribed in Western Canada (the English Language Arts Protocol, 1997) and Wales (Welsh Office, 1995) explicitly acknowledge the role of a language awareness acquired as an early language learning experience which had influenced pupils before joining a language class at the age of five or even earlier. Significantly, in bilingual countries, or societies with a bilingual or bidialectic language policy, the impact of a linguistic experience on children's development is seen as a positive contribution, helping their general growing conceptualization and their learning of all other subjects. The English Orders are less specific on this (DfE, 1995).

The variety of definitions of Language Awareness confirms the expectations associated with LA. They range from 'underpinning language mastery' (Kingman, 1988), to 'facilitating second language development and detecting deviance' (Gass, 1983), activating the social domain for 'communication awareness (Garrett and James, 1991) and taking in the recognition that 'bilingualism helps literacy by encouraging an analytical knowledge of language (Bialystok and Ryan, 1985). Official syllabus requirements and time constraints in the classroom require a choice of priorities. Indeed, claims that explicit teaching of LA/KAL can substantially contribute to improving learners' language performance have to be taken on trust since it is difficult to arrive at hard evidence. Because, when using language, even an intuitional awareness can be almost instantly converted into performance it is difficult to distinguish between what progress is due to explicit teaching and what has been 'picked up' by the user. The respective contributions made by an intuitive language awareness and directed conscious awareness to progress in language performance as opposed to the acquisition of competence cannot readily be measured with accuracy. This is because, however elementary, language performance is immediately available to users. Mathematical awareness on its own, on the other hand, for example awareness of difference in size, does not provide the child with the mathematical ability to compare size by measuring the objects.

Even so, perceptible changes in language performance, in the sense of using language for a particular purpose by choosing an extended or different vocabulary, can be identified after directed language education. Examples of word association 'creations' by pupils modelled on those acquired after reading or discussing an unknown text in class or after following and giving instructions during a woodwork session were collected in several classrooms in Alberta (Bilash and Tulasiewicz, 1995), Hertfordshire (Tulasiewicz and Jago, 1998) and Freiburg (Oomen-Welke and Karagiannakis, 1996) teaching Language Awareness.

TEACHER PREPARATION

In Britain, not much has come of the Kingman suggestion that all teachers of language should experience a common period of language education, even though many educators feel that this could provide a base for the preparation of teachers able to use Language Awareness as part of their classroom repertoire. The revolutionary changes in teacher education, especially in England and Wales, have not helped in attempts to introduce yet another element into existing PGCE and BEd courses (Adams and Tulasiewicz, 1995b). Even so, Language Awareness as part of intercultural awareness and education can be found in some teacher preparation courses taught by those committed to the cause of Language Awareness in such centres as Cambridge, Freiburg in Germany and Białystok in Poland. (This is not intended as a complete list.) However, although many mother tongue and foreign language undergraduates receive an introduction to linguistics, explicit Language Awareness has not found a secure place in initial teacher preparation courses, although it could alert them to their roles in a multicultural and multilingual classroom.

In-service courses, on the other hand, which take up the topic, to which the authors have contributed through collaboration in an informal international Language Awareness Study Group (see the *Language Awareness Newsletter*, edited by George Labercane and colleagues in Calgary), some of whose members have also contributed to this volume are available. Members have run pilot programmes in schools in England and abroad which introduce Language Awareness elements into pupils' regular language syllabuses, at the same time developing materials for use in schools which would constitute a more firmly contoured, distinct, Language Awareness element in the curriculum (Jago, 1998). On the other hand, though there have been small-scale studies of individual pupils' progress with language in which members of the Study Group have been involved, a research programme that would assess the benefits of a regular injection of explicit Language Awareness on language development is still at the discussion stage. The difficulties with setting up such programmes arise from the need to involve teachers already heavily committed to delivering prescribed syllabuses on which their pupils, as in England and Wales, are being tested, the need to produce explicit Language Awareness syllabuses, and problems arising from measuring changes in linguistic attitudes (such as language perception) and language performance. Assessing academic competence in specific language areas is much easier.

There is evidence that mother tongue and modern foreign language teaching syllabuses are beginning to include an element of language study which may be extended so as to introduce

Language Awareness in order to improve language skills (Adams and Tulasiewicz, 1995a; Bilash and Tulasiewicz, 1995; Tulasiewicz, 1989, 1993, 1997; Tulasiewicz and Jago, 1998). Language lessons dealing with such topics as 'language and power', however, which formed part of the original Knowledge about Language discussions are rare, and may have to make room for teaching traditional grammar. The periodical, *Language Awareness*, has since 1992, published articles on various aspects of language which provide a large variety of interpretations of the topic of Language Awareness, incorporating both school education and research. They range from what can be recognized as 'grammar translation' teaching to historical linguistics.

The claim that using the Language Awareness – language education – approach in mother tongue lessons but referring to more than one language makes it into a tool that can help to improve the ability to handle the mother tongue, of which a comprehensive command is the undoubted first priority of compulsory schooling in all countries, can be justified. Language Awareness can also serve mother tongue users who are 'language aware' themselves as an aid with their learning of modern foreign languages. As has been suggested this can be done by creating language teaching approaches that involve the introduction of comparative elements of language use from two or more language systems to run in parallel for part of the statutory time given over to learners' language development.

Bibliographies

Parts I and III

Adams, A. (1993) 'English', in A. King and M. Reiss (eds), *The Multicultural Dimension of the National Curriculum*. London: The Falmer Press.

Adams, A. (1996) 'Language awareness and information technology', *Curriculum and Teaching*, 11 (2).

Adams, A. and Tulasiewicz, W. (1995a) 'Beyond simple skills', *Education*, 186 (1).

Adams, A. and Tulasiewicz, W. (1995b) *The Crisis in Teacher Education: A European Concern?* London and Washington, DC: The Falmer Press.

Alatis, J. (ed.) (1970) 'Twenty-first annual round table. Bilingualism and language contact', Monograph Series *Language and Linguistics* No. 23, Washington, DC: Georgetown University Press.

Allworth, E. (1980) *Ethnic Russia: The Dilemma of Dominance*. New York, Oxford: Pergamon Press.

Almond, G.A. and Verba, S. (1963) *The Civic Culture: Political Attitudes and Democracy in Five Nations*. Princeton, New Jersey: Princeton University Press.

Ammon, U. (ed.) (1989) *Status and Function of Languages and Language Varieties*. Berlin, New York: Walter de Gruyter.

Ammon, U. (1991) 'The status of German and other languages in the European Community', F. Coulmas (ed.), *op. cit.*

Baker, C. (1993) *Foundations of Bilingual Education and Bilingualism*. Clevedon, Philadelphia and Adelaide: Multilingual Matters Ltd.

Barbour, S. (1994) 'Language and nationalism: Britain and Ireland, and the German-speaking area', in M.M. Parry, W.V. Davies and R.A.M. Temple (eds), *op. cit.*

Baron, D.E. (1992) *The English-only Question: An Official Language for Americans?* New Haven, London: Yale University Press.

Baron, S.W. (1947) *Modern Nationalism and Religion*. New York: Harper.

Bialystok, E. and Ryan, E. (1985) 'A metacognitive framework for the development of first and second language skills', in D. Forrest-Presley, G. Mackinnon and T. Waller (eds), *Metacognition, Cognition and Human Performance*. New York: Academic Press.

Bilash, O. and Tulasiewicz, W. (1995) 'Language Awareness and its place in the Canadian curriculum', in K. McLeod (ed.), *Multicultural Education: the State of the Art*. Winnipeg, Manitoba. CASLT.

Board of Education (1921) *The Teaching of English in England* [The Newbolt Report]. London: HMSO.

Breatnach, R.A. (1964) 'The Irish revival reconsidered', *Studies*, 53.

Brock, C. and Tulasiewicz, W. (1988) 'Western Christianity, educational provision and national identity: an editorial introduction', in W. Tulasiewicz and C. Brock (eds), *Christianity and Educational Provision in International Perspective*. London, New York: Routledge.

Bullock, A. (1975) *A Language for Life* [The Bullock Report]. London: HMSO.

Carroll, D.W. (1986) *Psychology of Language*. Monterey, CA: Brook/Cole Publishing Co.

Cazden, C.B. (1972) *Child Language and Education*. New York: Holt, Rinehart and Winston.

Cazden, C.B. (1976) 'Play with language and meta-linguistic awareness: One dimension of language experience', in J.S. Bruner, A. Jolly and K. Sylva (eds), *Play: Its Role in Development and Evolution*. Harmondsworth: Penguin.

Chevalier, J.C. and Janitza, J. (1989) *Rapport de la mission de réflexion sur l'enseignement du français, de la litterature et des langues vivantes et anciennes*. Paris: Centre National de Documentation Pédagogique (mimeo).

Chomsky, N. (1965) *Aspects of the Theory of Syntax*. Cambridge, MA: MIT Press.

Chomsky, N. (1986) *Knowledge of Language. Its Nature, Origin and Use*. New York, Praeger.

Clahsen, H. (1992) 'Learnability theory and the problem of development in language acquisition', in J. Weissenborn, H. Goodluck and T. Roeper (eds), *op cit*.

Condillac, E. de (1970) 'Essai sur l'origine des connaissances humaines', *Œuvres Complètes*, vol. 1, Geneva [first published 1746].

Connor, W. (1978) 'A nation is a nation, is a state, is an ethnic group, is a . . .', *Ethnic and Racial Studies*, 1.

Corson, D. (1993) *Language, Minority Education and Gender*. Clevedon, Philadelphia; Adelaide: Multilingual Matters Ltd; Toronto: Ontario Institute for Studies in Education.

Coulmas, F. (1991) 'European integration and the idea of the national language', in F. Coulmas (ed.), *A Language Policy for the European Union. Prospects and Quandaries*. Berlin, New York: Mouton de Gruyter.

Cox, B. (1991) *Cox on Cox*. London: Hodder and Stoughton.

Cox Report (1989) *National Curriculum English Working Group English from Ages 5 to 16*. London: Department of Education and Science.

Crystal, D. (1987) *Cambridge Encyclopedia of Language*. Cambridge: Cambridge University Press.

Cummins, J. (1979) 'Bilingualism and educational development in anglophone and minority francophone groups in Canada', *Interchange*, 9.

Cummins, J. (ed.) (1982) *Heritage Language Education: Issues and Directions*. Ottawa: Minister of State for Multiculturalism.

Cummins, J. (1984) 'Linguistic minorities and multicultural policy in Canada', in J. Edwards (ed.), *op. cit.*

Cummins, J. and Swain, M. (1986) *Bilingualism in Education. Aspects of Theory, Research and Practice*. London: Longman.

DES (1988) *Report of the Committee of Inquiry into the Teaching of the English Language* [The Kingman Report]. London: HMSO.

DfE (1995) *English in the National Curriculum*. London: HMSO.

Dodson, C.J. (1972) *Language Teaching and the Bilingual Method*. London: Pitman.

Dodson, C.J. (ed.) (1985) *Bilingual Education: Evaluation, Assessment and Methodology*. Cardiff: University of Wales Press on behalf of the University of Wales Faculty of Education.

Dunbar, R.I.M. (1996) *Grooming, Gossip and the Evolution of Language*. London: Faber and Faber.

Durkacz, V.E. (1983) *The Decline of the Celtic Languages: A Study of Linguistic and Cultural Conflict in Scotland, Wales and Ireland from the Reformation to the Twentieth Century*. Edinburgh: John Donald Publishers Ltd.

Dwyer, T.R. (1980) *Eamonn de Valera*. Dublin: Gill and Macmillan.

Eastman, C.M. (1984) 'Language, ethnic identity and change', in J. Edwards (ed.), *op. cit.*

Eastman, C.M. and Reese, T.C. (1981) 'Associated language: how language and ethnic identity are related,' General Linguistics', 21.

Edwards, J. (1977) 'Ethnic identity and bilingual education', in H. Giles (ed.), *op. cit.*

Edwards, J. (1979) *Language and Disadvantage*. London: Edward Arnold.

Edwards, J. (1984) 'Language, diversity and identity', in J. Edwards (ed.), *Linguistic Minorities: Policies and Pluralism*. London: Academic Press.

Edwards, J. (1985) *Language, Society and Identity*. Oxford: Blackwell.

Fairclough, N.C. (1989) *Language and Power*. London, New York: Longman.

Fairclough, N.C. (ed.) (1990) *Critical Language Awareness*. London: Longman.

Fishman, J.A. (1977) 'Language and ethnicity', in H. Giles (ed.), *op. cit.*

Flynn, S. and O'Neill, W. (eds) (1988) *Linguistic Theory in Second Language Acquisition*. Dordrecht etc: Kluwer Academic Publishers.

Gans, H. (1979) 'Symbolic ethnicity: the future of ethnic groups and cultures in America', *Ethnic and Racial Studies*, 2.

Garrett, P. and James, C. (1991) 'Language Awareness: a way ahead', in C. James and P. Garrett (eds), *Language Awareness in the Classroom*, London: Longman.

Gass, S. (1983) 'The development of L2 intuitions', *TESOL Quarterly*, 17.

Gass, S. M. and Selinker, L. (eds) (1991) *Language Transfer in Language Learning*. Amsterdam/Philadelphia: John Benjamin.

Gellner, E. (1964) *Thought and Change*. Chicago: University of Chicago.

Giles, H. (ed.) (1977) *Language, Ethnicity and Intergroup Relations*. London: Academic Press – see Chapters 1, 4 and 13.

Giles, H. and Johnson, P. (1981) 'The role of language in ethnic group relations', in J.C. Turner and H. Giles (eds), *Intergroup behaviour*. Oxford: Blackwell.

Goleman, D. (1996) *Emotional Intelligence: Why it Can Matter More Than IQ*. London: Bloomsbury.

Goodman, K. (1970) 'Reading: a psycholinguistic guessing game', in H. Singer and R.B. Ruddell (eds), *Theoretical Models and Processes of Reading*. Newark, DE: International Reading Association.

Gowers, E. (1973) *The Complete Plain Words*. London: HMSO.

Grace, G. (1978) *Teachers, Ideology and Control: A Study in Urban Education*. London: Routledge and Kegan Paul.

Green, J.N. (1994) 'Language status and political aspirations: the case of northern Spain', in M.M. Parry, W.V. Davies and R.A.M. Temple (eds), *op. cit.*

Grimes, B. (ed.) (1988) *Ethnologue. Languages of the World*. Dallas, TX: Summer Institute of

Linguistics (11th edn).

Haarmann, H. (1991) 'Language politics and the new European identity', in F. Coulmas (ed.), *op. cit.*

Habermas, J. (1974) *Theory and Praxis*. London: Heinemann.

Hagege, C. (1987) *Le français et les siècles*. Paris: Odile Jacob.

Halliday, M.A.K. (1967) 'Language and Experience', paper presented to the Nursery School Association conference on children's problems in language, Harrogate.

Halliday, M.A.K. (1973) *Explorations in the Functions of Language*. London: Arnold.

Hamburger, F. (1994) *Pädagogik der Einwanderungsgesellschaft*. Frankfurt am Main: Cooperative Verlag.

Haugen, E. (1972) 'Dialect language nation', in J.B. Pride and J. Holmes (eds), *Sociolinguistics, Selected Readings*. Harmondsworth: Penguin.

Hawkins, E. (1984) *Awareness of Language: An Introduction*. Cambridge: Cambridge University Press.

Hawkins, E. (1992) 'Awareness of language/Knowledge about language in the curriculum in England and Wales: An historical note on twenty years of curricular debate', *Language Awareness*, 1 (1).

Hayhoe, M. and Parker, S. (1994) *Who Owns English?* Buckingham, Philadelphia: Open University Press.

Henry, A. (1995) 'Raising awareness of politeness in business writing', *Language Awareness*, 4 (3).

Herbert, A.P. (1935) *What A Word!* London: Methuen.

Honey, J. (1983) *The Language Trap: Race, Class and the 'Standard English' Issue in British Schools*. Kenton: National Council for Educational Standards.

Humboldt, W. von (1979) *Werke*, vol. III, A. Flitner and K. Geil (eds), Stuttgart: Cotta.

Jago, M. A. (1998) 'Bilingual children in a monolingual society', in T. David (ed.), *Changing Minds II: Living and Learning in Early Childhood*. London: Paul Chapman.

Johanson, L. (1993) 'Code-copying in immigrant Turkish', in G. Extra and L. Verhoeven (eds), *Immigrant Languages in Europe*. Clevedon, Philadelphia, Adelaide: Multicultural Matters Ltd.

Joos, M. (1967) *The Five Clocks*. New York: Harcourt Brace and World.

Joseph, J.E. (1987) *Eloquence and Power, the Rise of Language Standards and Standard Languages*. London: Pinter.

King, A. and Reiss, M. (1993) *The Multicultural Dimensions of the National Curriculum*. London: Falmer Press.

Kingman Report (1988) *Report on the Committee of Inquiry into the Teaching of the English Language*. London: Department of Education and Science.

Kingman and the Linguists (1989) edited by Bourne, J. and Bloor, T., Birmingham: CLIE Publications. Special Issue.

Kloss, H. (1987) 'Abstandsprache und Ausbausprache', in U. Ammon, N. Dittmar and K.J. Mattheier (eds), *Sociolinguistics, An International Handbook of the Sciences of Language and Society*. Berlin: Walter de Gruyter, vol. 1.

Kodron, C. and Oomen-Welke, I. (eds) (1995) *Teaching Europe in Multicultural Society*. Freiburg: Fillibach Verlag.

Koch, H. (1991) 'Legal aspects of a language policy for the European Community. Language risks, equal opportunites and legislating on language', in F. Coulmas (ed.), *op. cit.*

Krashen, S.D. (1981) *Second Language Acquisition and Second Language Learning*. Hemel

Hempstead: Prentice-Hall.

Kron, F.W. (1996) 'Some thoughts on socio-critical educations with reference to language awareness', *Curriculum and Teaching*, 11 (2).

Lambert, W.E. and Tucker, G.R. (1972) *Bilingual Education of Children. The St Lambert Experiment*. Rowley, MA: Newbury House.

Language Awareness Newsletter (from 1993) Labercane, G. *et al.* (eds), Calgary: University of Calgary, Teacher Education.

Leopold, W.F. (1971) 'Patterning in children's language learning', in A. Bar-adon and W.F. Leopold (eds), *Child Language: A Book of Readings*. Englewood Cliffs, NJ: Prentice-Hall.

Lepschy, G. (1994) 'How many languages does Europe need?', in M.M. Parry, W.V. Davies and R.A.M. Temple (eds), *op. cit.*

Lodge, R.A. (1994) 'Was there ever a Parisian Cockney?', in M.M. Parry, W.V. Davies and R.A.M. Temple (eds), *op. cit.*

Luther, M. (1883) *D Martin Luthers Werke*. Weimar: Hermann Böhlau – see vol. II.

Mackay, D. and Thompson, B. (1968) *The Initial Teaching of Reading and Writing. Some Notes Towards a Theory of Literacy*. London and Harrow: Longman, Green and Co. Ltd.

MacLure, M., Phillips, T. and Wilkinson, A. (eds) (1980) *Oracy Matters: The Development of Talking and Listening in Education*. Milton Keynes: Open University.

McNeill, J. and Griffith, B. (in preparation) *Preserving the Mother Tongue: The Northland Cree Elders' View of the Wholeness of Language and the Oneness of Life*.

Marenbon, J. (1994) 'English, the government and the curriculum', in M. Hayhoe and S. Parker (eds), *op. cit.*

Mead, G.H. (1973) *Self, Language and the World*. D.L. Miller (ed.), Austin and London: University of Texas Press.

Muller, B. (1985) *Le Français d'aujourd'hui*. Paris: Klincksieck.

Oomen-Welke, I. (1994) 'Brückenschlag. Von anderen lernen – miteinander handeln', in *Deutsch im Gespräch*. Stuttgart: Klett.

Oomen-Welke, I. and Karagiannakis, E. (1996) 'Language variety in the classroom', *Curriculum and Teaching*, xi (2).

Parry, M.M., Davies, W.V. and Temple, R.A.M. (eds) (1994) *The Changing Voices of Europe*. Cardiff: University of Wales Press in conjunction with the Modern Humanities Research Association.

Paulston, C.B. (1992) *Sociolinguistic Perspectives on Bilingual Education*. Clevedon, Philadelphia, Adelaide: Multilingual Matters Ltd.

Pocock, J.G.A. (1971) *Politics, Language and Time: Essays on Political Thought and History*. New York: Atheneum Press.

Posner, R. (1994) in M. M. Parry, W. V. Davies and R.A.M. Temple, *op. cit.*

Poth, J. (1980) 'National languages and teacher training in Africa: A methodological guide for the use of teacher training institutes', [Educational studies and documents, 32]. Paris: UNESCO.

Pountain, C.J. (1994) 'Syntactic anglicisms in Spanish: exploitation or innovation', in M.M. Parry, W.V. Davies and R.A.M. Temple (eds), *op. cit.*

Responding to Kingman (1988) edited by Ashworth, E. and Masterman, L., Nottingham: Nottingham University School of Education.

Riagáin, P. (1991) 'National and international dimensions of language policy when the minority language is a national language. The case of Irish in Ireland', in Coulmas, F. (ed.), *op. cit.*

Richards, J.C. and Rodgers, T.S. (1995) *Approaches and Methods in Language Teaching.* Cambridge: Language Teaching Library. Cambridge University Press.

Roche, N. (1991) 'Multilingualism in European Community meetings – a pragmatic approach', in F. Coulmas (ed.), *op. cit.*

Ross, J. (1979) 'Language and the mobilization of ethnic identity', in H. Giles and B. Saint-Jacques (eds), *Language and Ethnic Relations.* Oxford: Pergamon.

Sachs, J. (1976) 'The development of speech', in E.C. Cateretta and N.P. Friedman (eds), *Handbook of Perception*, vol. 7 (*Language and Speech*). San Francisco, London: Academic Press; New York: Harcourt-Brace Jovanovich.

Saville, M. and Troike, R. (1971) *A Handbook of Bilingual Education.* Washington, DC: TESOL.

Skutnabb Kangas, T. (1981) *Bilingualism or Not: The Education of Minorities.* Clevedon, Philadelphia, Adelaide: Multilingual Matters Ltd.

Skutnabb Kangas, T. (1982) 'Arguments for teaching and consequences of not teaching minority children through the medium of their mother tongue, or Rise and decline of the "typical" immigrant child'. Paper presented to conference on the Practice of Intercultural Education, Brenkelen, The Netherlands.

Skutnabb Kangas, T. and Cummins, J. (1988) *Minority Education – from Shame to Struggle.* Clevedon, Philadelphia, Adelaide: Multilingual Matters Ltd.

Smith, A.D. (1991) *National Identity.* Harmondsworth: Penguin.

Spender, D. (1980) *Man Made Language.* London: Routledge and Kegan Paul.

Sprat, T. (1667) *History of the Royal-Society of London*, published in facsimile and edited with critical apparatus by J.I. Cope and H.W. Jones (1958), St Louis, MS: Washington University Studies.

Steiner, G. (1975) *After Babel.* Oxford, New York: Oxford University Press.

Stubbs, M. (1990) *Knowledge about Language.* London: Institute of Education.

Swain, M. and Lapkin, S. (1991) 'Additive bilingualism and French immersion education: the role of language proficiency and literacy', in A.G. Reynolds (ed.) *Bilingualism, Multilingualism and Second Language Learning.* Hillsdale, NJ: Lawrence Erlbaum.

Temple, R.A.M. (1994) 'Great Expectations? Hopes and fears about the implications of political development in Western Europe for the future of France's regional languages', in M.M. Parry, W.V. Davies and R.A.M. Temple (eds), *op. cit.*

Ten Brinke, S. (1976) *The Complete Mother Tongue Curriculum.* London: Longman.

Theroux, P. (1984) *The Kingdom by the Sea.* Harmondsworth: Penguin.

Trier, J. (1973) *Aufsätze und Vorträge zur Wortfeldtheorie.* A. Van der Lee and O. Reichmann (eds), The Hague and Paris: Mouton.

Trudgill, P. (1983) *Sociolinguistics: An Introduction to Language and Society.* Harmondsworth: Penguin.

Trudgill, P. (1984a) *Applied Sociolinguistics.* London: Academic Press.

Trudgill, P. (1984b) 'Irish', in *Language in the British Isles.* Cambridge: Cambridge University Press.

Tulasiewicz, W. (1985) 'Cultural identity and educational policy: the case of the German Democratic Republic', in C. Brock and W. Tulasiewicz (eds), *Cultural Identity & Educational Policy.* London, Sydney: Croom Helm.

Tulasiewicz, W. (1989) 'Knowledge or communication: towards a new role for modern foreign languages in the school curriculum', in W. Tulasiewicz and A. Adams (eds), *Teachers' Expectations and Teaching Reality.* London, New York: Routledge.

Tulasiewicz, W. (1993a) 'The European dimension and the National Curriculum', in A. King and M. Reiss (eds) *op. cit.*

Tulasiewicz, W. (1993b) 'Knowledge about language – Language Awareness: A new dimension in school language curriculum', *Curriculum and Teaching*, viii (1).

Tulasiewicz, W. (1994) 'Teaching modern languages – some thoughts from Britain', *Zeitschrift für internationale erziehungs – und sozialwissenschaftliche Forschung*, 11 (1).

Tulasiewicz, W. (1997) 'Language Awareness: A new literacy dimension in school language education', *Teacher Development, an International Journal*, 1 (3).

Tulasiewicz, W. and Jago, M. A. (1998) 'Making use of language awareness in language teaching', in *Festschrift for Elizabeth Halsall*. Hull: Hull University Press.

Tulasiewicz, W. and Tournier, M. (1995) 'La formation des enseignants et la prise en compte du multiculturalisme', *Recherche et Formation*, 18.

Tulasiewicz, W. and Zajda, J. (1996) 'Editors' introduction', *Curriculum and Teaching*, xi (2).

UNESCO (1953) *The Use of Vernacular Languages in Education*. Paris: UNESCO.

Vygotsky, L.S. (1962) *Thought and Language*. Cambridge, MA: MIT Press; New York: John Wiley.

Waldron, T.P. (1985) *Principles of Language and Mind*. London: Routledge and Kegan Paul.

Wardhaugh, R. (1987) *Languages in Competition: Dominance Diversity and Decline*. Oxford: Basil Blackwell in association with Deutsch.

Watts, R.J. (1991) 'Linguistic minorities and language conflict in Europe: learning from the Swiss experience', in F. Coulmas (ed.), *op. cit.*

Weinreich, U. (1953) *Languages in Contact, Findings and Problems*. New York: Linguistic Circle of New York.

Weisgerber, J.L. (1949) *Von den Kräften der Deutschen Sprache*. Düsseldorf: Pädagogischer Verlag Schwan – see vol. IV.

Weissenborn, J., Goodluck, H. and Roeper, T. (eds) (1992) *Theoretical Issues in Language Acquisition*. Hillsdale, NJ, Hove and London: Lawrence Erlbaum Associates Publishers.

Welsh Office (1995) *Welsh in the National Curriculum*. Cardiff: HMSO.

Whorf, B.L. (1956) *Language, Thought and Reality: Selected Writings of Benjamin Lee Whorf*, J.B. Carroll (ed.), New York and Cambridge, MA: MIT Press.

Wilkinson, A.M. (1965) *Spoken English*. Educational Review. Occasional Publication No. 2. University of Birmingham: School of Education.

Williams, R. (1981) *Culture*. London: Fontana.

Ziv, A. and Zajdman, A. (1993) *Semites and Stereotypes: Characteristics of Jewish Humor*. London, Westport, CT: Greenwood Press.

Part II

Académie de la Corse (1989) *Guide de l'enseignement de la langue et de la culture corses de la maternelle à l'université*. Ajaccio: Ministère de l'Education nationale.

Actes du Colloque, Petite Enfance et Politique de la ville (1993) *Petite enfance et développement des quartiers', mai*. Mulhouse and Paris: Syros.

Adams, A. (ed.) (1982) *New Directions in English Teaching*. Lewes: Falmer Press.

Adler, M.K. (1977) *Welsh and the Other Dying Languages in Europe: A Sociolinguistic Study*. Hamburg: Buske.

Aitchison, J. and Carter, H. (1994) *A Geography of Welsh*. Cardiff: University of Wales Press.

Ambrose, J. and Williams, C. (1981) 'On the spatial definition of minority', in E. Haugen,

J. McClure and D. Thomson (eds) *Minority Languages Today.* Edinburgh: Edinburgh University Press.

Ammar, S. (1988) 'L'Enseignement de l'Arabe en France: Enquêtes et Analyses.' Thèse de Doctorat d'Etat. Paris: Université de la Sorbonne Nouvelle.

Apeltauer, E. (1987) *Gesteuerte Zweisprachigkeit. Voraussetzungen und Konsequenzen für den Unterricht.* Munich: Hueber Verlag.

Aslan, Y. and Fuller, E. (1989), 'Azerbaijani intellectuals express concern over native language', *Report on the USSR*, 1 (9).

Auernheimer, G. (1990) *Einführung in die interkulturelle Erziehung.* Darmstadt: Wissenschaftliche Buchgesellschaft.

Babin, N. and Pierre, M. (1991) *Programmes, Instructions, Conseils pour l'école élémentaire.* Paris: Hachette Education.

Bade, K.J. (ed.) (1992) *Deutsche im Ausland – Fremde in Deutschland.* Munich: C.H. Beck.

Baker, C. (1985) *Aspects of Bilingualism in Wales.* Clevedon: Multilingual Matters.

Baker, C. (1992) *Attitudes and Language.* Clevedon: Multilingual Matters.

Ball, S.J. (1982) 'Competition and conflict in the teaching of English: a socio-historical analysis', *Journal of Curriculum Studies* 14 (1).

Ball, S.J. (1984) 'A subject of privilege: English and the school curriculum, 1906–35', in S.J. Ball and I.F. Goodson, *Defining the Curriculum: Histories and Ethnographies.* Lewes: Falmer Press.

Barnes, D. and Barnes, D. (1984) *Versions of English.* London: Heinemann.

Bartels, D. and Bartels, A. (1989) 'Language education programs for aboriginal peoples of the Siberian north: the Soviet experience', *Canadian Journal of Native Education*, 16 (1).

Bayrou, F. (1994) *Tout sur la nouvelle école: le nouveau Contrat pour l'école.* Paris: Ministère de l'Education nationale.

Berque, J. (1985) *L'Immigration à l'école de la République, Rapport au Ministre de l'Education nationale.* Paris: CNDP.

Berdychowska, B. (Director of the Office of National Minorities, the Ministry of Culture): interviewed by *Życie Warszawy*, 28 Nov. 1990 edition, details the amount of financial support disbursed by the Ministry of Culture and Art in 1991 for minority cultural activities in Poland (in Polish).

Belen'kiy, G.I. and Snezhnevskaya, M.A. (1985) 'Soderzhanie obucheniya literature [The literature curriculum]', in I.D. Zverev and M.P. Kashin *Sovershenstvovanie soderzhaniya obrazovaniya v shkole.* Moscow: Prosveshchenie.

Bilinsky, Y. (1981) 'Expanding the use of Russian or Russification?', *The Russian Review*, 40.

Board of Education (1910) *The Teaching of English in Secondary Schools.* London: HMSO.

Board of Education (1927) *Welsh in Education and Life.* London: HMSO.

Bolotov, V. A. (1991) 'Reforming teacher training in Russia', *ISSE Newsletter* [Institute for the Study of Soviet Education, Indiana University], 1 (1).

Bourgarel, F. *et al.* (1991) *Travailler en Z.E.P., CRDP de Versailles.* Paris: Hachette-Education.

Brumfit, C., Ellis, R. and Levine, J. (eds) (1985) *English as a Second Language in the United Kingdom.* Oxford: Pergamon Press and British Council.

Bruner, J. (1983) *Child's Talk: Learning to Use Language.* Oxford: Oxford University Press.

Bugajski, M. (1993) *Językoznawstwo normatywne.* Warsaw: Polskie Wydawnictwo Naukowe.

Butzkamm, W. (1993) *Psycholinguistik des Fremdsprachenunterrichts.* Tübingen: Francke

Verlag (2nd edn).

Bystrova, E.A. (1994) 'Teoriya i praktika prepodavaniya russkogo yazyka [Theory and practice in the teaching of the Russian language]', *Pedagogika*, 4.

Bystrova, L.P. (1992) 'Formirovanie samoobrazovatel'nykh umeniy [Creating the ability to educate oneself]', *Russkiy yazyk v shkole*, 1.

Cahiers Pédagogiques (1991) 'Hommes et Migrations à l'école: L'intégration', *1146*, septembre. Paris.

Cahm, E. (1972) *Politics and Society in Contemporary France 1789–1971*. London: Harrap.

Carter, R. (ed.) (1990) *Knowledge about Language and the Curriculum: The LINC Reader*. London: Hodder and Stoughton.

Carter, R. (1993) 'Proper English: language, culture and curriculum', *English in Education*, 27 (3).

Cavenagh, F A. (1930) *The Life and Work of Griffith Jones of Llandowror*. Cardiff: University of Wales Press Board.

Centro de Investigación, Documentación y Evaluación (1991) *El Sistema Educativo Español*. Madrid: Ministerio de Educación y Ciencia. Secretaría General Técnica. Servicio de Publicaciones.

Cervoni, J.-R. (1990) *Scola Corsa Bastia, 1970–90*. Bastia: Edizioni Scola Corsa.

CFBELMR (1993) [Comité français du bureau européen des langues moins répandues] *Quelle(s) Langue(s) pour nos Enfants*. Dublin: BELMR.

Chrysakopoulos, C. and Oomen-Welke, I. (1986) 'Griechische und türkische Muttersprachenklassen', *Diskussion Deutsch*, 90.

CNDP (1989) [Centre national de documentation pédagogique] 'Quatre Communautés immigrées', *Migrants-formation*, 21 March, Paris.

CNDP (1992) [Centre national de documentation pédagogique] *La maîtrise de la langue á l'école*. Paris: Ministère de l'Education nationale et de la Culture, Savoir Livre.

CNDP (1994) [Centre national de documentation pédagogique] 'L'Ecole dans la ville: ouverture ou clôture?' *Migrants-formation*, 97, June, Paris.

Comisión Coordinadora para a Normalización Lingüística (1993) *Unha lingua milenaria tras 10 anos da Lei de Normalización*. Vigo: Xunta de Galicia.

Commission on Nationality and Inter-nationality Relations of the Central Committee of the Communist Party of the Latvian SSR (1989), 'To master languages more deeply', *Soviet Education*, 31 (10) [Translated from 'Glubzhe ovladevat' yazykami', *Sovetskaya molodezh*, 7 Aug 1987].

Comrie, B. (1981) *The Languages of the Soviet Union*, Cambridge: Cambridge University Press.

Coote, E. (1596) *The English Schoole-Maister*. Menston: Scolar Press [facsimile (1968)].

Coupland, N. (1990) English in Wales: Diversity, Conflict and Change. Clevedon: Multilingual Matters.

Coupland, N., Williams, A. and Garrett, P (1994) 'The social meanings of Welsh English: teachers' stereotyped judgements', *Journal of Multilingual and Multicultural Development*, 15 (6).

Cox, B. (1990) 'Editorial', *Critical Quarterly*, 32 (4).

Cox, B. (1995) *The Battle for the English Curriculum*. London: Hodder and Stoughton.

Czerniewska, P. (1992) *Learning about Writing*. Oxford: Blackwell.

Davies, J. (1993) *The Welsh Language*. Cardiff: University of Wales Press.

Dawidziuk, M. (1991) 'Uncensored Belorussian publications', *Więź*, 2 (in Polish).

Departament d'Enseyament (1987) *Education in Catalonia*. Barcelona: Generalitat de Catalunya.

Departament de Cultura (1992) Leprête, M.: *La Lengua Catalana en la actualidad*. Barcelona: Generalitat de Catalunya

DES (1975) *A Language for Life* [The Bullock Report]. London: HMSO.

DES (1984) *English from 5–16 (Curriculum Matters 1)*. London: HMSO.

DES (1985a) *English from 5–16: The Responses*. London: HMSO.

DES (1985b) *Education for All* [the Swann Report]. London: HMSO.

DES (1989) *English for Ages 5–16* [The Cox Report]. London: HMSO.

DfE (1994) *Education Reforms in Schools*. London: HMSO.

Diez, M. *et al.* (1980) *Las Lenguas de España, Breviarios de Educación*. Madrid: Ministerio de Educación y Ciencia. Instituto Nacional de Ciencias de la Educación

Dixon, J. (1991) *A Schooling in English*. Milton Keynes: Open University Press.

Downing, J. (1984) 'Reading research and instruction in the USSR', *The Reading Teacher*, 37 (7).

Dudenenzyklopädie [the most recent edition] Mannheim: Dudenverlag – see especially vol. 1 for Spelling and vol. 4 for Grammar.

Durand-Prinborgne, C. (1990) 'Laïcité scolaire et signes d'appartenance religieuse', *Revue française de Droit administratif*, Janvier–Février.

Dziennik Ustaw (1993) Journal of Laws (Dz. U.), no. 34, item 150. Warsaw: Government.

Edwards, V. (1991) 'The Welsh speech community', in S. Alladina and V. Edwards (eds), *Multilingualism in the British Isles Vol. 1: The Older Mother Tongues of Europe, Africa, the Middle East and Asia*. London: Longman.

Eggar, T. (1991) 'Correct use of English is essential', *Times Educational Supplement*, 28 June 1991.

Eklof, B. (1993) 'Democracy in the Russian school: educational reform since 1984', in B. Eklof and E. Dneprov (eds), *Democracy in the Russian School: the Reform Movement in Education Since 1984*, Boulder CO/San Francisco/Oxford: Westview Press.

Elkonin, D.B. (1973) 'The USSR', in J. Downing *Comparative Reading. Cross-national Studies of Behavior and Processes in Reading and Writing*. New York: Macmillan.

Erben, J. (1980) *Deutsche Grammatik. Ein Abriß*. Munich: Hueber Verlag, (12th edn).

Erikson, E. (1963) *Childhood and Society*, New York: Norton (2nd edn).

Escarpit, R. (1979) 'Langue maternelle, langues étrangères,' *Le Français dans le Monde*, 142.

Evans, N. (1989) 'Gogs, Cardis and Hwntws: region, nation and state, 1840–1940', in N. Evans (ed.), *National Identity in the British Isles*. Harlech: Coleg Harlech Centre for Welsh Studies.

Ferguson, C.A. (1959) 'Diglossia', *Word*, 15.

Freudenreich, D. and Sperth, F. (1983) *Stunden Blätter. Rollenspiele im Literaturunterricht*. Stuttgart: Ernst Klett Verlag.

Fritzsche, J. *et al.* (1992) *Projekte im Deutschunterricht*. Stuttgart: Ernst Klett Verlag.

Geisler, W. *et al.* (1976) *Projektorientierter Unterricht*. Weinheim: Beltz Verlag.

Glinz, H. (1973) *Die innere Form des Deutschen. Eine neue deutsche Grammatik*. Bern and Munich: Francke Verlag. Bibliotheca Germanica 4 (6th edn).

Głowiński, M. (1990) *Nowomowa po polsku*. Warsaw: Polskie Wydawnictwo Naukowe.

Gogolin, I. (1994a) *Der monolinguale habitus der multilingualen Schule*. Münster: Waxmann Verlag.

Gogolin, I. (1994b) *Das nationale Selbstverständnis der Bildung.* Münster: Waxmann Verlag.

Goodwyn, A. (1992) 'English teachers and the Cox models', *English in Education*, 26 (3).

Goodwyn, A. (ed.) (1995) *English and Ability.* London: David Fulton.

Graff, G. (1987) *Professing Literature.* Chicago: Chicago University Press.

Grant, N. (1989) 'Mechanisms: policy formation and implementation', in M. Kirkwood (ed.), *Language Planning in the Soviet Union*, Basingstoke: Macmillan.

Green, B. (1995) 'Post-curriculum possibilities: English teaching, cultural politics, and the postmodern turn', *Journal of Curriculum Studies*, 27 (4).

Gregersen, F. (1994) 'Hvor dansk?', *Nydanske Studier* 19.

Griffiths, B. (1981) Preface to *Gwerin-eiriau Maldwyn.* Bangor: Llygad yr Haul.

Guiral, P. and Thuillier, G. (1982) *La vie quotidienne des professeurs de 1870 à 1940.* Paris: Hachette.

Haarder, B. (1991) 'Folkeskolen er dansk og taler dansk. Interview med undervisningsminister Bertel Haarder', *På let dansk*, 6, (1).

Hagström, B. (1987) 'Den färöiska tvåspråkigheten i sociologiskt och socialpsykologiskt perspektiv', in E. Wande *et al.* (eds), *Aspects of Multilingualism. Proceedings from the Fourth Nordic Symposium on Bilingualism, 1984. Acta Universitatis Upsaliensis. Studia Multiethnica Upsaliensia* 2, Uppsala: Uppsala University.

Hall, H. (1990) *Knowledge of the Catalan Language* (1975–1986). Barcelona: Generalitat de Catalunya, Departamento de Cultura.

Hannoun Report (1987) *L'Homme est l'espérance de l'Homme.* Paris: La Documentation Française.

Henrici, G. (1986) *Studienbuch: Grundlagen für den Unterricht im Fach Deutsch Fremd- und Zweitsprache (und anderer Fremdsprachen).* Paderborn: Schöningh Verlag.

Hessen, Der Kultusminister (1972) *Rahmenrichtlinien Sekundarstufe I Deutsch.* Wiesbaden: Government 1980.

Hetmar, T. and Jørgensen, J.N. (1993) 'Multilingual concepts in the schools of Europe: Denmark', *Sociolinguistica*, 7, Tübingen: Max Niemeyer Verlag.

HMI (1979) *Aspects of Secondary Education in England.* London: HMSO.

Hodgson, J.T. (1975) 'Changes in English teaching: institutionalization, transmission and ideology'. PhD thesis, London University.

Hoffmann, C. (1994) 'Language loss and language recovery: the case of the Rußland-deutsche', in M.M. Parry, W.V. Davies and R.A.M. Temple, *op. cit.*

Holmen, A. and Jørgensen, J.N. (eds) (1989) 'Enhedskultur – Helhedskultur. Artikler om dansk kulturel selvforståelse', *Københavnerstudier i tosprogethed*, 10. Copenhagen: Danmarks Lærerhøjskole.

Honowska, M. (1972) 'Język prasy osobliwy twór socjalny', *Biuletyn Polskiego Towarzystwa Językoznawczego*, XXX.

Howatt, A.P R. (1984) *A History of English Language Teaching.* Oxford: Oxford University Press.

Hughes, J.C. (1906) 'Llythyrau Ceiriog', *Cymru*, XXX 174–81.

INSEE (1990) [Institut national de la Statistique et des Etudes Economiques] *La Société française. Données sociales 1990.* Paris (ch 8: L'illettrisme).

INSEE (1993) [Institut national de la Statistique et des Etudes Economiques] *La Société française. Données sociales 1993.* Paris (ch 10: La population étrangère et son évolution).

Intxausti, J. (1995) *Euskal Herria: The Country of the Basque Language.* Vitoria: Gobierno

Vasco, Departamento de Cultura.

Ivanova, S.F. (1992) 'Kak nachinat' obuchenie ritorike? [How can we begin teaching rhetoric?]', *Russkiy yazyk v shkole*, 1.

Jenkins, D.E. (1908) *The Life of Thomas Charles of Bala*, 3 vols, volume III. [No publisher].

Jones, B.M. (1987) 'Do we have diglossia in Wales?' Paper presented at the Annual Linguistics Symposium of the University of Wales, Cardiff: SECAP.

Jørgensen, J.N. (ed.) (1991) 'Det danske sprogs status år 2001. Er dansk et truet sprog?', *Københavnerstudier i tosprogethed*, 14. Copenhagen: Danmarks Lærerhøjskole.

Jørgensen, J.N. (1994) '"Ethnic" and "societal" factors of immigrants' underachievement in the schools of the Nordic countries', in *Report from the Bradford Conference on Under-achievement in Education*, 2–4 February 1993, Bradford, UK.

Jørgensen, J.N. and Holmen, A. (eds) (1990) 'Modersmålsundervisning i mindretalssprog', *Københavnerstudier i tosprogethed*, 13. Copenhagen: Danmarks Lærerhøjskole.

Jørgensen, J.N. and Kristensen, K. (1995) 'On boundaries in linguistic continua', *Language Variation and Change*, 2, Cambridge: Cambridge University Press.

Jospin, L. (1989a) Loi d'Orientation sur l'Education. *Loi du 10 juillet 1989*. Paris: Government.

Jospin, L. (1989b) 'Ecole et Immigration: le Rôle des CEFISEM,' *Bulletin Officiel*, 43. Paris: Government.

Journal officiel de la République française (1994) *Dictionnaire des termes officiels de la langue française*. Paris: Imprimerie nationale.

Keosten, K. (1989) *Poland-national country: Dilemmas and reality. Nations: How did they rise and obtain their independence?* Warsaw: Polskie Wydawnictwo Naukowe (in Polish).

Klemensiewicz, Z. (1947) 'Poprawnoiść i pedagogika językowa', *Język Polski*, XXVII.

Klemensiewicz, Z. (1981) *Historia języka polskiego*. Warsaw: Polskie Wydawnictwo Naukowe.

Klyueva, N.P. and Chupasheva, O.N. (1994) 'Olimpiada po russkomu yazyku dlya uchashchikhsya srednikh uchebnykh zavedeniy [Competition in Russian for pupils of secondary educational establishments]', *Russkiy yazyk v shkole*, 5.

Kreindler, I. (ed.) (1982) 'The changing status of Russian in the Soviet Union', *International Journal of the Sociology of Language*, 33.

Kristiansen, T. (1990) *Udtalenormering i skolen. Skitse af en ideologisk bastion*. Copenhagen: Gyldendal.

Kristjánsdóttir, B. (1990) 'I virkeligheden handler vi alle kulturligt', in J.N. Jørgensen and A. Holmen (eds), *To kulturer i klasseværelset, Københavnerstudier i tosprogethed*, 9. Copenhagen: Danmarks Lærerhøjskole.

Kristjánsdóttir, B. and Jørgensen, J.N. (1998) 'Acquisition of literacy in multilingual contexts in Danish schools', in A.Y. Durgunoglu and L. Verhoeven (eds), *Acquisition of Literacy in a Multilingual Context: A Cross-Cultural Perspective*, Mahwah, NJ: Erlbaum Press.

Kron, F.W. (1998 in preparation) 'The emotional intelligence factor in language awareness'.

Kultusministerkonferenz. *Beschluß der KMK: Unterricht für Kinder ausländischer Arbeitnehmer* (for the texts of the 14/15 May 1964 discussion and the December 1971 Resolution see: Mahler, 1974).

Kurkowska, H. (1977) 'Polityka językowa a zróżnicowanie społeczne współczesnej polszczyzny', *Socjolingwistyka I Polityka językowa*. Katowice: Uniwersytet Śląski.

Kurkowska, H. (1981) 'Próba charakterystyki socjolingwistycznej współczesnego języka polskiego', in *Współczesna polszczyzna. Wybór zagadnień*. Warsaw: Polskie Wydawnictwo Naukowe.

Kuzmin, M. (1992) 'The rebirth of the national school in Russia', *Soviet Education Study Bulletin*, 10 (1).

Lamb, B. (1995) 'The students who need to put in a good word'. *Times Educational Supplement*, 31 March 1995.

Lawson, J. and Silver, H. (1973) *A Social History of Education in England*. London: Methuen.

Leonard, S.A. (1962) *The Doctrine of Correctness in English Usage 1700–1800*. New York: Russell & Russell.

Lewis, E.G. (1987) 'Attitudes towards the planned development of Welsh', *International Journal of the Sociology of Language*, 66.

Lingen, R.W. (1847) *Report of the Commission of Inquiry into the State of Education in Wales*, Vol. 1, London: HMSO.

Linke, A. (1993) 'Sprache und Geschlecht – Ein Einblick in den Forschungsbereich', *Praxis Deutsch*, 122.

Linke, A. and Oomen-Welke, I. (1995) *Herkunft, Geschlecht und Deutschunterricht*. Freiburg im Breisgau: Fillibach Verlag.

List, G. (1981) *Sprachpsychologie*. Stuttgart *et al.*: Kohlhammer.

Litermus, P. (Białystok School Superintendent): (1992) Bulletin no. 909, covers the session of the Parliamentary Commission on National Minorities and Ethnic Groups, 9 December (in Belorussian).

Lørring, L. (1988) Course notes: Course 00-509 1988, Royal Danish School of Educational Studies in Copenhagen (personal communication).

Luchtenberg, S. (1992) 'Language Awareness: Ein Ansatz fur interkulturelle sprachliche Bildung', *Interkulturell*, 3 and 4.

Luchtenberg, S. (1995) *Interkulturelle sprachliche Bildung*. Münster: Waxmann Verlag.

Lührs, K. (1985) *Spracherwerb und Sprachenlernen*. Cologne: Pahl-Rugenstein.

Lunzer, E. and Gardner, K. (1982) *Learning From the Written Word*. Edinburgh: Oliver and Boyd.

Mahler, G. (1974) *Zweitsprache Deutsch*. Donauwörth: Auer (see pp. 191 and 196).

Mais, S.P.B. (1914) 'Some results of English teaching at public schools', *The Journal of English Studies*, II (3).

Majewicz, A. (1986) 'A new Kashubian dictionary and the problem of the linguistic status of Kashubian (an insight from outside the field)', in *Collectanea linguistica in honorem A. Heinz*. Wrocław: Ossolineum.

Majewicz, A. (1989) *Języki świata i ich klasyfikowanie*. Warsaw: Polskie Wydawnictwo Naukowe.

Mańczak, W. (1995) 'Czy istnieje kaszubski język?', *Język Polski*, LXXV.

Marenbon, J. (1987) *English, Our English*. London: Centre for Policy Studies.

Mathieson, M. (1975) *The Preachers of Culture*. London: Allen & Unwin.

Mejding, J. (1994) *Den grimme ælling og svanerne? – om danske elevers læsefærdigheder*. Copenhagen: Danmarks Pædagogiske Institut.

MEN (1992) *Minimum Programowe przedmiotów ogólnokształcących w szkołach podstawowych i średnich obowiązujące od 1 września* (see pp 10–20, 35–39, 104–113). Warsaw: Fundacja Rozwoju Edukacji Narodowej.

Michael, I. (1970) *English Grammatical Categories*. Cambridge: Cambridge University Press.

Michael, I. (1979) 'The historical study of English: a preliminary enquiry into some questions of method', *History of Education*, 8 (3).

Mihalisko, K. (1989) 'Language revival: what would it require in Belorussia?', *Report on the USSR*, 1 (11).

Ministry of Education (1988) *The Folkeskole, Primary and Lower Secondary Education in Denmark*. Copenhagen: Undervisningsministeriet.

Mittins, W.H. (1991) *Language Awareness for Teachers*. Milton Keynes: Open University Press.

Mitter, W. (1992) 'Education in Eastern Europe and the former Soviet Union in a period of revolutionary change – an approach to comparative analysis', in M. Kaser, and D. Phillips, (eds), *Education and Economic Change in Eastern Europe and the Former Soviet Union*. Wallingford: Triangle Books.

Møller, A. (1988) 'Sprogpolitik og sprogplanlægning efter hjemmestyrets indførelse', in J.N. Jørgensen *et al.* (eds), *Bilingualism in Society and School. Copenhagen Studies in Bilingualism*, vol. 5. Clevedon, Avon: Multilingual Matters.

Muckle, J. (1988) *A Guide to the Soviet Curriculum: What the Russian Child is Taught in School*. Beckenham: Croom Helm.

Muckle, J. (1990) *Portrait of a Soviet School under Glasnost'*. London: Macmillan.

OECD / OCDE (1989) *L'Ecole et les cultures*. Paris: Centre pour la recherche et l'innovation dans l'enseignement.

Oliphant, J. (1903) *The Educational Writings of Richard Mulcaster*. Glasgow: James Maclehose and Sons.

Oomen-Welke, I. (1985) 'Innenansicht einer Türkenklasse: Erfahrungen und Reflexionen aus der Arbeit in einem [nationalen Modell]', *Deutsch lernen – Zeitschrift für den Sprachunterricht mit ausländischen Arbeitern*, 2.

Oomen-Welke, I. (1990) 'Türkische Hauptschüler im Mittleren Neckarraum', *Lernen in Deutschland*, 3.

Oomen-Welke, I (1993) 'Deutscher Unterricht als (inter-)kulturelle Praxis', in A. Bremerich-Vos (ed.), *Handlungsfeld Deutschunterricht im Kontext*. Frankfurt am Main: Diesterweg.

Ozouf, J. (1967) *Nous les maîtres d'école, Autobiographies d'instituteurs de la Belle Epoque*. Paris: Julliard.

Pakhnova, T.M. (1993) 'Khudozhestvennye teksty na urokakh russkogo yazyka [Artistic texts in Russian language lessons]', *Russkiy yazyk v shkole*, 3.

Parekh, B. (1989) 'Hermeneutics of the Swann Report', in G.J. Verma (ed.), *Education for All: A Landmark in Pluralism*. London: Falmer Press.

Peate, I.C. (1981a) 'Ychwaneg o Eiriau Llafar Cyfeiliog', in B. Griffiths (ed.), *Gwerin-eirau Maldwyn*. Bangor: Llygad yr Haul.

Peate, I.C. (1981b) 'Geirfaír Saer', in B. Griffiths (ed.), *Gwerin-eirau Maldwyn*. Bangor: Llygad yr Haul.

Peate, M.R. (1995) 'Oracy issues in ESL teaching in Key Stage 2: using the language master as a bridge between non-standard and standard English', in Mahendra K. Verma *et al.* (eds), *Working with Bilingual Children*. Clevedon: Multilingual Matters.

Peate, M.R. (1996a) 'The Other Languages of Wales', in P.W. Thomas (ed), *World Minority Languages*, Department of Welsh, Cardiff: University of Wales Press.

Peate, M.R. (1996b) 'The Blue Books and after: William Williams and his legacy', *The Welsh Journal of Education*, Cardiff: University of Wales Press.

Peel, R. and Hargreaves, S. (1995) 'Beliefs about English: trends in Australia, England and the United States', *English in Education*, 29 (3).

Peers, E.A. (1914) 'English composition: A constructive essay', *The Journal of English Studies*, III (1).

Pelz, M. (ed.) (1989) *Lerne die Sprache des Nachbarn – Grenzüberschreitende Spracharbeit zwischen Deutschland und Frankreich*. Frankfurt am Main: Diesterweg.

Prost, A. (1968) *Histoire de l'Enseignement en France 1800–1967*. Paris: Armand Colin.

Protherough, R. (1989) *Students of English*. London: Routledge.

Protherough, R. and Atkinson, J. (1991) *The Making of English Teachers*. Milton Keynes: Open University Press.

Protherough, R. and King, P. (eds) (1995) *The Challenge of English in the National Curriculum*. London: Routledge.

Raybould, W.H. (1995) 'The Welsh perspective on working with bilingual children in the primary school', in Mahendra K. Verma *et al.* (eds), *Working with Bilingual Children*. Clevedon: Multilingual Matters.

Reboul-Scherrer, F. (1989) *La vie quotidienne des premiers instituteurs (1833–82)*. Paris: Hachette.

Reid, E. (1990) 'Culture and language: teaching ESL in England', in B. Harrison (ed.), *Culture and the Language Classroom*. London: Modern English Publications and British Council.

Risager, K., Holmen, A. and Trosborg, A. (eds) (1993) *Sproglig mangfoldighed – om sproglig viden og bevidsthed*. Roskilde: Association Danoise de Linguistique Appliquée.

Rocznik Statystyczny (1993) prepared by Główny Urząd Statystyczny. Warsaw: Zakład Wydawnictw Statystycznych.

Rosen, H. (1981) *Neither Bleak House nor Liberty Hall*. London: Institute of Education.

Rosen, H. and Burgess, T. (1980) *Languages and Dialects of London School Children*. London: Ward Lock.

Russkiy yazyk v shkole (1985) 'Ob opyte raboty po russkomu yazyku v obshcheobrazovatel'nykh shkolakh RSFSR po usovershenstvovannoy programme v 1984–85 uchebnom godu [On experience in the teaching of Russian in accordance with the improved syllabus in the general-education schools of the RSFSR in 1984–85]', 5.

Russkiy yazyk v shkole (1994) 'Metodicheskie rekomendatsii po provedeniyu attestatsii uchiteley-slovesnikov [Methodological recommendations for implementing attestation of language and literature teachers]', 5.

Sambor, J. (1985) 'Nowomowa język naszych czasów', *Poradnik Językowy*, 6.

Sampson, G. (1921) *English for the English*. Cambridge: Cambridge University Press.

Satkiewicz, H. (1990) 'O zasadach aktualnej polityki językowej', *Poradnik Językowy*, 3.

Schmitt, G. (1980) 'Deutschunterricht in Vorbereitungsklassen und Förderkursen – Konzeption für einen didaktischen Baukasten', *Ausländerkinder*, 2.

Schmitt, G. (1992) 'Bilinguismusforschung – pädagogisch gesehen', *Interkulturell*, 3 and 4. Freiburg Pädagogische Hochschule Forschungsstelle Migration und Integration (Zwei- und Mehrsprachigkeit).

Schnapper, D. (1991) *La France de l'intégration, Sociologie de la Nation en 1990*. Paris: Gallimard.

Schuster, K. (1994) *Einführung in die Fachdidaktik Deutsch*. Baltmannsweiler: Burgbücherei Schneider (4th edn).

Secretaría General de Política Lingüística (1991) *Comparecencia a petición propria de la Secretaría General de Política Lingüística ante la Comisión de Instituciones e Interior del Parlamento Vasco*. Vitoria: Gobierno Vasco.

Secretaría de Estado de Educación (1992) *Lengua Castellana y Literatura – Primaria*. Madrid: Ministerio de Educación y Ciencia.

Secretaría de Estado de Educación (1992) *Lengua Castellana y Literatura – Secundaria Obligatoria*. Madrid: Ministerio de Educación y Ciencia.

Shayer, D. (1972) *The Teaching of English in Schools 1900–1970*. London: Routledge & Kegan Paul.

Smułkowa, E. (1988) 'The Belorussian linguistic links in the light of time and territorial aspects', in J. Tomaszewski, E. Smułkowa and H. Majecki (eds), *Polish-Lithuanian-Belorussian Studies*. Warsaw: Polskie Wydawnictwo Naukowe (in Polish).

Spuller, E. (1988) *Au Ministère de l'Instruction publique, 1887, Discours, allocutions, circulaires*. Paris: Hachette.

Suddaby, A. (1985) 'V.F. Shatalov – the new Makarenko', *Soviet Education Study Bulletin*, 3 (1).

Suddaby, A. (1988) 'The Makarenko tradition in Soviet education today', *Soviet Education Study Bulletin*, 6 (1).

Sutherland, J. (1989) 'Soviet education since 1984: the school reform, the innovators and the APN', *Soviet Education Study Bulletin*, 7 (1).

Tansley, P. (1986) *Community Languages in Primary Education*. Windsor: NFER-Nelson.

Tarrow, N. B. (1985) 'The autonomous Basque community of Spain: language, culture and education', in C. Brock and W. Tulasiewicz (eds), *Cultural Identity and Educational Policy*. London and Sydney: Croom Helm.

Taszycki, W. (1964) Rola Uniwersytetu Jagiellońskiego w dziejach języka polskiego. Wykład wygłoszony w UJ podczas inauguracji roku akademickiego 1963–64 (Inaugural lecture). Kraków: Polskie Wydawnictwo Naukowe.

Thomas, A. (1973) *The Linguistic Geography of Wales: A Contribution to Welsh dialectology*. Cardiff: University of Wales Press for the Board of Celtic Studies.

Thomas, A. (1987) 'A spoken standard for Welsh', *International Journal of the Sociology of Language*, 66.

Thomas, C.H. (1982) 'Registers in Welsh', *International Journal of the Sociology of Language*, 35.

Thornton, G. (1986) *APU Language Testing 1979–1983*. London: DES.

Tkachenko, E. (1994) 'Education reform in Russia', *Institute for the Study of Russian Education Newsletter*, 3 (1 and 2).

Tomaszewski, J. (1991) *The National Minorities in Poland in the Twentieth Century*. Warsaw: Spotkania Editions (in Polish).

Undervisningsministeriet (1984) *Bekendtgørelse af 20. november 1984 om folkeskolens undervisning af fremmedsprogede elever*. Copenhagen: Undervisningsministeriet.

Undervisningsministeriet (1992) *Sproglig viden og bevidsthed. Kvalitet i uddannelse og undervisning. KUP-rapport no. 16*. Copenhagen: Undervisningsministeriet.

Urbańczyk, S. (1977) 'Hierarchia kryteriów poprawności językowej we współczes nym języku polskim', in S. Urbańczyk (ed.), *Wariancja normy we współczesnych słowiańskich językach literackich*. Wrocław: Ossolineum.

USSR (1984) *New Frontiers of Social Progress*. Moscow: Novosti.

Valsiner, J. (1988) *Developmental Psychology in the Soviet Union*, Brighton: Harvester Press.

Verma, G.J. (1989) *Education for All: A Landmark in Pluralism*. London: Falmer Press.

Vigouroux-Frey, N. and Convey, F. (1994) 'France', in C. Brock and W. Tulasiewicz (eds), *Education in a Single Europe*. London: Routledge.

Vygotsky, L.S. (1986) *Thought and Language*, trans. and ed. A. Kozulin, Cambridge, MA.: MIT Press [original version *Myshlenie i rech'*. Moscow/Leningrad 1934].

V'yushkova, L.N. (1993) 'Obuchenie chteniyu na urokakh russkogo yazyka [teaching reading in the Russian class]', *Russkiy yazyk v shkole*, 3.

Webber, S. and Webber, T. (1994) 'Issues in teacher education', in A. Jones (ed.), *Education and Society in the New Russia*. Armonk, NY: M.E.Sharpe.

Welsh Language Board (1995) *An Outline Strategy for the Welsh Language*. Cardiff: Welsh Language Board.

Western Canadian Protocol for Collaboration in Basic Education (1997) *The Common Curriculum Framework for English Language Arts*. Edmonton: Edmonton Draft (Government).

White, J. (1986) *The Assessment of Writing: Pupils aged 11 and 15*. Windsor: NFER-Nelson.

White, J. (1990) 'On literacy and gender', in R. Carter (ed.), *Knowledge about Language and the Curriculum: The LINC Reader*. London: Hodder and Stoughton.

Wierzbicki, P. (1987) *Struktura kłamstwa*. London: Aneks.

Wilkinson, A.M. with Davies, A. and Atkinson, D. (1965) *Spoken English*. Birmingham: Birmingham University School of Education.

Wilkinson, A.M. (1990) *Spoken English Illuminated*. Milton Keynes: Open University Press.

Williams, C. (1982) 'The spatial analysis of Welsh culture', *Etudes Celtiques*, 19.

Wright, L.B. (1935) *Middle-class Culture in Elizabethan England*. Chapel Hill: North Carolina University Press.

Zimmern, A. (1900) 'Literature as a central subject', *The Journal of Education*, September.

Żurauski, A.I. (1967) *The History of Belorussian Literary Language*, vol. 1. Minsk (in Belorussian).

Żurauski, A.I. and Kramko, I. (1973) *The Mutual Relations Between Early Belorussian Literary Language and Other Slavonic Languages*. Minsk (in Belorussian).

Index